The Asbury Theological Seminary Series in Christian Revitalization Studies

This volume is published in collaboration with the Center for the Study of World Christian Revitalization Movements, a cooperative initiative of Asbury Theological Seminary faculty. Building on the work of the previous Wesleyan/Holiness Studies Center at the Seminary, the Center provides a focus for research in the Wesleyan Holiness and other related Christian renewal movements, including Pietism and Pentecostal movements, which have had a world impact. The research seeks to develop analytical models of these movements, including their biblical and theological assessment. Using an interdisciplinary approach, the Center bridges relevant discourses in several areas in order to gain insights for effective Christian mission globally. It recognizes the need for conducting research that combines insights from the history of evangelical renewal and revival movements with anthropological and religious studies literature on revitalization movements. It also networks with similar or related research and study centers around the world, in addition to sponsoring its own research projects.

A key feature in revitalization literature is the exploration of the distinctive path of holiness in the renewal of the imago Dei in a fallen humanity which is represented in the life and ministry of John Wesley. The theme comes into focus in the collection of perspectives on Wesleyan thought presented here as a festschrift honoring the contributions of Professor Herbert B. McGonigle to that heritage. The chapters address several disciplines which reflect decisive influence from Wesley's message of the holy life, including the history of Pietism and evangelicalism, missiology, ecclesiology and sacramental theology, homiletics, and interreligious concerns (with focus on Christianity and Islam). These chapters also bring honor to the life and research of Professor McGonigle, a scholar of the Church of the Nazarene in Great Britain who is known for his important research in Wesley studies, his work as first Director of the Wesley Research Centre at Manchester, and as chair of the Wesley Fellowship in Great Britain. Finally, by its presentation in this series, the volume offers important insight for contemporary research in revitalization studies.

J. Steven O'Malley, Editor
The Pietist and Wesleyan Studies Series

The Path of Holiness

Perspectives in Wesleyan Thought in Honor of Herbert B. McGonigle

Edited by
Joseph Cunningham and
David Rainey

Asbury Theological Seminary Series:
The Study of World Christian Revitalization Movements in
Pietist/Wesleyan Studies

EMETH PRESS
www.emethpress.com

The Path of Holiness Perspectives in Wesleyan Thought in Honor of Herbert B. McGonigle

Copyright © 2014 Joseph Cunningham and David Rainey

Printed in the United States of America on acid-free paper. All rights reserved. No part of this book may be reproduced, or stored in a retrieval system or transmitted in any form or by any means, electronic, mechanical, photocopying, recording, scanning or otherwise, except as permitted by the 1976 United States Copyright Act, or with the prior written permission of Emeth Press. Requests for permission should be addressed to: Emeth Press, P. O. Box 23961, Lexington, KY 40523-3961   http://www.emethpress.com.

Library of Congress Cataloging-in-Publication Data

The path of holiness : perspectives in Wesleyan thought in honor of Herbert B. McGonigle / edited by Joseph Cunningham and David Rainey.
   pages cm
 ISBN 978-1-60947-083-8 (acid-free paper)
 1. Wesley, John, 1703-1791. 2. Wesleyan Church--Doctrines. 3. Methodist Church--Doctrines. I. McGonigle, Herbert Boyd, honouree. II. Cunningham, Joseph, 1981- editor. III. Rainey, David, 1950- editor.
 BX8495.W5P38 2014
 230'.7--dc23
                    2014031241

Contents

Introduction / 1

Part I—Methodological & Historical

Chapter 1
    "Using John Wesley Today: Some Suggested Principles" / 7
        By Henry Rack

Chapter 2
    "The Wesleys and the Evangelical Tradition" / 27
        By Tom Noble

Chapter 3
    "Methodists and Moravians: The Shaping of Evangelical Spirituality" / 43
        By Ian Randall

Part II—Missional

Chapter 4
    "The Future of Wesleyan Missional Theology: Reconciliation and the Eucharist" / 63
        By David Rainey

Chapter 5
    "The DNA of Mission-Shaped Discipleship" **/ 75**
        By Phil Meadows

Chapter 6
    "John Wesley's Mission of Evangelism" / 95
        By Ron Benefiel

Part III—Biblical

Chapter 7
    "Holiness and Community in 1 John" / 127
        By Kent Brower

Part IV—Practical

Chapter 8
    Praedicare Verbum Dei: John Wesley's Theology of Preaching" / 145
        By Joseph Wood
Chapter 9
    "What has Athens to do with Oxford? A Study in Wesleyan Theology and Virtue Ethics" / 163
        By Joseph Cunningham

Part V—Interreligious

Chapter 10
    "John Wesley's Engagement with Islam" / 175
        By Kenneth J. Collins

About the Contribuors / 197

Introduction

The Path of Holiness:

Perspectives in Wesleyan Thought in Honor of Herbert B. McGonigle

This book serves to honor the life and work of Dr. Herbert B. McGonigle, former principal and lecturer emeritus of Nazarene Theological College, Manchester. His lifelong commitment to scholarship and teaching as well as his service for the Church of the Nazarene in Great Britain have made a lasting contribution both to the field of Wesley Studies and to numerous students who have gone on to parish work and other forms of ministry. His record of service and research indicates this. He was appointed director of the newly established Manchester Wesley Research Centre in 2003. Co-founder as well as chair of the Wesley Fellowship, Dr. McGonigle has authored numerous books and articles including "Pneumatological Nomenclature in Early Methodism," *Wesleyan Theological Journal*, vol. 8 (Spring 1973), *Sufficient Saving Grace: John Wesley's Evangelical Arminianism* (Paternoster, 2001), and *Christianity or Deism: John Wesley's Response to John Taylor on the Doctrine of Original Sin* (Moorley's Print and Publishing, 2012). Recognized internationally for his expertise in Wesley Studies, Dr. McGonigle is a scholar of first rate, a beloved teacher, and an unwavering mentor to the students and colleagues privileged to study and work with him.

This book is a collection of essays by scholars who have either studied with or worked alongside of Dr. McGonigle. The areas of research represented in the volume range from biblical studies and practical theology, to systematic theology and theological methodology, as well as historical and interreligious theology. Most books of this sort are written with a thematic focus. In this instance, each of the essays can be read independently of the others, but with a central unifying theme: holiness. When the Methodist tradition emerged during the long-eighteenth century in Britain, it did so as a revival movement. John Wesley, with his brother Charles Wesley, organized, galvanized, and expanded Methodism into a religious society within and beyond the Church of England. They embraced the mantle of preaching the gospel and spreading scriptural holiness across the land. While their ministerial designs were uniform, the eclectic nature of Wesley's interests is indicated by his variegated publishing record. He commented on Scripture in his *Explanatory Notes* (1755/65). He explored the history and origins of Methodism in relation to contemporary society in treatises like *An Earnest Appeal to Men of Reason and Religion* (1743) and *A Plain Account of the People Called Methodists* (1749). He published *Sermons on Several Occasions* (1746) and distributed numerous copies to his preachers for their spiritual edification and for the benefit of those to whom they preached—a decisively pastoral move. He even published on electricity (*The Desideratum: Or Electricity Made Plain and Useful*, 1759) and medicine (*Primitive Physick*, 1747) as well. But what motivated and unified his writing and preaching endeavors was a deep-seated calling to share the faith of holy living - a theological theme which he had discovered over the course of encounters with other evangelical groups like the Pietists, Puritans, and Moravians - with all who would listen. Wesley was a theologian to be sure, a cultural critic of sorts, and a pastor at heart. The essays given to honor Dr. McGonigle reflect Wesley's theological, evangelical, biblical, and pastoral concerns as well as the unifying theme of holiness which binds together Wesley's commitments.

The first chapter in the volume by Dr. Henry Rack explores methodologically the practice of using and applying the historical Wesley to theological questions of significance today. Dr. Rack's study addresses five main themes of continuous significance throughout Wesley's life and works: Wesley's often discussed "empiricism;" the problem of religious language and religious belief with respect to insiders and outsiders of evangelical faith; the question of tolerance toward varying opinions and belief within the Christian tradition as understood by Wesley; church order; and the nature of religious conversion and the process of salvation. According to Dr. Rack, using Wesley responsibly today and applying his teachings and principles to contemporary concerns, though fraught with historical and contextual limitations, ought to take seriously these five themes, holiness among them, which have proven to be perennially significant both throughout Wesley's works, as well as throughout the history of scholarship concerning Wesley's works.

In chapter two, Dr. Thomas Noble explores John Wesley's place within the context and history of Evangelicalism as a unified religious movement whose roots run deep in church history. Dr. Noble discusses the Moravian and puritan influences, as well as the impact of Luther and Calvin on later Evangelicalism. Dr. Noble concludes that Methodism, with its emphasis on spreading holiness and evangelizing the lost and broken, is both thoroughly evangelical and situated within a vibrant tradition of thoughtful intellectual engagement. Dr. Noble's work is followed in chapter three by Dr. Ian Randall's essay that considers and evaluates the Moravian influence on Methodist spirituality according to four primary foci: conversion, the Bible, the cross, and activism. Similar to Dr. Noble, Dr. Randall likewise explores the connections between Methodist and evangelical spirituality and the importance of deepening our understanding of that connection through continued scholarship on Evangelical history and spirituality.

The fourth and fifth chapters focus on missiology in relation to Wesleyan thought. Dr. Rainey recognizes the significance of grounding a Wesleyan theology missions within a distinctively Wesleyan discourse and Eucharistic practice, as well as the importance of retrieving the historical-theological John Wesley which must be distinguished from the Wesley of history. Dr. Meadows also emphasizes the importance of Wesleyan theology engaging missions. Using the analogy of gene therapy, Dr. Meadows establishes a fourfold framework for mission in terms of holiness, spiritual discipline, fellowship, and everyday works of mission, in an essay especially geared toward the application of Wesleyan missiology to pastoral ministry and discipleship. Both essays sense the need for ongoing discussion on how the Wesleyan tradition might continue to contribute to missiology as a functional specialty of Wesleyan theology, though missiology is often overlooked as such. This theme is echoed in chapter six, in which Dr. Ron Benefiel discusses Wesley's evangelism. In addition to the social context for Wesley's ministry, Dr. Benefiel argues that Wesley's model of evangelism is inherently incarnational and kenotic, and that Wesley's commitment to evangelism and spreading holiness was central to his ministerial practices. Appended to the chapter is an excerpt from Wesley's works concerning class-membership, as well as partial transcriptions of previously unpublished letters from the John Rylands Library, Manchester.

In chapter seven, Dr. Kent Brower discusses the notions of holiness, community, and controversy both within and behind the world of the text of 1 John. The essay demonstrates the overarching significance of holiness for the community represented in 1 John, though frequent use of holiness terminology is absent from the text. In this respect, 1 John echoes theological sentiments gleaned and expressed centuries later by John Wesley during his ministry in Britain and beyond, a ministry which, not unlike the experience of the Johannine community, brooked controversy over how best to practice and apply principles of holy living.

Chapter eight focuses on John Wesley's theology of preaching. Here, Dr. Joseph Wood explores the concept of *praedicare verbum Dei*, used by Wesley in his sermon called "Prophets and Priests." Dr. Wood suggests that Wesley's distinction between the role of priest and prophet – a distinction grounded in the writings of Richard Hooker – provides justification for Wesley's decision to support and incorporate the practice of lay preaching into the Methodist movement, though it was severely criticized by many of his religious contemporaries. Dr. Wood also shows that Wesley's theology of preaching was grounded in a pneumatology of inspiration, in which the call of preaching was understood to transcend the office of ordained minister, insofar as the call was authentic and fruitful of fostering scriptural holiness. Chapter nine considers the concept of holiness in Wesley's thinking, especially the Methodist doctrine of Christian perfection as "perfect love," in relation to classical virtue. Dr. Joseph Cunningham shows that Christian perfection – when read through lens of virtue ethics and the teleological nature of humanity in relation to enjoyment of God as our highest good – engages a number of themes in contemporary theology and provides a useful template for holy living, despite lingering systematic and epistemological problems.

Finally, in chapter ten, Dr. Kenneth J. Collins applies Wesley's understanding of salvation to the question of interreligious faith, focusing specifically on the relation between Christianity and Islam. The overarching argument he makes is that Wesleyan discourse, despite historical biases and limitations, is fertile with possibilities for fruitful and continuous dialogue between faith traditions concerning humanity's reconciliation with the divine.

To be sure, each essay may be read autonomously. However, taken together, they provide a mosaic of Christian thought and life from the Wesleyan perspective. The path to holiness, to Wesley, requires reconciliation with God experienced inwardly and manifested outwardly through charitable living and spiritual commitment evinced through participation in the body of faith. Whether Wesleyan discourse is placed in conversation with questions of historical, systematic, biblical, practical, or interreligious significance, what unites each specialism underneath the banner "Wesleyan," is the centrality of holiness to Wesleyan discourse—holiness without which none can experience true peace, love, and joy in relation to the divine. Dr. McGonigle recognized this in his research. But more than an abstract concept to be intellectually understood, the connection between inward and outward holiness guided his commitments as an educator and scholar and as pastor and theologian. More than an academic interest, it was his vocation. The path of holiness is humanity's journey into the life of God as the divine abides in the soul of humanity. This truth is exemplified in Dr. McGonigle's work on the life, thought, and legacy of John Wesley, but most importantly, it is evident in the kind of life he has always led in relation to those privileged to call him colleague and friend.

With Deep Gratitude,

David Rainey
Manchester, UK

Joseph Cunningham
Saginaw, Michigan, USA

Part I

Methodological & Historical

Chapter 1

Using John Wesley Today: Some Suggested Principles

By Henry D. Rack

Introduction

There have been and are continuing to be impressive and illuminating examples, particularly in the United States, of works which develop a distinctive Wesleyan theology. These are generally either more or less comprehensive systems of theology or else expositions of Wesley's teaching on particular topics which it is believed can be applied to present-day theological concerns such as (for example) feminism, ecology or medicine.[1]

There are, as most modern writers on Wesleyan theology are well aware, problems involved in lifting theological ideas developed in a particular historical and intellectual context in the past and attempting to apply them to the radically different circumstances of today. The problem is starkly put, for example, by William J. Abraham in an attempt to apply Wesley's view of overseas missions after what he describes as the collapse of the intellectual, political and ecclesiastical world in which it was originally formulated.[2] Postmodern attitudes to history and the alleged impossibility of recovering the mentalities of the past have complicated this problem still further.

But in any case I do not claim to be a theologian but rather a church historian who has chiefly studied eighteenth-century Methodism and evangelicalism with a special interest in biographical and spiritual developments in their historical context. I have done so in an attempt to understand rather

---

[1] A comprehensive recent example of the latter is William J. Abraham and James W. Kirby, eds., *The Oxford Handbook of Methodist Studies* (Oxford: Oxford University Press, 2009).

[2] William J. Abraham, "Saving Souls in the Twenty-First Century: A Missiological Midrash on John Wesley" in *Wesleyan Theological Journal*, vol. 38, no. 1 (2003):7-20.

than to evaluate Wesley's teaching or to adapt it for present-day purposes. Yet even mere historians, when they are also concerned Christians, cannot avoid from time to time standing back from their stance of empathetic reconstruction of the past to ask what may still be of more lasting truth and value in Wesley's teaching. It is unnecessary to attempt to develop another Wesleyan theology of the kind referred to earlier—a project for which in any case I do not consider myself theologically qualified. Rather, I think it is possible (and profitable) to try to discern what seem to be some fundamental principles or insights which are not, or at least need not be limited to Wesley's eighteenth-century context or the exact shape taken by the problems he was attempting to solve. The subjects I have in mind seem to me to be of perennial concern and relevance and Wesley's fundamental approach to them need not in principle, I would argue, be time-bound. The selection which follows, though the product of half a century's study of Wesley, is no doubt influenced by personal interests and concerns and are not, I am sure, exhaustive. Indeed I have considered others but reluctantly omitted them for lack of space and competence. The following, then, is a list of five subjects to be explored: (1) Wesley's often-discussed empiricism. This includes his appeal to "experience" as conditioning our approach to theology and church life as well as his openness to development and change in belief and policy. (2) The problem of religious language in approaching religious belief and in our attitudes to people whose views and language differ from our own. (3) Toleration. Here we can explore Wesley's attempt to distinguish between essential, fundamental Christian truths on which we can agree and what he called "opinions" on which he believed we can and should tolerate differences. (4) Church order. Here we can ask, as Wesley did, what should determine its shape? Where lies the priority between inherited order and the demands of evangelism and pastoral care? We may also assess the merits of his evident partiality for a societary religious ethos and a "connexional" polity for church organisation. It should be pointed out that comments on possible later applications here are confined to Britain for the evolution of Methodist church order elsewhere, notably in America, has necessarily followed a different pattern. (5) The nature and process of salvation. Arguably this was central to Wesley's concerns and he could be seen as attempting to combine views on justification and sanctification which had often been seen in Christian history as mutually exclusive and underlying major divisions between churches. Here, too, we have to consider his teaching on "perfection" which was and continues to be highly controversial.

Empiricism

This involves several issues. First there is, historically at least, Wesley's relationship to the Enlightenment which is also an aspect of the recurring debate over whether Methodism was a modernizing or reactionary movement and whether Wesley had an "enlightened" or "superstitious" mentality. The balance between these alternatives may be variously struck, recent tendencies being rather more favorable to his "reasonableness" than used to be the case.[3]

Second, in philosophical terms, and again historically, Wesley was clearly an empiricist of a fairly strict kind, though opinions on the sources for this in his case have shifted. It used to be generally assumed that he drew on Locke and especially on Peter Browne, but more recently emphasis has been on his debt to Oxford Aristotelianism.[4] This seems to be supported by Wesley himself in his sermon on "The Discoveries of Faith" where he dismisses innate ideas and appeals to a scholastic axiom derived from Aristotle that "There is nothing in the understanding which was not first perceived by one of the senses."[5]

This empiricism appears in his survey of science and in his *Primitive Physick* where he professes only to describe appearances and symptoms and refuses to speculate on ultimate causes. In form at least he appears to extend this "empiricism" to religious knowledge by positing a species of "spiritual senses."[6] Here, however, he is careful to claim that the ordinary senses cannot give knowledge of the "invisible world." Such knowledge requires the action of God and it appears that it is God who "hath appointed *faith* to supply the defects of sense...its office begins where that of sense ends."[7] It has been argued that "perceptible inspiration" for Wesley begins with God's "gracious relationality," which enables humans to receive the gift of faith. When embraced, "faith served as our faculty...for perceiving the testimony of the Spirit."[8]

---

[3] For a discussion see Henry D. Rack, "'A Man of Reason and Religion?' John Wesley and the Enlightenment" in *Wesley and Methodist Studies*, vol. 1 (2009): 2-17. For an examination of Wesley's supernaturalism see Robert Webster, "Methodism and the Miraculous: John Wesley's Contribution to the *Historia Miraculorum*" (D. Phil. diss., Oxford University, 2006).

[4] Rex Matthews, "'Reason and Religion Joined': A Study in the Theology of John Wesley (D.Theol. Diss.,Harvard University, 1986). Mark T. Mealey, "'Tilting at Windmills' John Wesley's Reading of John Locke's Epistemology" in *John Wesley Tercentenary Essays*, ed. Jeremy Gregory, *Bulletin of the John Rylands Library* vol. 85 (2003): 331-46.

[5] J. Wesley, "Sermons," ed. Albert Outler, vol.4 of *The Bicentennial Edition of the Works of John Wesley* (Nashville, Tennessee: Abingdon Press, 1987), 29. Hereafter abbreviated, Works [BE].

[6] J. Wesley, "An Appeal to Men of Reason and Religion" in *Works [BE]*, 4:30

[7] J. Wesley, "Sermons," *Works [BE]*, 4:30.

[8] Joseph W. Cunningham, "Pneumatology through Correspondence. The Letters of John Wesley to 'John Smith' (1745-48)" in *Wesley and Methodist Studies*, vol. 1(2009): 21-22.

Third, in important respects for the sources of authority for Christian truth, Wesley follows what was by his time an established Anglican tradition of reliance on a combination of Scripture, tradition and reason. He apparently saw scripture as the primary authority with tradition and reason as valuable for interpreting it. Yet on Scripture he was not really a literalist or "fundamentalist." (That much-abused term, essentially deriving from an early twentieth –century controversy, should not be applied to the more flexible world of eighteenth-century approaches to the Bible). It is striking, for example, to find that while Isaac Watts thought the Psalms needed Christianizing, Wesley perhaps went even further in saying that some of them were not fit for use by Christians. Hence he omitted some of them from his American Sunday Service.[9]

This said, Wesley lived in a predominantly pre-critical age, and the crude but disturbing criticisms levelled at the Bible's accuracy and authority by Deists did not encourage more balanced critical views among the more orthodox.[10] To the then customary triple authority of Scripture, tradition and reason, Wesley appears to add a fourth in experience. This was certainly a significant source of knowledge, including religious knowledge, for him. Thus he frequently emphasized in his teaching on "assurance" that this derived not simply from the practical and visible evidence of a changed life but also (and indeed primarily) from the Holy Spirit directly "witnessing with our spirit."[11] Yet it would be a mistake to suppose that Wesley was claiming that "religious experience" was the primary ground for belief in God and source for doctrine. There was, in the early twentieth century, a certain vogue for seeing Wesley as a kind of precursor of Schleiermacher, attempting to base religion on intuition and feeling.[12] There is, indeed, a passage in a letter to his brother Charles on his favourite doctrine of perfection, saying that if there were no "living witnesses" of that experience he would have to abandon the doctrine.[13] He

---

[9] Isaac Watts on the Psalms said he wished "To make them always speak the common sense of a Christian": Preface to *The Psalms of David* , quoted in Bernard L. Manning, *The Hymns of Wesley and Watts* (London: Epworth Press, 1942), 80. Wesley says that he left out many Psalms and omitted parts of others as being "highly improper from the mouth of a Christian Congregation." See Preface to *The Sunday Service of the Methodists in America* (1784), reprinted James F. White, ed., *John Wesley's Prayer Book* (Cleveland, Ohio: OSL Publications, 1991).

[10] For a recent carefully nuanced discussion of Wesley's attitude to the "inerrancy" and "infallibility of the Bible see Randy L. Maddox, "The Rule of Christian Faith, Practice and Hope: John Wesley on the Bible" in *Methodist* Review, vol. 3 (2011) reprinted in *Epworth Review*, vol. 38, no. 2 (2011): 6-37.

[11] See J. Wesley's sermons on "The Witness of the Spirit" and "The Witness of our own Spirit" in *Works [BE]*, 1: 267-313.

[12] For an example of such an attempt see George Eayrs, *John Wesley, Christian Philosopher and Church Founder* (London: Epworth Press, 1926). This may well have oversimplified Schleiermacher's theology as well, since it needs to be seen in the contemporary German intellectual context.

[13] J. Wesley to C. Wesley, 12 February 1767 in John Telford, ed., *The Letters of John Wesley* (London: Epworth Press, 1931), vol. 5:41. (Hereafter, Wesley, *Letters*).

had always insisted that the doctrine was rooted in Scripture and arguably laid more emphasis on visible contemporary examples as evidence for the doctrine in later years, especially in the wake of what he saw as a revival of the "work" from the late 1750s into the early 1760s, controversial though the perfectionist group led by Maxfield and Bell turned out to be.[14] But in the letter to Charles he seems to make it clear that what he was saying was not that his belief in the doctrine rested on experience as an authority but that if there were no living witnesses he would have to conclude that he had misunderstood the teaching of Scripture. The evidence of the living witnesses would simply prove that his understanding of Scripture was correct. One is reminded of his appeal to God to produce visible convulsions in Bristol in 1739 in response to the preaching of salvation for all to prove it was scripturally correct against Calvinism.[15]

The role of experience, then, is to help to settle the interpretation of Scripture rather than to be an equal, let alone superior authority. It is, indeed, apparently equal with tradition as an aid to interpretation and one senses that after his early high church period Wesley may well have seen it as of great importance for such interpretation – more so, perhaps, than is usual among theologians. Hence his fascination with collecting evidence of religious experience for his doctrines and beliefs, including apparently supernatural events. It could be argued that any theology which continues to have life in it ultimately includes a basis in religious experience and not simply in Scripture, tradition and reason.

Empiricism in terms of experience does indeed seem to have an important role in Wesley's career in terms of his response to his own and other people's experiences – perhaps theirs more than his own – as a significant factor influencing developments and changes in his teaching and policy. One can see this acknowledged by Wesley explicitly or implicitly on such issues as the perfectionist doctrine already mentioned and his views on toleration and churchmanship to be discussed later. Some may wish to go further than Wesley in basing religious belief on religious experience though this is subject to considerable difficulties as the interpretation of such experiences is always shaped by the person's existing religious traditions and environment as the contrasts between Catholic and Protestant (including distinctive Methodist) experiences show. Nevertheless, Wesley's eclecticism and constant adaptation of the ideas of others in response to the experience of changing needs and situations became a major underlying principle in his career which has a lasting relevance.

---

[14] For a recent examination of this episode see David Stark, "'The Peculiar Doctrine Committed to our Trust:' Ideal and Identity in the first Wesleyan Holiness Revival" (Ph.D. diss., Manchester University, 2011.)

[15] J. Wesley, *A Plain Account of Christian Perfection* (1767), including *Thoughts on Christian Perfection* (1763), *Further Thoughts on Christian Perfection* (1763) and *Brief Thoughts on Christian Perfection* (1763), reprinted in *A Plain Account of Christian Perfection* (London: Epworth Press, 1952). For the Bristol incident see Wesley's journal for 26 April 1739 in Wesley, *Works [BE]*, 19:51.

Problems of Language

Wesley became, at least in principle, remarkably free of dogmatic pronouncements in terms of doctrinal formulas, particularly in his later years. Here it would no doubt be a mistake, or at least an exaggeration, to claim for him a place in anything like the apophatic tradition of theology, i.e. the acute recognition of the inadequacy (indeed the non-application) of our human concepts and language for capturing and characterising the divine. This is commonly associated with the Eastern Orthodox tradition in theology and while there have been recurring claims for the influence of the eastern Fathers on Wesley's theology this has been mainly confined to his holiness teaching.[16] His increasing toleration of diverse "opinions" on various matters, so long as there is agreement on a common basic Christianity, will be discussed in the next section. What is of interest in the matter of religious language is a recurring recognition by Wesley in his later years that beliefs which are apparently different and even apparently contradictory may in fact be concealing a common experience of God or at least a different but acceptable variety of such experience under the variabilities and inadequacies of language. That is to say, Wesley seems to have become aware that words can only imperfectly capture the subtleties of religious experience and indeed are inadequate to do justice to the reality of God and his dealings with humanity. A parallel sense of the limitations of understanding as well as of experience might be seen in his refusal to speculate on the hidden causes behind scientific and medical phenomena noted earlier.

Where religious discourse was concerned, Wesley's reluctance to make fine distinctions in divinity, evident in his later years, in part reflects a widespread eighteenth-century revulsion against the intricacies and fine-drawn distinctions of seventeenth-century Protestant scholasticism which still attracted dogmatic evangelical Calvinists like Augustus Montague Toplady. It was against this kind of Calvinism that Wesley reacted strongly in his 1770 Minutes of Conference which led to Calvinist suspicions that he was lapsing into "salvation by works." Wesley had, for example, dismissed distinctions between being rewarded for the sake of our works and for their "merit" as mere hair-splitting though salvation in reward for our "merits" had commonly been regarded by protestants as a Roman Catholic error.[17]

But already, in 1767, he had reflected that a man may be saved who "cannot express himself properly on imputed righteousness" or who "has not

---

[16] See, e.g. the claims made by Albert Outler in his introduction to Wesley's sermons in *Works [BE]*, 1:74-75 and for later references and discussions in relation to Wesley's soteriology, T.A. Noble, "East and West in the Theology of John Wesley" [paper from the 2003 Tercentenary Conference, 'John Wesley, Life, Legacy and Legend'] in *The Bulletin of the John Rylands University Library of Manchester*, vol. 85, nos. 2-3 (2003): 359-372.

[17] "Minutes of Conference" (1770) in *Works [BE]*, 10:393-94. See also Henry D. Rack, *Reasonable Enthusiast. John Wesley and the Rise of Methodism*, 3rd ed. (London: Epworth Press, 2001), 391-92.

clear conceptions" of salvation or justification by faith can be saved. Even a man like William Law who actually denied justification by faith could be saved. Discussing differences of language Wesley concluded "he that feareth God and worketh righteousness is accepted with Him." In a sermon "On Living without God"(1790) he also says that he cannot affirm that people changed in heart and life can have no benefit from Christ's death if they lack clear views of the fall, justification by faith, or the atonement. For he believes that God "respects the goodness of the heart rather than the clearness of the head" and will not damn those lacking clear ideas and conceptions.[18] Interestingly, Charles Wesley acknowledged in 1748 that a young man was "in Christ before me but he not using my expressions hindered my perceiving it."[19]

These remarks of the Wesleys were a remarkable departure from the more theologically dogmatic type of evangelicalism. It was those Calvinists John saw as being obsessed by orthodox formulas rather than the achievement of holy lives that he inveighed against to John Fletcher. Holiness, he wrote, is more important than "correct" doctrines of "Absolute Decrees, of Irresistible Grace, of Infallible Assurance."[20] He was scathing in his condemnation of "what are vulgarly called gospel sermons...a mere *cant* word." Let but a "pert, self-sufficient animal , that has neither sense nor grace, bawl out something about Christ and His blood or justification by faith and his hearers cry out 'what a fine gospel sermon'." He prefers plain sermons on "good tempers and good works."[21]

One very striking example of Wesley's sense of the limitations of language can be found in his sermon on the Trinity. While he affirms the scripturally-evidenced "fact" of the Trinity he does not insist on any particular view of the relationship between the Persons or the inner character of the triune God or even the term "Trinity" itself.[22] What is remarkable here, and has attracted surprisingly little comment, is that Wesley's lack of dogmatism on this subject came in a century which had seen heated debate on the doctrine. Furthermore, a section of Dissent had drifted into ant-trinitarianism and in 1772 the Feathers Tavern Petition by Anglicans to relax the terms of subscription to the Thirty-Nine Articles included men with doubts about the Trinity.

Toleration

The instances cited in the last section of Wesley's increasingly relaxed attitude over niceties of theological language and doctrinal correctness, which he had come to see as subordinate to the achievement of a holy life, also raise the question of his views on religious toleration.

---

[18] J. Wesley journal for 1 December 1767 in *Works [BE]*, 22:114.
[19] C. Wesley, *Journal*, ed. Thomas Jackson (London: Wesleyan Methodist Book-Room, 1849), 2:25.
[20] J. Wesley, *Letters*, 5:83.
[21] J. Wesley, *Letters*, 6:326.
[22] J. Wesley's sermon on the Trinity (1775) in *Works [BE]*, 2:377-78.

Here again he reflected both a more general contemporary tendency and changes from his own earlier attitudes in response to observation and experience. He had once been an advanced high churchman influenced by Nonjurors and had insisted on the necessity of episcopal ordination for valid ministries and sacraments. The Nonjurors were those who had refused to swear allegiance to William and Mary when they displaced James II. They had also developed advanced sacramental and liturgical doctrines and practices beyond those of the Book of Common Prayer. The Wesleys at Oxford and for a time afterwards were influenced by the Manchester Nonjuror bishop Dr. Deacon via his disciple John Clayton who was their associate in the so-called "Holy Club."[23] But by the late 1740s Wesley had already concluded that no one pattern of church government had been enforced by the apostolic church but that a variety of patterns had emerged by a kind of natural process.[24]

He also acknowledged that acquaintance with Presbyterians who had "the root of the matter" in them had forced him to accept them as fellow-Christians. Despite his continuing adherence to high sacramental views he acknowledged that baptism did not always convey saving grace and that even if it had done, subsequent backsliding required that "you must be born again." He allowed that believers' and infant baptism were both acceptable options and even that baptism itself was not strictly necessary to salvation, otherwise (impossibly) Quakers would be damned.[25]

Wesley's fullest exposition of his principles of what he called "The Catholic Spirit" is in a sermon with that title.[26] Here he follows an Anglican tradition going back to the sixteenth century to the effect that people can agree on "fundamentals" but agree to differ on "adiaphora" or "things indifferent". Wesley preferred to express this distinction as being between "essential doctrines" and "opinions."[27] He wished to avoid both dogmatism and indifferentism. For him "essential" doctrines were broadly "evangelical" and one is to avoid both "speculative latitudinarianism" (indifference to all doctrines and "opinions") and "practical latitudinarianism" (indifference to all public wor-

---

[23] Henry D. Rack, "The Wesleys in Manchester" in *Proceedings of the Charles Wesley Society*, vol. 8 (2002): 6-23. See also Geordan Hammond, "Restoring Primitive Christianity: John Wesley and Georgia 1735-37" (Ph.D. diss., Manchester University, 2007).

[24] J. Wesley, *Works [BE]*, 10:156-57, 202-203 (Conferences of 1745 and 1747). See Rack, *Reasonable Enthusiast*, 293-94.

[25] J. Wesley, "Farther Appeal to Men of Reason and Religion," Part III, *Works [BE]*, 11:250 on Presbyterianism; *Works [BE]*, 26:425 on baptism. For these and other issues over Wesley's views of, and relationships with, contemporary Dissent, see Henry D. Rack, "John Wesley and Eighteenth-century Dissent" in *A Thankful Heart and a Discerning Mind: Essays in Honour of John Newton*, ed. Mervyn Davis (Gloucestershire: Lonely Scribe, 2010), 40-56, 61-78.

[26] J. Wesley, *Works [BE]*, 2:79-95. See also Wesley's sermon "A Caution against Bigotry" in *Works [BE]*, 2:61-78.

[27] For this Anglican tradition see *The Study of Anglicanism*, ed. Stephen Sykes and John E. Booty (London: SPCK, 1988), 164, 222,224, 234. See also J. Wesley, *Works [BE]*, 2:376, and Letters, 4:297.

ship and modes of church government). One is, in other words, to be firm in one's own beliefs yet tolerant of those of others.

But what are "opinions"? Wesley took a generous and practical view of those matters on which we may agree to differ. "Whatever is compatible with love of Christ and a work of grace I term an opinion." He says that even holding to the Calvinist doctrine of "Particular Election and Final Perseverance" is compatible with love and grace. In practice he often vehemently opposed those doctrines but here we are concerned with his stated principles. Earlier, writing to Bishop Warburton he had elaborated further, including the remarkable claim that "Right opinions is at best but a very slender part of religion (which properly and directly consists in right tempers, words and actions) and frequently it is no part of religion; for it may be where there is not religion at all..." Earlier still, to James Clark, he had written that "orthodoxy or right opinion was never more than a slender part of religion , and sometimes no part at all...The religion of a child of God is righteousness, peace and joy in the Holy Ghost". "Religion in other words is the love of God and man, producing all holiness of conversation..."[28] This, in effect, resembles his later allowance that differences of language do not necessarily mean differences over the achievement of holiness and his earlier assertion to "John Smith" in 1746 that " even faith itself " is not "an end but a *means* only ...The end of the commandment is love...let this love be attained, by whatever means, and I am content."[29]

For continuing application of Wesley's principles of toleration today, we are bound to ask how far he was prepared to take his toleration of religious differences. The principle he laid down only applied to Christians of various kinds. He did not extend the courtesy to Deists or ant-Trinitarians like Dr John Taylor of Norwich.[30] What, too, was his attitude to adherents of other religions, those termed in Wesley's day "the heathen"? Whatever he might think of the range of opinions offered on this subject today, ranging from salvation seen as exclusively through Christ alone to the claim that all religions are in reality simply different ways of approaching the same God, it is worth observing that Wesley drew back from simply condemning "the heathen" to damnation. In his sermon on "Faith" in 1788 he defines the various levels of faith: of a materialist , a Deist, heathen and "Mahometans," of Jews, of Roman Catholics, of Protestants. This lists the value of the "faith" in ascending order. Thus he rates the faith of heathens and "Mahometans" to that of Deists. They are only required to live up to the light they have and some may well have the "essentials of true religion" by the "inward voice" of God.[31]

---

[28] J. Wesley, *Letters*, 4:297 (1765); 4:347(1762); 3:203 (1756).

[29] J. Wesley, *Works [BE]*, 26:203. See further below, section 5, for the significance of this statement for Wesley's view of the process of salvation.

[30] See J. Wesley's attack on Taylor's *Scripture Doctrine of Original Sin* (1735-36) in *The Doctrine of Original Sin* in *Works* (London: Wesleyan Conference Office, 1872), 9:196-444 and G. T. Eddy, *Dr Taylor of Norwich: Wesley's Arch-Heretic* (Peterborough: Epworth Press, 2003).

[31] J. Wesley, *Works [BE]*, 3:494.

16   *The Path of Holiness*

In a sermon "On Charity" (1784) he asks whether, since love of God derives from faith in Christ, "the whole heathen world is excluded from all possibility of salvation" he argues that he that believeth not shall be damned" (Mark 16:16) applies only to those to whom the gospel is preached and "we are not required to determine anything touching their final state." This we leave to God's judgement but "this we know, that he is not the God of the Christians only, but the God of the heathen also..." He is "merciful to those calling upon him with the light they have and accepts those fearing God and working righteousness."[32] Or again, in a sermon "On Living Without God" (1780) he distinguishes between Christianity and morality, observing that morality without Christianity is of no value to God "to those that are under the Christian dispensation..." "But I have no authority from the Word of God 'to judge those that are without'. Nor do I conceive that any man living has a right to sentence all the heathen and Mahometan world to damnation." They are left to him "who is the God of the heathen as well as the Christian, and who hateth nothing that he hath made..."[33]

This attitude was not peculiar or original to Wesley. It reflects long-standing teaching in the Catholic world on "invincible ignorance" and what some Protestants called "uncovenanted mercies." The former doctrine can be seen, for example, in St Thomas Aquinas and both occur in seventeenth century Anglican writers that Wesley may well have read. Indeed he used the phrase "invincible ignorance" in the sermon on "The Catholic Spirit."[34]

Wesley was not always consistent in the application of his own principles, especially in his hostility to Roman Catholics and Calvinists. On the former he reflected long-standing English political prejudices against granting Catholics full civil rights rather than purely religious antipathy and he was certainly against physical persecution or denial of their right to their own worship. On the latter and others disagreeing with him he sometimes claimed he did not condemn them for their "opinions" but for their attempts to force them on other people.[35]

But the distinction Wesley attempted to make between essential doctrines and "opinions" was open to difficulties. One person's "opinions" might be another's essential doctrine. Thus to the Baptist Gilbert Boyce Wesley had not only allowed for believers' and infant baptism but even (as was noted earlier) maintained that baptism itself was not strictly necessary to salvation. But Boyce claimed that Scripture "fully determined to one side only" i.e. be-

---

[32] J. Wesley, *Works [BE]*, 3:295-96.
[33] J. Wesley, *Works [BE]*, 4:174.
[34] J. Wesley, *Works [BE]*, 2:84 and note; citations in *OED* under the phrase include a work of 1711 and in a commentary on the Thirty-Nine Articles.
[35] For a discussion of his views of Roman Catholics see Henry D. Rack, *Reasonable Enthusiast*, 309-12; and for an expulsion from the Manchester society and the charge of being "Pope John" (a case where he claimed it was only for forcing their opinions on others) see John Byrom, *Remains* II (2) in Chetham Society (old series) vol. 44 (1857), 629-31, not referred to in Wesley's journal.

lievers' baptism.³⁶ Yet despite this recurring problem, it is arguable that it is only on the basis of some such distinction as Wesley's that it is possible to achieve ecumenical cooperation and even closer theological understanding as well as well as mutual toleration between different forms of Christianity and schools of thought. And Wesley's sentiments on the "heathen" remain a challenge to all forms of religious bigotry. For we are all subject to the judgement and mercy of a God "who is God of the heathen as well as Christian, and who hateth nothing that he hath made…"

Church Order

In Philip Pulman's recent controversial but thought-provoking *The Good Man Jesus and the Scoundrel Christ*, the "Christ" figure (portrayed as Jesus's twin brother) is advised that to implement Jesus's teaching of the Kingdom two things are necessary. One is "to make history the handmaid of posterity and not its governor." The other is that although Jesus thought the kingdom was coming so soon that no church was necessary, in fact "God wants the church to be the image of the Kingdom. Perfection does not belong here…Jesus, in his purity, is asking too much of people…"³⁷ One is reminded of the early twentieth-century Catholic Modernist, Alfred Loisy, who wrote that "Jesus preached the kingdom, and it was the church that came, enlarging the form of the gospel "and that "the church is as necessary to the gospel as the gospel to the church and that the two are really one."³⁸ Uncomfortable and indeed subversive though these remarks may seem to be they fairly reflect the discomfort that Christians as well as non-Christians have often felt at the contrasts between Jesus's teaching and the subsequent record of the churches.

What was Wesley's view of the church and its role? As is well-known he always denied that he was creating a new church and liked to claim that he was simply organizing Methodism as an auxiliary to the Church of England, though he also liked to claim that it was "peculiar to the people called Methodists" that they could become Methodists while remaining members of a variety of churches.³⁹ Yet it seems fair to say that Wesley's followers became in practice more and more self-sufficient. Indeed the deed of declaration in 1783, as Frank Baker remarked, implied that "Wesley was setting up Methodism as a separate institution…"⁴⁰

On the other hand it is important to recognize that there were "Church Methodists" in England who were hostile to Wesley's late ordinations and to Methodists receiving sacraments from their own preachers rather than in

---

³⁶ J. Wesley, *Works [BE]*, 26:420, 421, 425.
³⁷ Philip Pulman, *The Good Man Jesus and the Scoundrel Christ* (Edinburgh: Canongate Books, 2010), 97, 170-71.
³⁸ Alfred F. Loisy, *The Gospel and the Church* (London: Isbister, 1903), 166, 151.
³⁹ J. Wesley, "Thoughts upon a late Phenomenon" (1788) in *Works [BE]*, 13:266.
⁴⁰ Frank Baker, *John Wesley and the Church of England* (London: Epworth Press, 1970), 229. Baker offers a well-balanced account of the tensions in Wesley between adherence to the Church and willingness to "vary" from it.

their parish church. Recent research on the condition of the eighteenth-century Church of England and its clergy has considerably revised their traditionally bad reputation and suggested that they responded more flexibly and effectively to changing times than has often been allowed. This in turn may suggest that Wesley's "irregularities" as an Anglican clergyman may not be as extreme and un-Anglican as is often assumed.[41]

Yet despite Wesley's often-expressed devotion to the Church of England, some of his statements and action suggest that, consciously or unconsciously, he was developing a radical new view of the nature and role of church order. Perhaps, as I have suggested, the fact that he did not see himself as organizing a church enabled him to feel free to organize Methodism in any way he wished, regardless of ecclesiastical precedent, and in doing so to produce what was potentially a fresh and original attitude to church order.[42] Beginning as a stiff high churchman, refusing to acknowledge the validity of non-episcopal ministries, by the 1740s he was moving well away from this position. As we have seen, at the 1745 Conference he had allowed that in the early church a variety of types of ministry had developed without a single divinely-ordained pattern. By 1761 he was denying that there had been any unbroken apostolic succession of bishops.[43] In the 1740s, too, he had concluded from his personal reading of Lord King and Bishop Stillingfleet that he was following early church precedents in claiming that although a mere presbyter he was a "primitive episkopos" with the right to ordain though he did not excercize the supposed right until the 1780s.[44]

It is true that when he did begin to ordain he appears to have adopted a form of three-fold ministry consisting of deacons, elders or presbyters and superintendents, which he saw as one of the patterns appearing in the early church. But despite its apparent equation with a bishop, the superintendent was precisely what it said – an overseer, not a separate and higher order of ministry with the unique power to ordain. For Wesley's claim was that a pres-

---

[41] For revisionist views of the eighteenth-century Church of England see, for example, John Walsh, C. Colin Haydon and Stephen Taylor, eds., *The Church of England c.1689 to c.1833* (Cambridge: Cambridge University Press, 1993) and Jeremy Gregory and Jeffrey C. Chamberlain, eds., *The National Church in Local Perspective* (Woodbridge: The Boydell Press, 2003). For the Wesleys in this revised perspective see Jeremy Gregory, "'In the Church I will Live and Die'. John Wesley, the Church, and Methodism" in *Religious Identities in Britain, 1688-1832*, ed. William Gibson and Robert Ingram (Aldershot and Burlington, NJ: Ashgate, 2005); Jeremy Gregory, "Charles Wesley and the Eighteenth Century" in *Charles Wesley: Life, Literature and Legacy*, ed. K.G.C. Newport and Ted A. Campbell (Peterborough: Epworth Press, 2007), 18-39. For a recent study of Charles Wesley's support for "Church Methodism" see Gareth Lloyd, "Charles Wesley: A New Evaluation of his Life and Ministry" (Ph.D. diss., University of Liverpool, 2002), chapter 8 especially 247-85.

[42] Rack, *Reasonable Enthusiast*, 238, 402.

[43] J. Wesley, *Letters*, 4:140-41.

[44] John to Charles Wesley 19 August 1785 in Wesley, *Letters*, 7:284.

byter could ordain.[45] The much-discussed issue of Wesley's ordinations, their significance and validity, need not be pursued further here. What is much more important for my present purpose is to ask whether Wesley's order of priorities and claims for his Methodist behavior and organization implied a more radical attitude to the whole question of church order than has been commonly recognized. It is perhaps surprising that there has not been more discussion of the implications of a celebrated passage in his correspondence with the pseudonymous "John Smith" in 1746.

"Smith" had charged that Wesley did a great deal of harm by "setting aside order." To this Wesley responded: "What do you mean by order? A plan of church discipline? What plan? The primitive? Or our own?" But then "What is the end of all *ecclesiastical order*? Is it not to bring souls from the power of Satan to God? And to build them up in his fear and love? Order, then is so far valuable as it answers these ends and if it answers them not, it is nothing worth." Keeping to the usual parish-bound Anglican ministry has not reached the neglected masses as Methodist methods have done. He added that "where the knowledge and love of God are, *true order* will not be wanting..."[46] Wesley was laying down the fundamental principle that what is necessary for preaching the gospel and exercizing pastoral care must take precedence over any system of church order. To follow through this principle is far-reaching and liable to make uncomfortable reading for church leaders.

No doubt Wesley's downright assertion of evangelistic priorities over "order" was the product of his reaction to the practical needs of Methodism and in response to criticisms of his irregularities. But it has been argued by Professor Hempton that the piecemeal organization which Wesley developed for Methodism appears to be in tune with contemporary fashion. Partly following Frederick Dreyer, Hempton claims that one of the ways in which Methodism reflected Enlightenment values was in the principle of free association, exemplified in the English taste for voluntary organizations. This, as applied to church organization, contrasted strongly with systems of church order laid down on the basis of dogma or church tradition such as divine right episcopacy or Presbyterianism.[47]

Wesley certainly had an early predilection for religious societies for mutual cultivation of the spiritual life, but it has to be added that his Methodist organization, though to be classed as voluntary rather than official or based on dogmatic principles, was from another point of view dominated and controlled by Wesley. It is significant that after his death the Methodist leader-

---

[45] For discussions of Wesley's actions see Baker, *John Wesley and the Church of England* , chapters 9 and 15. See also Rack, *Reasonable Enthusiast*, 293-96, 523-26.

[46] J. Wesley, *Works [BE]*, 26:205-206.

[47] David Hempton, *Methodism: Empire of the Spirit* (New Haven: Yale University Press, 2005), 50-52; Frederick Dreyer, *The Genesis of Methodism* (London: Associated Universities Presses, 1999), 93, 96-105. For the English associationist culture see Peter Clark, *British Clubs and Societies 1580-1800. The Origins of an Associationist World* (Oxford: Clarendon Press, 2000), though unfortunately he chose to say little about religious associations (See 33-35, 55-57 for exceptions).

ship in Britain resolved not "to appoint another king in Israel" and developed government by committees instead. Government by a limited number of superintendents in a quasi-episcopal system as recommended in the "Lichfield Plan" of 1794 was rejected. The committee model at least allowed for debate and the airing of minority views, so reducing the risk of abuses of power by a single ruler or elite.[48] The paradox here was perhaps that Wesley's legacy was that of a single authoritarian ruler but the impossibility of anyone inheriting that mantle (whether or not deemed desirable) made a different structure of authority inevitable. Indeed Wesley's own establishment of the Conference as his successor and leaving open the role of the President had pointed the way. It has to be emphasized, however, that what has just been described and commented on applies only to Britain. In America his legacy was, partly from necessity, partly by choice, differently handled.[49] The point being emphasized here is that the implications for any settled system of church order by Wesley's priorities as stated to "John Smith" are disturbing, even revolutionary. They deserve to be regarded as a perpetual challenge to church leaders and not least to Methodists.

Wesley did not, perhaps, fully live up to his own ideal. The essential features of his system had all emerged by the late 1740s and at that stage conformed to the principles he had laid down to "Smith" and was not significantly modified thereafter. Indeed he frequently adjured his followers to observe and not to attempt to mend his rules.[50] But what was well-designed to meet some of the weaknesses of contemporary Anglican and Dissenter church structures did not necessarily fit later and changing times. There were, for example, complaints in the later nineteenth century that the short-term postings of Methodist ministers were not suited to the long-term pastoral needs of urban situations and city missions with extended appointments were developed as a consequence.

Other aspects of Wesley's system were also open to debate. Two other characteristics have attracted particular attention and have caused tension, perhaps almost from the start. One is its "connexionalism" which Wesley strongly defended. That is to say, the concept of a nationwide system of societies linked together by common rules and a common system of oversight. What Wesley resisted was the localized independence of most Dissenter churches of his day and the self-sufficiency of the Anglican parish. But there were always countervailing pressures towards localism in Methodism and in

---

[48] For the phrase "another king in Israel" see the Halifax Circular of 30 March 1791 in Rupert E. Davies et al., eds., *History of the Methodist Church in Great Britain* (London: Epworth Press, 1988), vol.4: 241-42. For the Lichfield Plan see op. cit., 257-59.

[49] For a study of the ethos and significance of the American system see Russell E. Richey, *The Methodist Conference in America* (Nashville, Tennessee: Kingswood Books, 1996). For the English Methodist Conference during Wesley's lifetime see the introduction to *The Methodist Societies: The Minutes of Conference*, Henry D. Rack, ed. *Works [BE]*, 10.

[50] J. Wesley, *Letters*, 4:171, 180, 194.

the nineteenth century there was also resistance to Wesleyan ministerial dominance and the result was a series of secessions with less centralization and more lay representation.

The other feature of Methodism which could cause tension was its societary ethos, exemplified in the long term by the class meeting and in earlier years by the more exacting bands and select bands for pursuing perfection. Methodist membership was defined by membership of the class and this provoked much debate in the nineteenth century. Some preferred communicant membership as in other churches. On the other hand there have been attempts in more recent years to revive the class meeting or modern equivalents as a means to revive Methodist dynamism. Wesley's advocacy of the class and other small group meetings for cultivating piety was based on his belief that "the Bible knows nothing of solitary Christianity" and "no holiness but social holiness." The latter aphorism in its original context clearly did not refer to what we might term "social service" or a "social gospel" though we shall see later that such applications of Methodist aspirations to holiness were certainly not excluded.[51]

My concern in this discussion has not been to criticize or defend particular aspects of Methodism or its institutions but to emphasise Wesley's fundamental principle. That principle was to subordinate particular schemes of "order" to the requirements of evangelism and pastoral care. To pursue this principle consistently is to be permanently open to the uncomfortable challenges of change.

The Nature and Process of Salvation

The background to Wesley's views on this lie far back in Christian thought and reflect the recurring tension between the role of divine grace and human effort in the process of salvation. It can be seen, for example, in the classic confrontation between St Augustine and Pelagius, between Catholics and Protestants during the Reformation, Calvinists and Arminians in the seventeenth century, Jesuits and Jansenists in the same period and evangelical Calvinists and their critics (including Wesley) in the eighteenth century.

What seems to have been a common Anglican position by the early eighteenth century was a compromise expressed, for example, by Bishop Gibson of London in 1730: "faith in Christ is the foundation of a Christian's *title* to heaven" but that "repentance and good works are necessary conditions of

---

[51] The "solitary religion" quotation was from a "serious man" during Wesley's Oxford period: see Henry Moore, *Life of Rev. John Wesley* (London: John Kessler, 1825), vol.1, 162. "No holiness but social holiness" is from the preface to *Hymns and Sacred Poems* (1739) in J. Wesley, *Works*, 14:321 and Sermon 24 "Sermon on the Mount" IV in J. Wesley, *Works [BE]*, 1: 533-34, cited by Randy L. Maddox in "The Role of Christian Faith" (above, note 10), 17 and note 69. For a recent study of the class meeting see Andrew F. Goodhead, "A Crown and a Cross: The Significance, Development and Decline of the Methodist Class Meeting in Eighteenth-century England" (Ph.D. diss., Sheffield University, 2007).

obtaining it..."⁵² This balanced the need for grace with the need to respond to grace by holy living and as Gibson made clear avoided both the excessive emphasis on faith alone among the Puritans and the excessive emphasis on good works alone among some eighteenth century moralists. A similar view to that expressed by Gibson appears to underlie Wesley's disciplined search for holiness in his Oxford period, as he came to see in later life after initially dismissing it as a vain search for salvation by works in the immediate aftermath of his Aldersgate experience in 1738. Experience and further reflection later convinced him that this was a mistake. Hence the modifying footnotes to his negative estimate of his missions to Georgia and the famous account in his journal for 24 May 1738 of his earlier religious life when he published the new edition of 1774-75. These included the admissions that even before Aldersgate he had "the faith of a servant, though not that of a *son*."⁵³

What is remarkable is that although Wesley's pre-conversion Arminian-based "holy living'" piety was often shared by other future evangelicals, most of them turned Calvinist after their conversions whereas Wesley developed a form of evangelical Arminianism. He asserted that the possibility of salvation was open to all and combined belief in the need of justification by grace through faith with the necessity of the subsequent development of holiness to the point of "perfection." As early as 1746 he had declared to Thomas Church that the "main doctrines" of Methodism were repentance, faith and holiness. "The first of these we account, as it were, the porch of religion, the next the door, the third religion itself." ⁵⁴ Wesley saw justification by faith less as the central doctrine of Christianity than as the beginning of an extended pilgrimage whose real goal was perfection.

Portraying this goal as achievable in our present life, either by a gradual process of discipline or as a sudden gift or as a combination of both led to Wesley being suspected by Calvinist evangelicals of slipping back into a "popish" salvation by "works." Wesley defended himself by asserting that even the allegedly "perfect" depended every moment on divine grace.⁵⁵

---

⁵² [Edmund Gibson], *The Great Work of our Redemption by Christ and the Several Branches of it Represented...under the Second Head of the Bishop of London's Second Pastoral Letter* (London: J. Roberts, 1731), 29. Though see Jeffrey .S. Chamberlain, "Moralism, Justification and the Controversy over Methodism" in *Journal of Ecclesiastical History*, vol. 44 (1993): 652-78, which shows that eighteenth-century preaching was not merely moralistic despite significant differences from Methodism.

⁵³ J. Wesley's journal in *Works [BE]*, 18:215 and his note.

⁵⁴ J. Wesley, *Works [BE]*, 9:227.

⁵⁵ Wesley's most careful exposition of the relationship between grace and human effort, the necessity of both and the way in which human effort is always informed by and dependent upon grace is in the sermon "On Working out our own Salvation" in *Works [BE]*, 3:199-209. After the unguarded assertion of the value of works in the controversial minutes of the 1770 Methodist Conference, at the 1771 Conference it was affirmed that "we have no confidence but in the alone merits of our Lord and Saviour Jesus Christ for justification or salvation" and that although Christians should do good works as they are able, they "have no part in meriting or purchasing our salvation", *Works [BE]*, 10:403.

In 1935 George Croft Cell, reacting against what he saw as the humanist trends of his time reasserted Wesley's reformation credentials. But he also made the memorable claim that Wesley had accomplished the remarkable feat of healing the historic theological rift between Catholics and Protestants by creating a "necessary synthesis of the Protestant ethic of grace with the Catholic ethic of holiness..."[56] Though Wesley undoubtedly drew on both sides of the historic theological divide, one must hesitate to credit him with the achievement of theological originality and sophistication of this magnitude. Yet it is reasonable to allow that he was indeed drawing on the two different traditions and trying to reconcile them so as to benefit from the strengths and avoid the weaknesses each had shown.

What made his teaching even more controversial, and not only to evangelicals, was his rash use of the term "perfection" which, as he had frequently to explain, did not make such an extreme and unqualified claim as the term appeared to imply. In response to the extreme claims of some perfectionist revivalists in the early 1760s, he attempted to explain and justify what he claimed had been his consistent teaching for many years past in his *Plain Account of Christian Perfection* (1767). As well as allowing for the survival of what he termed "infirmities," it appears that he was only able to claim the possibility of an imperfect "perfection" by using a very limited definition of the sin which he claimed was overcome. This was sin as "a voluntary transgression of a known law which it was in our power to obey."[57] That this limited definition was inadequate and open to dangers is obvious and it appears from Wesley's and his followers' descriptions of what the experience was like is that it amounted to an uninterrupted sense of love towards God and other people. This may help to explain the paradox of Wesley asserting both that perfection could be received in a moment by faith and that it could be worked up to by discipline and improved upon – presumably extended and deepened – after being first received.[58] The doctrine was controversial within as well outside Methodism and has continued to be so. Wesley's successors were often uncomfortable with the doctrine, played it down or divided into those who emphasised an instant "second blessing" and those preferring an indefinite growth in holiness. Variations on the former position fed into nineteenth-century "holiness" movements and were one source of later Pentecostalism.[59]

---

[56] George Croft Cell, *The Rediscovery of John Wesley* (New York: Henry Holt, 1935), 361.

[57] J. Wesley, *Works [BE]*, 25:289, 318 in 1731 but repeated in 1772 in *Letters*, 5:322. How Wesley could argue for a limited "perfection," using this definition of sin while also recognizing a less questionable and more penetrating notion of it is well expressed by Colin W. Williams, *John Wesley's Theology Today* (London: Epworth Press, 1960), 170.

[58] For a further exposition of this point of view see Rack, *Reasonable Enthusiast*, 398-400.

[59] See, for example, John L. Peters, *Christian Perfection in American Methodism*, (Nashville, Tennessee: Abingdon Press, 1956).

Wesley might have avoided much controversy and misunderstanding had he not used the term "perfection" especially as he was forced to qualify it. It is true that the term had a long pedigree in Catholic spirituality and on some of this he drew. But he always affirmed that he found the doctrine in Scripture and his peculiar claims for what can be achieved in this life and for a possible instant blessing are hardly what Catholic spiritual writers had in mind. Wesley himself often used the less problematical term "holiness" and it was this that he justifiably claimed had been the purpose of his spiritual quest since his Oxford days. The aim of Methodism was, he once remarked "to reform the nation and in particular the church and to spread Scriptural holiness over the land."[60]

We need not enter here into the long and controversial history of Wesley's perfectionism and the theological problems it raises, but if we are looking to him for lasting and fruitful principles, they are probably to be found in a vision of the Christian life as a pilgrimage in quest of a holy life. This may form a bridge between different forms of Christianity as the definition, scope and applications of "holiness" and the means to achieve it can cover a wide variety of traditions and methods in spirituality. For those in the evangelical tradition accustomed to see what Wesley called the "door" as the way to become a "born-again" Christian via a particular kind of conversion experience as the route to receiving justification by faith, Wesley's view of salvation offers a salutary challenge. To repeat – he saw justification as only the first step towards achieving what he saw as real Christianity in terms of the progressive achievement of holiness. In doing so he increasingly recognized that behind differing forms of language what mattered was this achievement, "by whatever means."

Although the subject cannot be pursued in detail here (though some would certainly wish to add this to my five Wesley insights of lasting significance) it should be recognised that Wesley's notion of "holiness" was neither narrowly individualistic nor exclusively "spiritual." One of his early aphorisms was "no holiness but social holiness." In its original context we have seen that this referred to the need to share and nourish one's spiritual life in company with others, particularly in small groups. [61]It is, however, clear that a sense of the need for a social application of a practical kind in terms of charitable giving and personal service to the poor was an early concern in Wesley's own life in Oxford. That concern was frequently expressed in his later career.[62]

In general terms it seems clear that Wesley saw this concern as an application of his notion of holiness or perfection in its aspect as love of neighbour

---

[60] "Large Minutes" of 1763 in *Works [BE]*, 10:845.

[61] See above, note 51.

[62] For this concern see John Walsh, "John Wesley and the Community of Goods" in *Studies in Church History*, Subsidia 7 (Oxford: Blackwell, 1990), 25-59. Manfred Marquardt, *John Wesley's Social Ethics* (Nashville, Tennessee: Abingdon Press, 1992). See also Richard Heitzenrater, ed. *The Poor and the People Called Methodists* (Nashville, Tennessee: Abingdon Press, 2002).

as well as God. The fact that this did not involve any anachronistic notion of a "social gospel" or "welfare state" does not invalidate seeing this as a principle of much wider application in the changed circumstances of later times. Though his care for the poor has often been criticized as merely individual charity dictated by the narrow horizons of his day, this is to underestimate its significance. In fact it was not purely individualistic but implemented, at least in part, in terms of voluntary collective effort through Wesley himself and local Methodist societies. One significant example was that of Strangers' Friend Societies in several towns, run by Methodists but for the benefit of non-Methodists.[63]

What certainly has long-term relevance is Wesley's conspicuous concern for the poor, including his insistence that they were not necessarily to be blamed for their plight and that they should be helped individually and treated with courtesy. His attitude may be seen as informing the "preference for the poor" as a Christian principle which has informed more recent church-based initiatives. It also contrasts with the recurring attempts to distinguish between the "deserving" and "undeserving" poor which informed many official and voluntary (including evangelical) attempts to deal with poverty in the nineteenth century. That suspicious and censorious attitude has recently revived in some peculiarly dogmatic and unlovely forms in the demonizing of the poor as scroungers and wilful dependents on welfare benefits.[64]

Conclusion

One conclusion from the Wesley principles discussed here is that in each case they exhibit connections between beliefs which have often been pursued separately and commonly perceived as mutually contradictory or incompatible with each other. In Wesley's case they seem to exist rather in creative tension with beneficial results. There is an interesting exposition by David Hempton of one aspect of this, to the effect that Methodist dynamism came from the tension (evident also within Wesley himself) between "enthusiasm" and "enlightenment." [65] Unlike the dogmatism and exclusiveness of his early life, the mature Wesley as theologian and religious leader and much else became what might be termed a "both-and" rather than an "either-or" Christian. Such an attitude, it may be suggested, is a healthy and fruitful principle for Christians in every age to follow rather than the bigoted exclusiveness which has too often disfigured the life of Christianity.

---

[63] On the Stranger's Friend Societies see, Luke Tyerman, *Life and Times of the Rev. John Wesley, M.A.* 2nd ed. (London: Hodder and Stoughton, 1872), vol. 3:252-54. See Edgar T. Selby, "The Journals of James Chubb" in *Proceedings of the Wesley Historical Society*, vol. 29 no. 2 (1953): 32-35.

[64] For further discussion of the scope of Wesley's social concerns see Rack, *Reasonable Enthusiast*, 361-70, 447-49.

[65] Hempton, *Methodism: Empire of the Spirit*, chapter 2, especially 41, 52-53.

Chapter 2

The Wesleys and the Evangelical Tradition

By T. A. Noble

Introduction

The Evangelical tradition is generally thought to have its origin in that movement in eighteenth-century Britain and her North American colonies know as the "Evangelical Revival" or the "Great Awakening." The Wesley brothers and George Whitefield were the leading figures in England. In New England, it was Jonathan Edwards, in Scotland Ebenezer and Ralph Erskine, in Wales, Howel Harris and Daniel Rowland. George Whitefield was the itinerant who preached powerfully throughout the British dominions, but all of them were conscious of being part of the widespread movement. Isaac Watts arranged to re-publish Jonathan Edwards' work, *A Faithful Narrative*, about the revival in Northampton, Massachusetts from 1733 to 1735, a work which helped to shape the revivals in England and Scotland.[66] And the movement was consciously linked not only across these countries but also across denominations. George Whitefield, though a clergyman of the Church of England, was welcomed to preach at the Cambuslang revival in Presbyterian Scotland,[67] and also among the Congregationalists of New England. By the end of the century, Thomas Chalmers and Charles Simeon emerged as the leading Evangelical figures in the Churches of Scotland and England respectively. William Wilberforce, the Tory MP encouraged by Wesley to undertake his

---

[66] See Frank Lambert's slightly jaundiced account, *Inventing the 'Great Awakening'* (Princeton: Princeton University Press, 1999).

[67] See the published thesis of that Nazarene, then Presbyterian scholar, Arthur Fawcett, *The Cambuslang Revival: The Scottish Evangelical Revival of the Eighteenth Century* (Edinburgh: Banner of Truth, 1971). Fawcett was a predecessor of Herbert McGonigle as minister of the Uddingston Church of the Nazarene in Lanarkshire.

fight against slavery, and Hannah More, whose writings were widely influential, were notable among the Evangelical laity. The Baptist pastor and cobbler, William Carey, took the lead in launching British Evangelicals into the world-wide missionary movement which was to change the whole demography of global Christianity. Meanwhile in the newly independent North American colonies, Francis Asbury led the remarkable Methodist advance. All of these together were the major leaders in the Evangelical movement throughout the English-speaking world which has had such an immense impact on world Christianity and continues to be vibrant and growing today.

It is true that the term "Evangelical" was not much used by Wesley himself since it only came into use to refer to the heirs of the revival later in the century. It is also true that the word has been subject recently to definitional debate—especially in the United States. It is presumed by some that Evangelicalism is an American form of religion taking its rise after the Second World War,[68] a perspective which is compounded by the tendency to equate Evangelicalism simplistically with fundamentalism or to see it as merely a development from the fundamentalism which emerged between the world wars. This essay seeks to overcome such a myopic distortion of church history by providing a more nuanced appraisal of the origins of Evangelicalism.

Defining Characteristics of the Tradition

David Bebbington and Mark Noll are very helpful here in widening our horizons. It is true that Bebbington's definitive study, *Evangelicalism in Modern Britain*,[69] limits the story largely to the British Isles. But Bebbington also gives a longer perspective in that he extends the time line back to the 1730s, the beginning of the Evangelical Revival, and he offers a working definition of Evangelicalism which has become almost standard. Evangelical Christians, he suggests, may be identified by four characteristics: conversionism, activism, biblicism and crucicentrism. Mark Noll's more recent work, *The Rise of Evangelicalism*, combines wider horizons both geographically and chronologically.[70]

Bebbington's four characteristic marks are very helpful in setting wider parameters than those which we might apply to Fundamentalism. It is true that Fundamentalism qualifies by all four of these characteristics to be included within Evangelicalism. However it has to be said that while they may be sincere Evangelicals, their particular concerns tend to distort the Evangelical faith. Starting from a narrow version of the idea of biblical inerrancy

---

[68] See among many examples, Mark Ellingsen, *The Evangelical Movement: Growth, Impact, Controversy, Dialog* (Minneapolis, Minnesota: Augsburg Fortress Press, 1989).

[69] David Bebbington, *Evangelicalism in Modern Britain: A History from the 1730s to the 1980s* (London: Routledge, 1989).

[70] Mark A. Noll, *The Rise of Evangelicalism: The Age of Edwards, Whitefield and the Wesleys* (Downers Grove, Illinois: InterVarsity Press, 2010). There are also numerous other attempts to define what constitutes the Anglo-Saxon Evangelical movement which we do not need to repeat here.

propagated particularly by American Calvinists of the old Princeton school (the Hodges and Warfield), they have added to that a very wooden interpretation of Genesis 1, resulting in the false "science" of "creationism" (not to be confused with the Christian doctrine of *creatio ex nihilo*), the adoption of the fanciful scheme of dispensationalism invented in the nineteenth century by John Nelson Darby, and more recently, the adoption of a certain political stance. The last of these contributes to the alignment of so-called "liberal" and "conservative" views in theology with liberal and conservative views in politics, a sad polarization from which the church in America needs to be delivered. These positions, while sincerely held by many good people on both sides of the polarization, become too easily more of an ideology to argue for than a faith by which to live.

And yet it has to be said that all Evangelicals should be deeply concerned with truth and with the mission of the Church to proclaim the truth. Bebbington's four characteristic marks of Evangelicalism, traced over a history of two and half centuries, help us to see the wider picture, and the Wesleys certainly meet those qualifications. John Wesley's famous "conversion" at Aldersgate Street and the life-long thrust of his ministry thereafter that his hearers should be *born again* certainly make him a "conversionist."[71] His amazing exertions over five decades of continuous preaching, writing, travelling, and ministry to the poor constitute an "activism" second to none. His focus on the Bible as *homo unius libri* make it clear that for him the Bible is the final authority in all matter of faith and doctrine. And his proclamation of justification by faith was certainly centered in "Christ crucified." As for Charles, all four characteristics apply also to him, particularly the last. His Christ-centered hymns focus our attention on "the blood of his cross" (Col. 1:20). It was appropriate that Billy Graham, one of the leading Evangelicals of the twentieth century, should make one of Charles's hymns a theme song in his "crusades": "And can it be that I should gain an interest in the Saviour's blood?" That other Evangelical hymn-writer and poet, William Cowper, similarly focussed on the deliberately shocking metaphor from the book of Revelation when he extended it to write, "There is a fountain filled with blood, drawn from Emmanuel's veins."

And yet the question must be posed whether Bebbington's four characteristics are theologically adequate. They are certainly helpful for the historian trying to set limits on a historical movement. Bebbington argues that Evangelicalism so defined began in the eighteenth century, and it is true that the Evangelical Revival of the eighteenth century exhibits some new features compared with what went before. Most notable perhaps was the new focus on "the new birth" and the passion for evangelism and mission which accompanied it. There was a deep conviction of coming judgment and a deep concern that every person needed to be delivered from "the wrath of God against all ungodliness and wickedness" (Rom. 1:18). One thinks of Jonathan Edwards'

---

[71] See Kenneth J. Collins and John Tyson, eds., *Conversion in the Wesleyan Tradition* (Nashville, Tennessee: Abingdon Press, 2001).

sermon of 1741 on "Sinners in the Hands of an Angry God."[72] But for the Evangelical preachers, not only Edwards but also Whitefield and especially the Wesleys, that wrath was the form which the passionate love of God took when confronted with the sickening evil of human sin. And in the deeper mystery of his love, God had provided "the Lamb of God who bears away the sin of the world" (John 1: 29). Paradoxically he had provided his own propitiation by which our sins are wiped out. But given that in Christ, "we have been reconciled to God," the Church has been entrusted with the mission of exhorting all to "be reconciled" (II Cor.: 18-20). It was that passion to preach this gospel to every creature (Matt. 16:15 AV) and to "make disciples of all nations" (Matt.28:19, NRSV) which perhaps differentiated the Evangelical movement of the eighteenth century from what went before it.

The Heritage from the Puritans and Pietists

And yet we have to say that the eighteenth-century Evangelicals were the heirs of those who went before them, notably the English Puritans and the German Pietists. Isaac Watts, who has been called the last of the Puritans, was a significant personal link. But it is important to understand that Puritanism began within the Church of England. In its origins in the Elizabethan era, it was a movement to further "purify" the Church of England to make it more like Calvin's "Reformed" church in Geneva. Puritans were not unique in their deep piety: that also characterized many of their opponents within the Church. What distinguished them was their desire to abolish bishops, liturgy and vestments. It has been said that the Reformation was essentially a Reformation of worship and that was one of Puritans' prime concerns. Following Zwingli, Calvin and the Swiss Reformation, many Puritans wanted to ban from worship anything not explicitly found in Scripture – such as choirs, organs, and non-biblical liturgy and ceremonial – and to confine worship to prayer and preaching, and to metrical psalms and paraphrases of other Scripture passages all of which (unlike other hymnody) were held to be directly inspired by the Holy Spirit. In addition, many Puritans expressed a desire for expository biblical preaching such as was to be found in the Presbyterian tradition of Scotland, the kind of preaching which produced deep conviction and spiritual conversion. After the English Civil War the Puritans seemed to have triumphed (although sadly by force of Cromwell's arms), but with the Restoration of the monarchy and the Elizabethan Settlement of the Church of England in 1660, they were ejected from their parishes in 1662 and became the "Dissenters" – the three "Nonconformist" denominations of Presbyterians, Congregationalists and Baptists.

Like Watts, Edwards, as a New England Congregationalist, was in the Puritan tradition (although Watts was a revolutionary in adding hymns to the metrical psalms). And although Whitefield was a clergyman of the Church of

---

[72] For an account of the theology of Jonathan Edwards, see Stephen R. Holmes, *God of Grace and God of Glory* (Edinburgh: T & T Clark, 2000).

England, his dramatic preaching was welcomed (as we have seen) by Presbyterians in Scotland and Congregationalists in New England, and he stood in the same Calvinist tradition. With the Wesleys it was rather more complicated. Or perhaps we should say that they were much more "ecumenical" or "catholic" or "eclectic" in their theology. Certainly there was a strong Puritan influence. Both their grandfathers had been Puritan ministers put out of the Church of England in the Great Ejection. Robert Monk has documented the Puritan influence on Wesley.[73] The Puritan influence was even stronger for George Whitefield. He had been part of the Holy Club at Oxford and had become there a "serious Christian," but it was after he left Oxford that Whitefield had his evangelical conversion through the influence of the Puritan tradition.[74] It was to be expected therefore that Whitefield and the brothers should be allies in the early days of the revival, and it was Whitefield who persuaded John Wesley to be (as he said) "more vile" by adopting field-preaching. Despite the theological dispute which quickly arose on predestination, they still regarded themselves as allies in the cause of the gospel, Whitefield requesting that John Wesley should preach at his funeral. And Wesley insisted that his doctrine of justification by faith was virtually the same as Calvin's: "I think on justification just as Mr Calvin does... In this respect I do not differ from him an hair's breadth."[75]

All of that made the Wesleys fellow Evangelicals, but they differed from those in the Calvinist Puritan tradition in that the primary influence which led them to evangelical faith was that of Lutheran Pietism. Pietism arose in the seventeenth-century Lutheran church in Germany as a reaction against spiritual lethargy. Long sermons, "academic" in the wrong sense, were in essence, extended arguments for Lutheran dogmatics, rather than biblical expositions which spoke to the people and prompted conversion. Johannes Arndt, followed by Jacob Spener, had invented *collegia pietatis*, small groups of lay people praying together and discussing the Bible to apply its teachings to their lives. The Moravians, although they could trace their heritage back before Luther to the teachings of Jan Hus in the late fourteenth century, had become part of the Pietist movement. Moving from Moravia to settle on the lands of Count Zinzendorf in eastern Saxony, they established the community of Herrnhut in 1722, and experienced a revival which they attributed to the work of the Holy Spirit. They were pioneers of the modern missionary movement, and it was a group of Moravian missionaries on their way to the British colony of Georgia which first impressed John Wesley. On his return to London, it was the Moravian, Peter Böhler, who was the mentor leading John Wesley to justifying faith, and it was through that influence that Wesley

---

[73] Robert Monk, *John Wesley: His Puritan Heritage* (Nashville, Tennessee: Abingdon Press, 1966).
[74] See Arnold Dallimore, *George Whitefield*, vols. 1 & 2 (Edinburgh: Banner of Truth, 1970 & 1980); and Frank Lambert, *Pedlar in Divinity: George Whitefield and the Transatlantic Revivals, 1737–1770* (Princeton: Princeton University Press, 1993).
[75] J. Wesley, Letter to John Newton of 14 May 1765, in John Telford, ed., *The Letters of John Wesley* (London: Epworth Press, 1931), vol. 4:298. (Hereafter, Wesley, *Letters*).

found himself in a religious meeting in Aldersgate Street within the old city of London, where "one was reading Luther's preface to the Epistle to the Romans," through which Wesley came to "trust in Christ and Christ alone for salvation."

Rooted in the Reformation

Clearly then, Wesley stood in the tradition of both Luther and Calvin in coming to see "justification by faith" as the heart of the gospel. This provides clues for true appreciation of what it means to be in the Evangelical tradition. Although Evangelicals in the English-speaking lands have a particular subculture, the Evangelical tradition is neither a British nor an American invention: it is the tradition of the Reformation. Indeed it is unfortunate that in the English-speaking world the Reformation tradition has been designated by using the word "Protestant." That was originally a *political* word, referring to the "Protest" of some of the German princes of the so-called Holy Roman Empire at the Diet of Speyer in 1529 at what seemed to be an attempt by imperial government to ban reforms in the Church. But the *theological* word adopted by the Lutherans to refer to their churches after the Reformation was "Evangelical." The Church now reformed was known (as it still is today) as *die Evangelische Kirche*. The choice of terminology was significant, for what it highlighted was the central concern of that branch of the Church catholic to be centred on the *evangel*—the gospel. In the succeeding centuries, many Protestant denominations in Europe and America have shifted away from this Reformation faith and heritage, being influenced by Deism and the later so-called "Liberalism," two movements which re-shaped Christian theology to fit with elements of Enlightenment and "modernity." Against this background therefore, it is right to think of Evangelicals today as heirs to the doctrines of the Reformation and indeed (like the Reformers) to the Nicene faith of the Fathers, and who seek the vital spiritual life which characterized both the Reformation and the later Evangelical Revival.

Evangelicals are therefore first and foremost committed to the gospel. The eighteenth-century Evangelical Revival was not the beginning of the Evangelical movement: rather, as the name tells us, it was its "revival." True, there were new features. First, they inherited from Puritans and Pietists a greater emphasis on the new birth than is found in the Reformers. Luther certainly talks in one place about his discovery of the truth of justification by faith as like being born again,[76] but Calvin speaks of "regeneration" as a synonym for repentance, and sees it not as a moment at the beginning of the Christian life, but as something which continues life-long. And he tells us almost nothing of his own conversion.[77] For Wesley and his contemporaries, as for the Pietist and Puritans, conversion or the new birth (regeneration) was thought of as

---

[76] *Weimar Ausgabe*, 54: 185-86. (Cf. *Luther's Works*, vol. 34, Lewis Spitz and Helmut Lehman, eds. (Minneapolis, Minnesota: Fortress Press, 1960), 336-37)

[77] See François Wendel, *Calvin* (Glasgow: Collins, 1963), 37-45; and T.H.L. Parker, *John Calvin* (London: Lion, 1975), 15-27, and Appendix 2, 192-196.

the initial moment of Christian faith. This was connected to the second new emphasis, on evangelism, leading eventually to the world-wide missionary movement. But these new developments do not make the Evangelical Revival the beginning of the Evangelical tradition; that began with the Reformation.

It is appropriate then to define Evangelical Christianity by drawing on the four great "alones" which are said to sum up the Reformation faith across all its varieties: Lutheran, Reformed and Anabaptist. The first of these, *sola fide*, arose right at the beginning of the German Reformation in Luther's wrestling spiritually and exegetically with the meaning of justification. His great breakthrough was in differentiating justification from sanctification. This Reformation distinction is perhaps somewhat more clear-cut than it is in Paul's own writings, but what it correctly captures is that we are *declared* righteous or holy through faith before we are *made* righteous or holy. This was the conundrum Luther wrestled with: how God could be just and yet justify or acquit the *ungodly*. The answer was that God's righteousness is not that justice by which he condemns the guilty, but rather that faithfulness to his covenant promises by which he redeems his people from their sins. Redemptive action rather than vengeance characterized God's righteousness. But this led to the question whether faith was not in itself a kind of good work by which we merit our justification. Luther's answer was that even faith was the gift of God, implying that our salvation is totally a gift which we do not merit in any way: that is to say, that it was *sola gratia*. Here the Reformation was truly Augustinian. Augustine did not grasp the doctrine of justification by faith as it was later clarified by Luther, but he did insist against Pelagius that salvation was entirely by grace. From his perspective, God's prevenient grace (*gratia praeveniens*) prepared the will (*voluntas praeparatur a Deo*) so that the elect freely but inevitably believe and enter in. Persons were then gradually transformed through the grace infused into them by the sacraments until eventually at the last judgement, individuals were declared truly righteous and holy. For the Reformers, salvation was similarly *sola gratia*, but God, through grace, gave the faith by which the believer was justified not at the end, but at the beginning of the life of faith.

But it is really with the third of the "alones" that we come to the heart of the gospel as the Reformers understood it. Against all the mediators they saw in the religion of the pre-Reformation Church – earthly priests and heavenly saints – they insisted that there was "one Mediator between God and man, the man Christ Jesus" (I Tim 2:5). Salvation therefore was *a solo Christo* (by Christ alone) for there was "no other name under heaven given among men, whereby we must be saved" (Acts 4:12, AV). Their focus was particularly on "Christ crucified," his death on the cross for our sins, and picking up the doctrine of the Atonement as it had been formulated since Anselm, they focussed on the satisfaction provided by that propitiation. Going further than Anselm, they not only insisted that Christ satisfied God's justice so that we need not be punished, but taught that Christ bore our punishment in our place. He alone therefore was "the Lamb of God who bore away the sin of the world."

Solus Christus can therefore be seen as the true theological heart of the Reformation.

Finally, many Reformation theologians came to assert that Christian theology must be drawn from Scripture alone (*sola Scriptura*). The Swiss Reformers may have begun with this when they began to reform the Church according to their reading of the Bible, but Luther came to this, the formal principle of the Reformation, *after* he had formulated the three material principles. It was only when he discovered that the Pope would not embrace what Luther understood to be the true Pauline doctrine of justification by faith, that he formulated the methodological principle that traditions of the Church ought to be subject to Holy Scripture.

Unity and Diversity among Evangelicals

What is clear is that despite the passage of five hundred years, and across all the many varieties of traditions within the Evangelical tradition – Lutheran, Reformed, Anglican, Anabaptist, Methodist, Pentecostal – all are characterized by these uniting themes. Donald Dayton argued some years ago that the term Evangelical was no longer of any use because it included such a wide variety of traditions.[78] However, this is precisely what makes it so useful. Evangelicals recognize each other across denominations and across divisions over sacraments or ecclesiology or predestination precisely because they are all committed to these characteristics of Reformation theology. While Bebbington's characteristics are useful with respect to identifying Evangelicalism's historical development, it is these theological characteristics which bring us to the heart of what is distinctive about Evangelical theology.

It is clear therefore that the Wesleys were major leaders in the broad Evangelical tradition.[79] We have already alluded to their Evangelical doctrines of justification by faith and the new birth. Also part of the Evangelical faith of the Reformation was the Augustinian formulation of the doctrine of original sin. Wesley took up the cudgels to defend that against the Deist, John Taylor of Norwich, writing his longest theological treatise in order to answer Taylor point by point, and summarizing his doctrine too in a sermon included as Sermon 38 in his definitive body of sermons, *Sermons Preached on Several Occasions*.[80] However, it would be wrong to think of the Evangelical movement as

---

[78] See Donald W. Dayton, "Some Doubts about the Usefulness of the Category 'Evangelical'" in Donald W. Dayton and Robert K. Johnson, eds. *The Variety of American Evangelicalism* (Downers Grove, Illinois: InterVarsity Press, 1991), 251.

[79] On Wesley's connections with other Evangelicals in the Church of England see A. Brown-Lawson, *John Wesley and the Anglican Evangelicals of the Eighteenth Century* (Durham: Pentland Press, 1994).

[80] John Wesley, *Sermons Preached on Several Occasions* (London: Epworth Press, 1944), 502-513. See also Sermon 44 in *The Bicentennial Edition of the Works of John Wesley*, vol. 2, Albert Outler, ed. (Nashville, Tennessee: Abingdon Press, 1985), 170-185. Hereafter abbreviated, *Works [BE]*. See Herbert McGonigle's recent booklet, *Christianity*

only a theological tradition. While the eighteenth-century Evangelicals regarded it as vital to adhere to and proclaim the truth of the gospel in opposition to Deism, their main concern was not heresy but dead orthodoxy. Their concern was not only with truth, but with spiritual life. The Pietist influence particularly made them all too aware that an orthodox church may be a dead church in which there were few signs of spiritual vitality. They were aware that it was not enough to preach the Word but that the Word had to be preached in the power of the Spirit. Like Paul, Evangelical preachers wanted to be able to say, "For our gospel came to you not only in word, but also in power and in the Holy Spirit and with full conviction" (I Thess. 1:5). This was made very clear in Wesley's last sermon before the University of Oxford (which caused much offence). Entitled, "Scriptural Christianity," it was on Acts 4:31 (AV): "And they were all filled with the Holy Ghost."[81] And the distinctive Methodist emphases which he enumerated again and again were "repentance, faith and holiness."[82] The Methodist or Evangelical movement (often synonyms in the eighteenth century) was not only concerned with Nicene and Reformation orthodoxy, but with vital spiritual life and experience.

What is very clear then about the Evangelical tradition is the intimate connection between Evangelical doctrine and evangelism. To put that another way: the gospel and mission cannot be divorced. Mission for the Wesleys and other Evangelicals includes both evangelism and social action. It is focussed on the gospel that "Christ died for our sins in accordance with the scriptures" (I Cor. 15: 3), and it declares urgently that all need to repent and believe in Christ because of the reality of coming judgment.[83] But such preaching was not divorced from social action on behalf of the poor and those who suffer injustice. Evangelical agencies and missions have initiated a host of schools, friendly societies, and charitable works, as Evangelical history from the Wesleys themselves through Wilberforce, Shaftesbury, Booth, Livingstone and innumerable other preachers, missionaries and lay activitists makes very clear. Mission, centred in evangelism and Evangelical theology centred on "Christ crucified" are therefore intimately related. If Christian people fail to be passionately concerned with Evangelical truth, the truth of the gospel, they may continue to engage in social action, but they will lose the urgency of evangelism, and the Church will start to wither and decline. Conversely, if they preach the gospel but have no concern for social action, they will undermine the gospel by what will appear to be hypocrisy.

---

or Deism? John Wesley's Response to John Taylor's Denial of the Doctrine of Original Sin (Sheffield: The Wesley Fellowship, 2012).

[81] *Works [BE]*, 1:159-180.

[82] See Chapter 2 of Ted A. Campbell, *Wesleyan Beliefs* (Nashville, Tennessee: Kingswood, 2010), 63-85.

[83] No one was clearer or more graphic on that than Wesley. Cf. Sermon 15, "The Great Assize" in *Works [BE]*, 1:354-375.

Arminian Evangelicals

To the common Evangelical tradition however the Wesleys brought two particular linked emphases—their Arminianism, and included with that, their view of Christian sanctification. Herbert McGonigle has shown that, while John Wesley had some acquaintance with the writings of the Dutch theologian Arminius, his Arminianism came through that "high church" tradition of the seventeenth-century Church of England which rejected the five-point Calvinism really stemming from Theodore Beza and the Synod of Dort (1619). But unlike the followers of Arminius in the Netherlands, who later departed from the Evangelical faith at key points, John Wesley was (as McGonigle reminds us) an *Evangelical* Arminian.[84] Despite the claim of some Calvinists therefore who wish to restrict the word 'Evangelical' to their own narrow tradition, the vast majority of Evangelicals have been and are "Arminian."

It was also from that high church or Arminian tradition in the Church of England that the Wesleys inherited their particular understanding of Christian sanctification. Luther placed less emphasis on sanctification in case it undermined justification by faith reflected a subtle Pelagianism. One consequence of this is that some in the Lutheran tradition have fallen into antinomianism. Among the more extreme adherents to this position, it is held that the more one sins, the more magnified the pardoning grace of God.[85] By contrast, Calvin followed those Lutheran theologians who defined the "third use of the law" in the Formula of Concord: that it not only served to keep civil order and to bring us under conviction of our sins, but had a role in shaping the life of the Christian.[86] Some later Calvinists distorted his teaching in such a way that, believing themselves to be among the elect, they could sin with impunity.[87] To this issue of the holy life, the Wesleys brought into the Evangelical tradition their earlier influence from the "holy living" school of the Church of England. George Herbert, Bishop Jeremy Taylor of Armagh, and Wesley's contemporary, William Law, were the main voices. After his Aldersgate Street conversion, Wesley wrote to William Law rebuking him as a representative of this tradition that he had never made clear to his younger friend the Pauline and Reformation doctrine of justification by faith, and yet the Wesleys continued to pursue Christian holiness as the holy living school had taught them.

It was through this Arminian tradition that the Wesleys also developed a love for the early Fathers. From Clement of Alexandria in particular, as well as works known as the "Homilies" of Macarius, they developed their own doctrine of Christian perfection. The word itself is liable of course to serious

---

[84] Herbert McGonigle, *Sufficient Saving Grace: John Wesley's Evangelical Arminianism* (Carlisle: Paternoster Press, 2001).

[85] The author recalls T.F. Torrance reminiscing about such antinomians among graduate Lutheran fellow-students.

[86] See John Calvin's *Institutes*, I, vii, 12

[87] See Robert Burns' scathing satire on this in his poem, "Holy Willie's Prayer."

misunderstanding, and John Wesley only insisted on it because it was biblical. But their doctrine was seriously misunderstood by other Evangelicals as "sinless perfection" (and still is today), and it took John Wesley a life-time to work out a balanced formulation of this "imperfect perfection." However, since his doctrine is in line with the Greek Fathers of the Church and with the medieval spirituality of Bernard of Clairvaux and Thomas Aquinas, the Wesleys are significant ecumenical figures in the way in which they united the Evangelical faith of the Reformers, and the Greek and Latin piety of the Church catholic long before the decline that led to the Reformation.[88]

Further, although their interest was in the piety and spirituality of the Church of the Fathers and its medieval successors, they were also loyal to its central theological formulation of the Christian faith in the creeds. Wesley was clear in his adherence to the three creeds: the Apostles', Nicene, and Athanasian Creed, and that indeed was part of his commitment to the Church of England as reformed in the Reformation. The *Book of Common Prayer* which he frequently used listed the three creeds, thus reflecting the loyalty of the Reformers to the Nicene faith of the church catholic. For them the church catholic was a greater entity than what they regarded as the *Roman* Catholic or "papist" church of their day. Wesley's adherence to the Nicene faith, that faith articulated in the one creed officially adopted by a council of the whole Church at the councils of Nicaea (325 AD) and Constantinople (381 AD), was clearly set out in his "Letter to a Roman Catholic."[89]

In 1784, John Wesley had a conversation with the young Charles Simeon. Simeon's name is not so well known outside England, but he was as influential upon the Evangelicals who remained in the Church of England as Wesley was on the Methodists who left. More than anyone else, he shaped the Evangelical Anglican tradition which extends today down to John Stott and N.T. Wright. Simeon was a Fellow of King's College, Cambridge, and vicar of Holy Trinity Church in the town for over fifty years from 1782 till his death in 1836. In that time he nurtured a generation of young clerics, modelling expository preaching and teaching and promoted a trust to purchase "livings" where they could provide the same kind of Evangelical parish ministry. He regarded himself as neither an Arminian nor a Calvinist, or at least as a "moderate Calvinist" or a "Bible Christian." His account of what he said to the aged Wesley is well-known:

> Sir, I understand that you are called an Arminian; and I have been sometimes called a Calvinist; and therefore I suppose we are to draw daggers. But before I consent to begin combat, with your permission I will ask you a few questions...

In essence what he asked was whether Wesley adhered to the *solus Christus* and *sola gratia* of the Evangelical faith, and when Wesley's replies satisfied him fully, he responded:

---

[88] See T.A. Noble, *Holy Trinity: Holy People: The Theology of Christian Perfecting* (Eugene, Oregon: Wipf and Stock, 2013), 44-72.

[89] *The Works of John Wesley*, vol. 10, Thomas Jackson, ed., reprinted (Grand Rapids, Michigan: Baker, 2007), 80-86.

Then, Sir, with your leave, I will put up my dagger again; for this is all my Calvinism; this is my election, my justification by faith, my final perseverance: it is in substance all that I hold and as I hold it: and therefore, if you please, instead of searching out terms and phrases to be a ground of contention between us, we will cordially unite in those things wherein we agree.[90]

The Evangelical Tradition since Wesley

After the Wesleys died, the Evangelical tradition of which they were a part has grown and gone through various phases of development, shaping and being shaped by cultural change. First we may note that throughout the nineteenth century, Evangelical churches grew. By Wesley's death it is reckoned that there were about 140,000 members of the Methodist societies throughout the British Empire and the newly formed United States and growth continued steadily through the century. The pastoral work of itinerant preachers and the effectiveness of the newly invented camp meetings led to Methodism's becoming the largest denomination in America. Baptists and Congregationalists similarly grew and on both sides of the Atlantic. At the same time that it was growing, Evangelical Christianity continued the co-operation across denominations which characterized the leaders of the eighteenth-century revival, and this was formalized by the founding of the Evangelical Alliance in London in 1845, soon developing into an international body in which today 128 countries are represented.

Secondly, throughout the nineteenth century Evangelicals had a significant influence in political and social issues. Already at the beginning of the nineteenth century, Anglican Evangelicals were influential in Parliament. Simeon was attached to the so-called Clapham Sect, that group of wealthy Anglican MPs, bankers, lawyers and business men who lived in the London suburb of Clapham. They were the group who under Wilberforce secured the abolition of the slave trade in 1807 and the abolition of slavery itself throughout the British Empire in 1833. They were the leaders in campaigning for higher standard of integrity in political and public life. They supported Hannah More in the new movement to establish Sunday schools for the poor, they were led by Shaftesbury in fighting for better conditions for working people, and they supported Pitt, Peel and Gladstone in cleansing British political life from corruption and nepotism. By the end of the century, the "Nonconformist conscience" too had become a significant factor in the political and moral life of the nation.[91]

---

[90] The account in full is in the preface to Simeon's sermon, *Horae Homileticae*, p. xvii, and is quoted in full in Hugh Evan Hopkins, *Charles Simeon of Cambridge* (London: Hodder and Stoughton, 1977).

[91] See John Wolffe, *The Expansion of Evangelicalism: The Age of Wilberforce, More, Chalmers and Finney* (Downers Grove, Illinois: InterVarsity Press, 2007).

Thirdly, Evangelicals also took the lead in "Foreign Missions."[92] Anglicans founded the British and Foreign Bible Society and the Church Missionary Society as well as the colony of Sierra Leone as a home for freed slaves. Methodist missions had already begun in the West Indies in the 1780s under the leadership of Thomas Coke. In 1792, the Baptists had formed the Baptist Missionary Society, and in 1795 it was mainly Congregationalists who founded the London Missionary Society which was to send David Livingstone to Africa. Those who disapproved of the Evangelicals were strongly opposed to this controversial move to Foreign Missions, and in Scotland, Thomas Chalmers had to fight in the General Assembly before the Kirk eventually sent Alexander Duff to India in 1830. What Latourette called "the great century" of Christian missions was the outcome of the Evangelical Revival and it has resulted two centuries later in the great demographic shift in world Christianity which now finds the majority of the world's Christians outside Europe and North America. Roman Catholic expansion was clearly also a factor, but among Protestants, it was the Evangelicals, those faithful to the tradition of the Reformation and the eighteenth-century revival, who sowed the seed of such a great harvest. Later in the century, Hudson Taylor's China Inland Mission launched a new phase of "faith missions" and the Student Volunteer Movement led to hundreds of young graduates following C.T. Studd and the "Cambridge Seven" in offering themselves as missionaries. Their vision was captured in their famous watchword, "The evangelization of the world in this generation." It was the student movement, led by John R. Mott, which initiated the Edinburgh World Missionary Conference of 1910, leading to the launching of the ecumenical movement.

Fourthly, we may note the rise of "revivalism" as a new phase in Evangelicalism in the mid-nineteenth century. What was new was that, aware of impact of the revival of the previous century, it became an explicit aim to cultivate "revival" by discovering and practicing specific methods which would produce it. Particularly under the influence of Charles Finney, this focus on methods was accompanied by a new focus on the Holy Spirit. But rather than seeing revival as something which God alone brought about, what may be called a new technology of revival developed.[93] It was presumed by many that, if Christians prayed enough and fulfilled God's conditions, then revival would be sure to come. A whole new subculture developed in which the "altar call" and subjectively oriented "gospel songs" played a large part. This was largely an American development, but American revivalists such as Phoebe Palmer influenced the Booths, and the Second Great Awakening was held to

---

[92] See Andrew Walls, *The Missionary Movement in Christian History* (Edinburgh: T. & T. Clark, 1996), especially chapter 7, "The Evangelical Revival, the Missionary Movement, and Africa."

[93] See David Bebbington's comment on Finney's influence in Britain, *Evangelicalism in Modern Britain: A History from the 1730s to the 1980s* (New York: Routledge, 1989), 116. See also Charles Hambrick-Stowe, *Charles G. Finney and the Spirit of American Evangelicalism* (Grand Rapids: Eerdmans, 1996) and Marianne Perciaccante, *Calling Down Fire* (New York: University of New York Press, 2003).

reach its climax in 1859. From Dwight L. Moody in the 1870s to Billy Graham in the 1950s, American revivalism had a significant impact in Britain. However, it cultivated revival rather than true evangelism. Such forms of revivalism capitalized on a widespread Christian culture in which the masses were already familiar with the elements of the Christian faith. While this phenomenon continues in parts of the United States, with the "death of Christian Britain"[94] from the 1960s, it has ceased to be effective here, and even in the United States, it appears to be increasingly obsolescent. It is important not to identify this particular cultural expression of Evangelicalism and the Evangelical faith itself.

Fifthly, by the end of the nineteenth century, Evangelical Christianity was widely influential in popular culture, but confronted by various intellectual developments, particularly Darwinian evolution in the sciences, and in theology, the increasing influence from Germany of theological Liberalism and what was called Higher Criticism.[95] This was not an entirely new experience. Since the eighteenth-century, the Christian faith had lost its dominance in the intellectual life of Europe for the first time in a thousand years. Then it was Deism which had been the main opponent of Evangelical faith, but the German theologian Friedrich Schleiermacher, a son of Pietism, had tried to counter its influence by an apologetic new presentation of Christian faith in what became called the Liberal tradition, and by the end of the nineteenth century, this had issued in the Liberalism of Adolf von Harnack. Linked with the development of this so-called Liberal theology in Germany was the biblical criticism which subjected the biblical documents to rigorous criticism and appeared to undermine belief in their historicity and authority. Once a generation of leading Evangelical theologians such as Warfield, Orr, Denney and Forsyth passed away early in the twentieth century, the disastrously inadequate grass-roots fundamentalism captured attention. In addition to its adoption of dispensationalism, and what later became called "creationism," fundamentalism reacted against Walter Rauschenbusch's reduction of mission to social action in such an extreme way as to repudiate Evangelicalism's long commitment to ministry to the poor. In continental Europe meanwhile, a strong reaction against Liberalism was led by Karl Barth, who certainly identified himself as Evangelical, standing in the tradition of the Reformation. But in English-speaking Evangelicalism, a strong conservatism was suspicious of him (particularly traditional Calvinists within his own Reformed tradition), and no adequate response to new forms of the Liberal tradition, represented by figures such as Bultmann and Tillich, emerged until later in the century.

The emergence of the Evangelical movement from its fundamentalist phase between the two world wars came with the so-called "New Evangelicals" in the United States and the rise of the Intervarsity movement beginning in Britain. Billy Graham and Carl Henry, the first editor of *Christianity*

---

[94] See Callum G. Brown, *The Death of Christian Britain* (New York: Routledge, 2001).
[95] See David Bebbington, *The Dominance of Evangelicalism: The Age of Spurgeon and Moody* (Downers Grove, Illinois: InterVarsity Press, 2005).

Today, were the leading figures among the American New Evangelicals and the recovery of intellectual strength was furthered by the founding of a number of Evangelical seminaries. Evangelical biblical scholars such as George Eldon Ladd of Fuller Theological Seminary and F.F. Bruce of Manchester University demonstrated how biblical criticism could be exercised responsibly. Sadly, American Evangelicals were to be seriously divided in the 1970s by blood-letting over the issue of "inerrancy."[96] In the United Kingdom such a sad and debilitating division was avoided. There, John Stott was the leading public representative of the Intervarsity movement which sprang from student initiative in forming Christian Unions throughout British universities and eventually also in North America and throughout the Commonwealth. It was the vision of Douglas Johnson and other leaders of the Intervarsity Fellowship which led to the strategic founding of Tyndale House, Cambridge—a biblical research library which eventually produced a generation of leading biblical scholars committed to the Evangelical faith. This had a hidden but immense global impact.[97] Graham and Stott together led the Lausanne movement, a series of conferences in which global Evangelicalism recovered its commitment to social action without compromising the focus on evangelism. At the same time that Evangelical Christianity was recovering its nerve intellectually, the new focus on the Holy Spirit seen in the early twentieth-century Pentecostal movement spread to the established churches through the charismatic movement.

Conclusion

How would John and Charles Wesley view the global reach of Evangelical Christianity, if they could see it today? Enormous developments in society and culture since their death would no doubt astound them. But they would surely rejoice in the growth of the gospel around the world, the kind of growth which Charles envisioned in his great hymn,

> See how great a flame aspires,
> Kindled by a spark of grace!
> Jesu's love the nations fires,
> Sets the kingdoms on a blaze.[98]

At the same time, they would surely be saddened by the serious decline of the churches in Britain and Europe (including particularly, Methodism), while at the same time rejoicing in the robust and increasing strength of the Evangelical movement within their beloved Church of England. Perhaps what would

---

[96] See George Marsden's several works on American Evangelicalism and fundamentalism.

[97] See T.A. Noble, *Tyndale House and Fellowship: The First Sixty Years* (Leicester: InterVarsity Press, 2006).

[98] J. Wesley, *Works [BE]*, 7:341

sadden them most is the way in which their emphasis on Christian holiness is marginalized and deeply misunderstood across Evangelical Christianity.

And what would they say about the so-called "holiness churches"? No doubt they would be glad that these have tried to remain true to the doctrine of sanctification, and glad that they have played a part in world mission. But would they not call for a new vision? Would they not want to see a new vision which breaks from anti-intellectualism and sectarian provincialism, and which recaptures the profundity and power of the gospel? Would they not want to see a new focus on "Christ crucified"? Would they not want to see a new endowment with the "catholic spirit" which calls the whole Church of Christ to embrace the *evangel* – the New Testament gospel which not only proclaims forgiveness of sins and reconciliation to God, but also the transforming power the Holy Spirit? Would they not want us to recapture the vision of "Christianizing Christianity" and of embodying an Evangelical people who not only preach "scriptural holiness" clearly and thoughtfully, but who are impelled and energized by the outgoing redemptive power of "perfect love" to transform not only individual lives, but the very structures of increasingly sick and corrupt human society?

Chapter 3

Methodists and Moravians: The Shaping of Evangelical Spirituality

By Ian Randall

Introduction

Herbert McGonigle wrote in 2001, in *Sufficient Saving Grace*, about the "life-long delight of studying Wesleyan theology," and that delight has been very evident in his important work in this field.[99] It has, for him, been important to call attention to the roots of Wesleyan theology, and also to engage with varied understandings of Wesleyan developments.[100] In this essay I want to give attention to the place of the Moravians in the story of early Methodist piety.[101] "John Wesley," writes Phyllis Mack in *Heart Religion in the British Enlightenment*, "was an exponent of practical piety."[102] For Wesley, Methodism

---

[99] Herbert B. McGonigle, *Sufficient Saving Grace: John Wesley's Evangelical Arminianism* (Carlisle: Paternoster, 2001), xi. He has not only made contributions through writing, but in many other very significant ways. One aspect of ministry into which I was drawn by him was the work of the Wesley Fellowship. A high point for me was the 2004 Fellowship residential conference. As part of the conference, Herbert led us in a Wesleyan love feast, in which powerful testimonies were shared, and spontaneous prayers and singing occurred.

[100] McGonigle, *Sufficient Saving Grace*, 1-12, sets out work in the field.

[101] For a recent survey of Methodist spirituality, see I.M. Randall, "Methodist Spirituality" in *The Ashgate Research Companion to World Methodism*, W. Gibson, P. Forsaith and M. Wellings, eds. (Franham: Ashgate, 2013), 289-306.

[102] Phyllis Mack, *Heart Religion in the British Enlightenment: Gender and Emotion in Early Methodism* (Cambridge: Cambridge University Press, 2008), 32.

was not defined by a set of "opinions" or "the judgment of one man or another."[103] Central to his concern was authentic religious experience. Thus to examine Methodist spirituality is to look at the heart of Methodism. In a similar vein, Kenneth Cracknell and Susan White argue that "in many ways the Methodist movement was in its beginnings primarily a *spiritual renewal* movement."[104] Some Methodist authors have given sustained, detailed attention to the analysis of Methodist spirituality.[105] However, more remains to be done.

In 1988, in an article entitled "Opening the Ecumenical Door to Let the Riffraff in," Donald Dayton spoke of the "Presbyterianization of evangelicalism," a tendency in America for the Princeton tradition to dominate evangelicalism, so that evangelical history was interpreted according to Reformed categories.[106] Since then there has been an upsurge in scholarly work on the Wesleyan tradition. New developments have included the journal, *Wesley and Methodist Studies*. An important recent volume in the field is *The Ashgate Research Companion to World Methodism* (Farnham: Ashgate, 2013), edited by W. Gibson, P. Forsaith and M. Wellings.[107] However, there are still writers who wish to question the place of Methodism as a shaping force within evangelicalism. Thus Garry Williams, writing in a volume, *The Emergence of Evangelicalism* (2008), considered Reformed theology "the authentic evangelical mainstream of three centuries," but did not view John Wesley as foundational to evangelicalism, and saw Wesley's position on election as a theological "deviation."[108] Essayists in the volume were querying David Bebbington's work on evangelicalism, and in his response to the essays Bebbington noted that no author had written a chapter on Methodism.[109] I see evangelicalism as variegated, but a distinct stream of Christian spirituality.[110]

---

[103] John Wesley, "The Character of a Methodist" (1742), in Rupert Davies, ed., *The Bicentennial Edition of the Works of John Wesley*, vol. 9 (Nashville, Tennessee: Abingdon Press, 1989), 33-4. Hereafter this edition will be abbreviated as *Works [BE]*.

[104] Kenneth Cracknell and Susan J. White, "Methodist Spirituality" in *An Introduction to World Methodism* (Cambridge: CUP, 2005), 141. Italics original.

[105] Gordon Wakefield's work has been of great importance. Gordon Wakefield, *Methodist Devotion: The Spiritual Life in the Methodist Tradition* (London: Epworth Press, 1966); *Fire of Love: The Spirituality of John Wesley* (London: Epworth Press, 1976); *Methodist Spirituality* (Peterborough: Epworth Press, 1999).

[106] D.W. Dayton, "Opening the Ecumenical Door to Let the Riffraff in" in *The Ecumenical Review*, vol. 40, no. 1 (1988): 100.

[107] A notable contributor to Wesleyan studies has been the Nazarene Theological College, Didsbury, Manchester, where Herbert developed what has become a highly significant research community.

[108] Garry J. Williams, "Enlightenment Epistemology and Eighteenth-Century Evangelical Doctrines of Assurance" in *The Emergence of Evangelicalism: Exploring Historical Continuities*, M.A.G. Haykin and K.J. Stewart, eds., (Nottingham: APOLLOS, 2008), 374.

[109] David Bebbington, "Response" in *The Emergence of Evangelicalism: Exploring Historical Continuities*, Haykin and Stewart, eds., (Nottingham: APOLLOS, 2008), 424.

[110] I have developed this in *What a Friend we have in Jesus* (London: DLT, 2005).

Moravian and Methodist Connections

David Bebbington describes in *Evangelicalism in Modern Britain* how the decade beginning in 1734 "witnessed in the English-speaking world a more important development than any other, before or after, in the history of Protestant Christianity: the emergence of the movement that became Evangelicalism."[111] In a contrasting vein, John Kent, in *Wesley and the Wesleyans*, dismissed the "so-called evangelical revival" as a persistent myth, although he acknowledged that Wesleyanism grew because John Wesley "responded to the actual religious demands and hopes of his hearers."[112] Henry Rack's view, which connected the Evangelical Revival with the rise of Methodism, represents a widely accepted position.[113] The new spiritual impetus had strong links with earlier English Puritanism. Bebbington argues, however, that Puritans tended to view assurance of salvation as the fruit of spiritual struggle, whereas evangelicals "believed it to be general, normally given at conversion and the result of simple acceptance of the gift of God."[114] Not all Puritans took the same view of assurance, but there was a change with the eighteenth century. This has been linked with the Enlightenment period. Thus Jeremy Gregory notes how emphases in Wesley chimed in with wider emphases on "optimism, human potential, perfectibility, and the essential equality of humankind" and suggests that "Wesley's emphasis on evidence and experience can also be seen as echoing Enlightenment trends."[115]

Studies over the past few years have generally aligned themselves with the argument advanced by Bebbington that evangelicalism comprises those who stress conversion, the Bible, the cross of Christ, and activism.[116] Much attention has been paid to Anglo-American developments, but Colin Podmore rightly observes that the story of the movement begins in Central Europe following the Reformation period.[117] Count Nicholas Ludwig von Zinzendorf (1700-60), from Dresden in Germany, became the creative leader of the Renewed Unity of the Brethren, or the Moravian Church. In 1722 Zinzendorf, who had been educated in the Lutheran Pietist environment at Halle, opened his estate in south-east Saxony to Protestant refugees from Bohemia and Mo-

---

[111] David Bebbington, *Evangelicalism in Modern Britain: A History from the 1730s to the 1980s* (London: Routledge, 1995), 20.

[112] J. Kent, *Wesley and the Wesleyans: Religion in Eighteenth-Century Britain* (Cambridge: CUP, 2002), 1-2.

[113] Henry D. Rack, *Reasonable Enthusiast: John Wesley and the Rise of Methodism* (London: Epworth Press, 2002, 3rd edition), 158-250.

[114] Bebbington, *Evangelicalism*, 43.

[115] Jeremy Gregory, "The Long Eighteenth Century" in *The Cambridge Companion to John Wesley*, Randy L. Maddox and Jason E. Vickers, eds. (Cambridge: CUP, 2010), 38.

[116] Bebbington, *Evangelicalism in Modern Britain*, 2-17.

[117] C. Podmore, *The Moravian Church in England, 1728-1760* (Oxford: Clarendon Press, 1998), 5; cf. W.R. Ward, *The Protestant Evangelical Awakening* (Cambridge: CUP, 1992), chapters 2 and 4.

ravia.[118] Members of this group, escaping from persecution by the Roman Catholic Habsburgs, were part of the Unity of the Brethren (*Unitas Fratrum*) a movement with its origins in religious reform in Bohemia under Jan Hus.[119] With Zinzendorf's help, a community called Herrnhut (under "the Lord's Protection") was established for these "Brethren," and it became the scene in 1727 of a profound spiritual renewal, at which time the community numbered at least 220. Powerful spiritual assurance was a hallmark of what took place: Podmore speaks of a quasi-pentecostal experience.[120] In this study I want to examine the effect of Moravian thinking and practice on early Methodist spirituality.[121]

John and Charles Wesley first met the Moravians in 1735, sailing from England to Georgia, in America, where the brothers hoped to exercise a ministry. In 1732 Moravians had been sent by the Herrnhut community to reach out to slaves in the West Indies, and within ten years Moravian missionaries had gone to North America, Greenland, Surinam, South Africa, the Gold Coast, Algeria, Arctic Russia and Ceylon.[122] Moravians had established missionary work in Georgia a year before John and Charles went there and there were twenty-six Moravians on the ship with the Wesleys. Characteristically, John Wesley - always a keen investigator - began learning German so that he could speak to his fellow-travellers. One incident on the voyage (one often related) was when a violent storm started and many English passengers began to scream out in fear. The Moravians, it seems, calmly sang hymns together. John Wesley was profoundly impressed, recording in his diary that he asked one of the Moravians afterwards: "Was you not afraid?" He answered, "I thank God, no." Wesley then asked: "But were not your women and children afraid?" He replied: "No; our women and children are not afraid to die."[123]

On arrival in Georgia in February 1736, John Wesley sought out the Moravian Bishop, August Spangenberg, a former Professor at Jena University in Germany. Wesley wanted the conversation to be a personal one. Spangengberg replied that he could say nothing until he had asked Wesley some questions. As recorded in Wesley's journal, Spangenberg asked: "Have you the witness within yourself? Does the Spirit of God bear witness with your spirit that you are a child of God?" Wesley found himself unprepared to give a defi-

---

[118] For Zinzendorf see A. J. Lewis, *Zinzendorf: The Ecumenical Pioneer* (London: SCM, 1962).

[119] See I. Noble, "Jan Hus in Ecumenical Discussion" in *Journal of European Baptist Studies*, vol. 6, no. 2 (2006): 5-19.

[120] Podmore, *The Moravian Church in England*, 6.

[121] See I.M. Randall, "Christ Comes to the Heart: Moravian Influence on the Shaping of Evangelical Spirituality" in *Journal of European Baptist Studies*, vol. 6, no. 3 (2006): 5-23. I am grateful for the kind permission of Dr Keith Jones to make use of the material in *JEBS*.

[122] A. Freeman, "*Gemeine*: Count Nicholas von Zinzendorf's Understanding of the Church" in *Brethren Life and Thought*, vol. 47, nos. 1 and 2 (2002): 11.

[123] See J. Wesley's journal entry for 25 January 1736 in *Works [BE]*, vol. 18, Rupert Davies and Richard Heitzenrater, eds. (Nashville, Tennessee: Abingdon Press, 1988), 143.

nite answer. Spangenberg continued: "Do you know Jesus Christ?" Wondering how to respond, Wesley finally replied, "I know he is the Saviour of the world." To this Spangenberg replied: "True, but do you know he has saved you?" The best that Wesley could offer was, "I hope he has died to save me." He followed this with an attempt at a more convincing reply, but as he noted in his journal, "I fear they were vain words."[124] On the following day Wesley asked Spangenberg about the Moravian Church. Spangenberg described the Herrnhut community as comprising "about a thousand souls, gathered out of many nations. They hold fast the discipline, as well as the faith and practice, of the apostolical church."[125]

It is well known that a number of spiritual influences on John Wesley prior to this period can be traced. The Wesley family - especially his mother Susanna - was one. The family had been part of the Puritan movement. The High Church Jeremy Taylor was another influence. In 1726 Wesley read Thomas à Kempis and began to see that "true religion was seated in the heart."[126] William Law's writings, *On Christian Perfection* (1726) and *A Serious Call to a Devout and Holy Life* (1728) also influenced his spirituality. Wesley corresponded with Law.[127] John and Charles Wesley and George Whitefield were also part of the "Holy Club" in Oxford which would eventually be called "Methodists." There was, too, the (somewhat ambiguous) influence on John Wesley of more mystical streams of spirituality, expressed by German mystics or in books like *The Life of God in the Soul of Man*, by Henry Scougal, a Scottish Episcopalian. But the Moravian influence was more decisive.[128] In 1736, as Clifford Towlson argued in *Moravian and Methodist*, Spangenberg revealed to Wesley not only "a way of life" but also "the power by which that way could be assured."[129]

Conversion: To "Know the Saviour"

During the Wesleys' time in Georgia a close relationship between John Wesley and the Moravians continued. In February 1738, on his return to England, Wesley met another Moravian, Peter Böhler, who had been a Lutheran turned Moravian at Herrnhut in 1737, and was ordained in the following year. He was in his mid-twenties at the time he met the Wesleys and was spending time in England on his way to North America. John Wesley and Böhler met in

---

[124] See J. Wesley's journal entry for 8 February 1736 in *Works [BE]*, 18:146; cf. H. McGonigle, *John Wesley and the Moravians* (Ilkeston: Moorleys/ Wesley Fellowship, 1993), 6-7.

[125] See J. Wesley's journal entry for 9 February 1736 in *Works [BE]*, 18:147.

[126] See J. Wesley's journal entry for 24 May 1738 in *Works [BE]*, 18:243.

[127] See D.L. Jeffrey, ed., *A Burning and a Shining Light* (Grand Rapids: Eerdmans, 1987), pp. 143, 146.

[128] Bebbington, *Evangelicalism in Modern Britain*, 37-40. See also A. S. Wood, *The Burning Heart: John Wesley: Evangelist* (Exeter: Paternoster Press, 1978), chapter 3.

[129] Clifford Towlson, *Moravian and Methodist: Relationships and Influences in the Eighteenth Century* (London: Epworth Press, 1957), 41.

London on 7 February 1738. "A day much to be remembered," Wesley wrote.[130] Ten days later John and Charles set out for Oxford with Böhler. A major topic of conversation was salvation, or how one can know the Saviour. Böhler, in a report to Zinzendorf, conveyed the Moravian conversionist outlook:

> ... I travelled with the two brothers, John and Charles Wesley, from London to Oxford. The elder, John, is an amiable man; he acknowledges that he does not yet rightly know the Saviour and suffers himself to be instructed. He loves us sincerely. His brother, with whom you conversed frequently in London a year ago, is greatly troubled in spirit and knows not how he shall begin to know the Saviour.[131]

Charles was in poor health at the time, and on 24 February he sent for Böhler to pray about his suffering. Böhler recorded that he "prayed with him [Charles] for the salvation of his soul and body," and on a subsequent occasion Böhler "watched with Charles Wesley," who Böhler said was "very dangerously ill." On this occasion John Gambold, a member of the Oxford Holy Club who became a Church of England clergyman and later a Moravian, administered the Lord's Supper, and Böhler reported that Charles "was very happy and said that if he should die, he would go to the Saviour, at least as one who hungers and thirsts."[132] Moravian conversionism was having an impact.

In the meantime, John Wesley continued to spend time with Böhler. At times during their conversations, Wesley struggled to understand Böhler, as when he said "My brother, my brother, that philosophy of yours must be purged away." Kenneth J. Collins raises the possibility that the "philosophy" opposed by Böhler was Wesley's tendency to be guided "by rule and resolution."[133] On 5 March 1738 a more fruitful meeting with Böhler took place, at which Wesley – as he put it in his journal - was "clearly convinced of unbelief, of the want of 'that faith whereby alone we are saved'."[134] Herbert McGonigle comments that through Böhler "the Moravian influence on Wesley's understanding of salvation by faith and his own Christian experience was to be profound."[135] In Böhler's own report to Zinzendorf of the conversation of 5 March, the question of whether Wesley had the assurance of faith was, for Böhler, crucial. Responding to Böhler's questions about his "spiritual state," Wesley said that "sometimes he felt quite certain, but sometimes very fearful."

---

[130] See J. Wesley's journal entry for 7 February 1738 in *Works [BE]*, 18:223.

[131] Moravian Archives at Herrnhut, reproduced in W.N. Schwarze and S.H. Gapp, Peter Böhler and the Wesleys, *World Parish*, no. 2 (November, 1949), and cited in Towlson, *Moravian and Methodist*, 50.

[132] Cited in Towlson, *Moravian and Methodist*, 51.

[133] Kenneth J. Collins, *A Real Christian: The Life of John Wesley* (Nashville, Tennessee: Abingdon Press, 200), 56. See J. Wesley's journal entries for 18-19 February 1738 in *Works [BE]*, 18:226. heir conversations were in Latin, *Mi frater, mi frater, excoquenda est ista tua philosophia –*

[134] J. Wesley's journal entry for 4-5 March 1738 in *Works [BE]*, 18:228.

[135] McGonigle, *Sufficient Saving Grace*, 108.

Böhler told Zinzendorf that he "talked with him [Wesley] very fully" and urged him to "go to the opened fountain" – a reference to the blood of Christ, a central theme in Moravian spirituality.[136]

Their conversation was unsettling to Wesley to the point where he considered halting preaching: "Leave off preaching. How can you preach to others, who have not faith yourself?" Wesley asked Böhler what he thought about this, and perhaps to Wesley's surprise the answer Böhler gave was: "By no means." When Wesley asked what he should preach, Böhler replied: "Preach faith *till* you have it; and then, *because* you have it, you *will* preach faith."[137] Towlson comments that "this might seem dangerous advice, for it might lead either to self-deception or even to pretence," but Towlson argues that Böhler's meaning was clear: "If I have convinced you of the need for faith, preach it until it is no longer a mere intellectual conviction, but your own spiritual certainty."[138] Böhler followed up this conversation later on in March, and this time was able to speak to both the Wesleys. He described this meeting, in a letter to Zinzendorf: "I had a very full conversation with the two Wesleys, in order to impress upon their minds the Gospel, and in order to entreat them to proclaim the same to others as they had opportunity, at Oxford and elsewhere."[139] Böhler was not only a crucial influence but was quite deliberate in the way he exercised his influence.

The question of personal assurance of salvation was now the major issue with which John Wesley was wrestling. Linked with it, there were questions about whether conversion was instantaneous. As he reflected on his own lack of inner peace, John Wesley met and was impressed by three people to whom Böhler introduced him. These "living witnesses," said Wesley, testified at a meeting on 23 April that God had given them "in a moment such a faith in the blood of his Son as translated them out of darkness into light, out of sin and fear into holiness and happiness." Later Wesley would disagree with the Moravians on issues connected with assurance, but at this point his "disputing" ended. In distress he cried out: "Lord, help Thou my unbelief."[140] Böhler himself was not as sanguine about Wesley's response. Although Böhler was pleased with the testimonies given, and he noted that "John Wesley and the rest who were with him were as thought struck dumb by these narratives," when Böhler asked Wesley what he now believed, it seems that Wesley initially replied that "four examples did not settle the matter and could not convince him." Böhler then offered to bring eight more.[141] There was apparently no escape for Wesley.

The continued conversations with Böhler led to significant events in May 1738. John Wesley recorded on 3 May that his brother Charles had a long

---

[136] Cited in Towlson, *Moravian and Methodist*, 52.
[137] J. Wesley's journal entry for 4-5 March 1738 in *Works [BE]*, 18:228.
[138] Towlson, *Moravian and Methodist*, 52-3.
[139] Cited in Towlson, *Moravian and Methodist*, 53.
[140] J. Wesley, journal entry for 23 April 1738 in *Works [BE]*, 18:234. See also McGonigle, *John Wesley and the Moravians*, 8-9, 11.
[141] Cited in Towlson, *Moravian and Methodist*, 54-5.

conversation with Böhler and came to see clearly "the nature of that one true living faith" by which someone is saved.[142] John's journal for 24 May 1738 recorded events that took place at a religious society meeting in Aldersgate Street, London. Wesley wrote the following:

> In the evening I went very unwillingly to a society in Aldersgate Street [in the city of London], where one was reading Luther's Preface to the Epistle to the Romans. About a quarter before nine, while he was describing the change which God works in the heart through faith in Christ, I felt my heart strangely warmed. I felt I did trust in Christ, Christ alone, for salvation; and an assurance was given me that He had taken away *my* sins, even *mine*, and saved *me* from the law of sin and death…I then testified openly to all there what I now first felt in my heart.[143]

Later on that evening, John celebrated his experience in Charles' room, as with others they sang a hymn written by Charles.[144] A week earlier, Charles had gone from believing the message brought by the Moravians to experiencing it personally.[145] An important influence on Charles was William Holland, a member of the Church of England who had united himself with the Moravians.[146] The shaping of early Methodist spirituality in the area of conversion owed a great deal to Moravian experience.

The Bible: "O Give Me that Book!"

John Wesley referred to himself as a *homo unius libri*, a "man of one book." In the preface to his sermons (where he used this phrase) he spoke of the way of salvation as being "written down in a book," and he continued: "O give me that book! At any price give me the Book of God! I have it. Here is knowledge enough for me."[147] A number of influences contributed to Wesley's interpretation of the Bible and these influences varied over time.[148] In the period being examined here, Wesley was looking for an authentic faith affirmed by Scripture and experience. Böhler was able to refer to both sources of authority. Perhaps Heitzenrater slightly over-states the case when he says that Böhler had "a fairly easy task" convincing Wesley.[149] It is certainly the case, as Bullen argues, that Böhler's views sent Wesley back to Scripture. For example, when

---

[142] J. Wesley, journal entry for 3 May 1738 in *Works [BE]*, 18:237.
[143] J. Wesley, journal entry for 24 May 1738 in *Works [BE]*, 18: 249-50.
[144] McGonigle, *John Wesley and the Moravians*, 9-10.
[145] F.C. Gill, *Charles Wesley: The First Methodist* (London: Lutterworth Press, 1964), 65-71.
[146] Towlson, *Moravian and Methodist*, 64-5.
[147] Albert Outler, ed., *Works [BE]*, vol. 1 (Nashville, Tennessee: Abingdon Press, 1984), 105.
[148] See Donald A. Bullen, *A Man of One Book? John Wesley's Interpretation and Use of the Bible* (Milton Keynes: Paternoster, 2007).
[149] Richard P. Heitzenrater, "Great Expectations: Aldersgate and the Evidences of Genuine Christianity" in *Aldersgate Reconsidered*, Randy L. Maddox, ed., (Nashville: Kingswood Books, 1990), 64.

Böhler spoke of instantaneous conversion, Wesley said: "I searched the Scriptures again touching this very thing, particularly the Acts of the Apostles: but to my utter astonishment found scarce any instances there of other than *instantaneous* conversions; scarce any other so slow as that of St. Paul, who was three days in the pangs of the new birth."[150] "The influence of the Moravians," says Bullen, "challenged Wesley's long held views, not by challenging his understanding of the authority of the Bible, but by questioning his interpretation of it."[151]

The Bible featured prominently on the day of John Wesley's Aldersgate experience, although the reading of Luther's preface to the book of Romans was also significant. Wesley wrote on 24 May that he had been thoroughly convinced by Böhler about faith being a gift of God, and "by the grace of God" Wesley "resolved to seek it unto the end." He continued to seek "justifying, saving faith," he stated, "though with strange indifference, dulness, and coldness, and unusually frequent relapses into sin," until Wednesday, 24 May. At about five "this morning" (he was writing at the end of the day), he opened his New Testament and read: "There are given unto us exceeding great and precious promises, even that ye should be partakers of the divine nature." (2 Pet. 1: 4). Wesley later opened the Bible again and found these words: "Thou art not far from the kingdom of God." In the afternoon he went to St. Paul's. The anthem was, "Out of the deep have I called unto thee, O Lord: Lord, hear my voice. O let thine ears consider well the voice of my complaint. If thou, Lord, wilt be extreme to mark what is done amiss, O Lord, who may abide it? For there is mercy with thee; therefore shalt thou be feared."[152] Böhler had encouraged Wesley to read the Scriptures closely, which profoundly shaped Wesley's experience of 24 May.

Three weeks after his experience at Aldersgate, Wesley set off to visit Moravian settlements in Germany. In the course of a three-month trip, he and his companions met Zinzendorf and other Moravians at Herrnhut and elsewhere.[153] Wesley's understanding of salvation was deepened, especially by the preaching of Christian David, originally a carpenter from Moravia, whom Wesley described as "the first planter" of the church in Herrnhut. Wesley's journal recorded the biblical themes in talks by David:

> Four times also I enjoyed the blessing of hearing him preach... and every time he chose the very subject which I should have desired, had I spoken to him be-

---

[150] J. Wesley, journal entry for 24 May 1738 in *Works [BE]*, 18:249.
[151] Bullen, *A Man of One Book?*, 89.
[152] J. Wesley, journal entry for 24 May 1738 in *Works [BE]*, 18:249.
[153] Incidentally, parts of Wesley's journal reflect his interests as a traveller. Cologne, wrote Wesley, was "the ugliest, dirtiest city I ever yet saw with my eyes" and its cathedral a "huge misshapen thing." As Warren Smith comments, Wesley was seeking an understanding of "God's redeeming love" and the (Catholic) cathedral "held scant interest." Warren Thomas Smith, "Eighteenth-Century Encounters: Methodist-Moravian" in *Methodist History*, vol. 24, no. 3 (April 1986): 148-9. Cf. J. Wesley, journal entry for 26 & 28 June 1738 in *Works [BE]*, 18:258. During his journey he also visited Halle, the Lutheran Pietist centre.

52   *The Path of Holiness*

fore. Thrice he described the state of those who are 'weak in faith', who are justified... who have received forgiveness through the blood of Christ, but have not received the constant indwelling of the Holy Ghost. This state he explained once from, 'Blessed are the poor in spirit; for theirs is the kingdom of heaven'; when he showed at large, from various Scriptures, that many are children of God and heirs of the promises, long before their hearts are softened by holy *mourning*; before they are *comforted* by the abiding witness of the Spirit...."[154]

Wesley spent time with the Herrnhut leaders, including hours in conversation with Christian David (in German) when the latter described how, through study, he had been convinced that "all Scripture was given by inspiration of God."[155] Wesley observed the way Moravians allocated people to small groups called "classes" and "bands."[156] This owed much to Lutheran Pietism and especially Philipp Spener, who had proposed *collegia pietatis* or devotional meetings in which believers met to teach each other. Spener included as one of his six major ideas for renewing the churches the "earnest and thorough study of the Bible in private meetings."[157] Pietist study groups emphasized the right of lay people to interpret scripture.[158] Zinzendorf drew from these ideas as well as from the traditions of the Unity of the Brethren. He insisted that the core principles of the Moravians were "apostolic" or patterned after the primitive church of the New Testament.[159] Wesley noted that about 90 bands met in Herrnhut, most of them three times each week, for members to "confess their faults to one another, and pray for one another."[160] Kenneth J. Collins observes the impact that the Moravians had on Wesley's organizational structure: Wesley's Methodist classes and especially his bands were "an inheritance from the Moravians."[161] It has been argued by Eamonn Duffy that Wesley abandoned the ideal of "primitive" New Testament Christianity in favour of "real" Christianity, but at this point Wesley hoped that "THIS Christianity," as at Herrnhut, would "cover the earth."[162]

The Bible was used in a variety of ways at Herrnhut. Wesley wrote: "Every morning at eight is singing and exposition of Scripture; and commonly short

---

[154] J. Wesley, journal entry for 8 August 1738 in *Works [BE]*, 18:270.

[155] J. Wesley, journal entry for 12 August 1738 in *Works [BE]*, 18:273-4.

[156] J. Wesley, journal entry for 12 August 1738 in *Works [BE]*, 18:292.

[157] Ward, *The Protestant Evangelical Awakening*, 57.

[158] See J.N. Strom, "Problems and Promises of Pietism Research" in *Church History*, vol. 71, no. 3 (2002): 536-54.

[159] Freeman, "*Gemeine*: Count Nicholas von Zinzendorf's Understanding of the Church," 15.

[160] J. Wesley, journal entry for 12 August 1738 in *Works [BE]*, 18:292.

[161] Kenneth J. Collins, 'Wesley's life and ministry' in *The Cambridge Companion to John Wesley*, 51.

[162] E. Duffy, "Primitive Christianity Revived" in *Studies in Church History*, vol. 14 (1977): 287-300; cf. C.J. Podmore, "The Anglicans and the Brethren: Anglican Attitudes to the Moravians in the Mid-Eighteenth Century" in *Journal of Ecclesiastical History*, vol. 41, no. 4 (1990): 627; and J. Wesley, journal entry for 12 August 1738 in *Works [BE]*, 18:272.

prayer."[163] Podmore, who questions if preaching was central, nonetheless notes that an hour was set aside for Bible reading, and the official preaching part of the liturgy involved a sermon, as well as "quarter-hours" when brief homilies were given.[164] What the Moravian community managed to avoid, at least in the early period, was biblical teaching restricted to one minister. Christian David, after hearing a sermon by Johann Andreas Rothe, the Lutheran pastor of Berthelsdorf (where Zinzendorf lived), affirmed Rothe's view that one or two preachers alone could not serve the needs at Herrnhut, so in 1725 seven men and seven women, who were deemed appropriately gifted, were appointed as "helpers," a term that was equivalent to pastor.[165] When Wesley later began to appoint lay preachers they were often referred to as "helpers."[166] Wesley's sermons provided a guide to lay preachers, similar to the way in which large numbers of copies of manuscript sermons were circulated from Herrnhut to widely-scattered Moravian groups.[167] To the Moravians, the Bible was central to the life of faith. This is reflected in how they structured their class and band meetings. Their approach, which Wesley witnessed during his travels to Moravia, would have a formative impact on his ministry.

The Cross: "His Blood Availed for Me"

Although the whole Bible was important to the Moravians, the person of Jesus Christ and his sacrifice on the cross was central. Methodism shared a similar focus on the merits of Christ's sacrifice appropriated to the believer during personal conversion. Charles Wesley set this out in a classic hymn, "O for a thousand tongues to sing," a hymn intended "for the anniversary day of one's conversion." After the initial verses (the hymn had eighteen), the focus was on Christ's redemption:[168]

> O for a thousand tongues to sing
> My great Redeemer's praise,
> The glories of my God and King,
> The triumphs of his grace!

---

[163] J. Wesley, journal entry for 12 August 1738 in *Works [BE]*, 18:293.

[164] Podmore, *The Moravian Church in England*, 147-8.

[165] Freeman, "*Gemeine*: Count Nicholas von Zindendorf's Understanding of the Church," 13-14.

[166] Collins, "Wesley's Life and Ministry," 51. Collins suggests that Wesley "went beyond his pietist and Moravian colleagues in his extensive use of lay preachers," but it is worth asking how much he drew from the Moravians, here as elsewhere.

[167] G. Stead, "Moravian Spirituality and its Propagation in West Yorkshire during the Eighteenth-Century Evangelical Revival" in *Evangelical Quarterly*, vol. 71, no. 3 (1999): 243.

[168] F.C. Gill, *Charles Wesley: The First Methodist* (London: Lutterworth Press, 1964), 72.

> He breaks the power of cancelled sin,
> He sets the prisoner free;
> His blood can make the foulest clean;
> His blood availed for me.

The image of a "thousand tongues" with which to praise Christ came from Böhler, and a number of Charles' early hymns drew from Moravian writings.[169] When John Wesley visited Herrnhut he was impressed by a Swedish member of the community, Arvid Gradin, and he quoted Gradin's definition of "full assurance of faith" as "repose in the blood of Christ."[170] A focus on the wounds of Christ and his "wounded heart" produced intense devotion among Moravian believers.[171] This was expressed in Moravianism's "Blood and Wounds Theology." Zinzendorf concluded: "We will look for nothing else in the Bible but the Lamb and His Wounds."[172]

Although this devotion could lead to excessive and extreme practices, when mediated through the celebration of communion it was edifying. Although worship was not identical in each Moravian community, most communities recognized the Lord's Supper as the central liturgical element of worship. Wesley saw this in their practices as well: "On the first Saturday in the month, the Lord's Supper is administered. From ten in the morning till two, the Eldest [among the elders] speaks with each communicant in private concerning the state of his soul. At two they dine, then wash one another's feet, after which they sing and pray. About ten they receive in silence without any ceremony, and continue in silence till they part at twelve."[173] The service could also include the laying on of hands. Those assisting at communion might wear a white alb tied with a red girdle, intended as a reminder that, like those "robed in white" in the Book of Revelation. At the conclusion of the service the whole congregation might prostrate themselves. Several Roman Catholics who watched a Moravian-style Communion service at Fetter Lane, London, claimed to have "liked it very well."[174] Others who witnessed Moravian Eucharistic services described them in terms of being gathered into the passion of Christ and into the whole community of the faithful.[175]

John Wesley's views about the benefits of communion were formulated when he was a young Church of England priest, before his encounters with the Moravians. He held a high regard for communion, one which reflected both Calvinist and catholic influences, and his regard remained the same throughout his life. In a sermon preached in 1788 called "The Duty of Constant Communion" (which he noted had been written over fifty-five years

---

[169] Mack, *Heart Religion*, 43.
[170] McGonigle, *John Wesley and the Moravians*, 12.
[171] Bebbington, *Evangelicalism in Modern Britain*, 39.
[172] J.E. Hutton, *A History of the Moravian Church* (London: Moravian Publication Office, 1909), 265, 275-6, 322.
[173] J. Wesley, journal entry for 12 August 1738 in *Works [BE]*, 18:293.
[174] Podmore, *The Moravian Church in England*, 147.
[175] Stead, "Moravian Spirituality and its Propagation," 237.

before), Wesley urged the frequent observance of the Lord's Supper as "a plain command of Christ." In addition, there were "great benefits" in communion, notably "the forgiveness of our past sins and the present strengthening and refreshing of our souls." The Lord's Supper also, said Wesley, "gives strength to perform our duty, and leads us on to perfection." The reference to perfection is an important theme in Wesley's spirituality. To Wesley, communion was highly significant to the spiritual life, which is why he urged frequent observance of the Lord's Supper.

> Let every one therefore who has either any desire to please God, or any love of his own soul, obey God and consult the good of his own soul by communicating every time he can; like the first Christians, with whom the Christian sacrifice was a constant part of the Lord's day service. And for several centuries they received it almost every day: Four times a week always, and every saint's day beside. Accordingly those that joined in the prayers of the faithful never failed to partake of the blessed sacrament.[176]

In 1745 the Wesleys published *Hymns on the Lord's Supper*, which contained 166 items. As F.C. Gill notes, the hymns convey the depths and mystery of the Eucharist and are intended to nourish spiritual experience.[177]

Although it was not the Moravian influence which shaped Wesley high regard for the spiritual benefits of communion, Wesley's visit to Herrnhut and his observation of Moravian sacramental practice likely reinforced his convictions. Wesley does not mention in his comments on his visit the fact that he was apparently not invited to share in the Moravian celebration of the Lord's Supper, but this is stated (although a century later) by Daniel Benham, who wrote the biography of James Hutton, the first English Moravian. Benham wrote:

> When the congregation [at Herrnhut] saw Wesley to be *homo perturbatus*, and that his head had gained ascendancy over his heart, and being desirous not to interfere with his plan of effecting good as a clergyman of the English Church when he should become settled – for he always claimed to be a zealous English Churchman – they deemed it not prudent to admit him to that sacred service.[178]

As Herbert McGonigle comments, whether this rebuff played a part in altering John Wesley's opinion of the Moravians is not clear, but over the next two years Wesley accused the Moravians of an emphasis on "stillness" in spiritual experience which seemed to rule out human responsibility, of rejecting rather than encouraging the faith of those who did not have "full assurance," of teaching that people were free from God's law (antinomianism), and of preferring "modern mystics" to the early church fathers. On the question of who should be admitted to communion, Wesley believed that it should be open to

---

[176] J. Wesley, "The Duty of Constant Communion" in *Works [BE]*, vol. 3, Albert Outler, ed. (Nashville, Tennessee: Abingdon Press, 1986), 430.

[177] F.C. Gill, *Charles Wesley: The First Methodist* (London: Lutterworth Press, 1964), 123.

[178] D. Benham, *Memoirs of James Hutton* (London: 1856), 40.

those seeking "the liberty of the gospel." To Wesley, it was a "converting ordinance," a means by which people could experience faith and grow in grace.[179]

Activism: "to all the peoples of the world"

To what extent, finally, does the well-known activism of evangelical life and of Methodism in particular derive its power from Moravian influence? Zinzendorf wrote in 1738 about the task of going out "to all the peoples of the world."[180] "I look upon all the world," John Wesley similarly stated, "as my parish."[181] There is an echo here of Zinzendorf. The Moravians had been influenced by Zinzendorf's "Order of the Mustard Seed," with its promise to "carry the Gospel to the heathen beyond the seas." For Moravians the power to engage in active mission was from the Holy Spirit. Incidentally, the Spirit in early Moravian liturgy was described by the image "Mother." The *Te Matrem*, a prayer to the Holy Spirit, says: "O Mother! Whoever knows you and the Saviour glorifies you because you bring the gospel to all the world." As Craig Atwood notes, this aspect of Moravian theology has been played down by historians. Zinzendorf claimed, referring to the Holy Spirit, that "he did not know her before the year 1738."[182] Zinzendorf did not emphasise the Holy Spirit above Christ. Zinzendorf taught that "Our Saviour...will do all by His Spirit...when He comes and approaches the Heart with His Power."[183]

Concern for overseas missions was present in the Society for the Promotion of Christian Knowledge (1699). Also, David and John Brainerd worked among North American Indians. But the Moravians, with their commitment to conversion, a biblical Christianity, the cross and activism, offered a model of what might be termed a missional spirituality. Moravians spoke of converts being "awakened by the doctrine of Jesus's sufferings" and argued that the Moravian focus on narrating the story of Christ crucified touched people's hearts and indeed was an emphasis revealed by the Holy Spirit.[184] Mark Noll suggests that "a direct bestowal of energy from Moravianism and the converts of [George] Whitefield," together with stimulus from America – notably through Jonathan Edwards – contributed to "a period of dynamic evan-

---

[179] McGonigle, *John Wesley and the Moravians*, 14-18; Podmore, *The Moravian Church in England*, 64. As early as 1737 Spangenberg noted Wesley's view that through Holy Communion "a man can be converted." See D.L. Rights, "Moravian Archives at Herrnhut" in *South Atlantic Quarterly*, vol. 43, no. 4 (1944): 46. Cited in Towlson.

[180] J.C.S. Mason, *The Moravian Church and the Missionary Awakening in England, 1760-1800* (Woodbridge: The Boydell Press, 2001), 6.

[181] John Telford, ed., *The Letters of the Rev. John Wesley, A.M.*, vol. 1 (London: Epworth Press, 1931, reprinted 1960), 286. Hereafter abbreviated as *Letters*.

[182] C. Atwood, "The Mother of God's People: The Adoration of the Holy Spirit in the Eighteenth-century Brüdergemeine" in *Church History*, vol. 68, no. 4 (1999): 886-9.

[183] Zinzendorf, *Sixteen Discourses on Jesus Christ our Lord* (1750), cited in Stead, "Moravian Spirituality and its Propagation," 235.

[184] Mason, *The Moravian Church*, 168.

gelical expansion."[185] Although it took some time for Methodism to commit itself to world mission, some Anglicans, such as Bishop Thomas Wilson of Sodor and Man, were deeply impressed by Moravian initiatives. In 1739 Wilson asked Moravian Henry Cossart about Moravianism's mission in the West Indies, Greenland, the American colonies and the Baltics, and afterward commented: "I am ashamed to blush for myself, that in so many years I have taken so little pains in comparison, and done so little good."[186]

Moravian hymns also stimulated mission. The first Moravian hymnbooks included older hymns from the Unity of the Brethren and also hymns composed by contemporary authors such as Zinzendorf. John Wesley translated some of these into English. Many outlined salvation in Christ and expressed dedication to Christ's will. The following verse speaks of going out in "witness":[187]

> O ground us deeper still in thee
> And let us thy disciples be!
> And when we witness here below
> Let thy pure joy our hearts o'erflow.

As Moravian mission spread, new communities began to sing hymns in their own languages. An important book on the Moravian mission to Greenland noted that from about 1742 Greenlanders were singing, in the Inuit language, hymns replete with Christian teaching, such as a Moravian hymn about the "Saviour's Blood and righteousness."[188] As Nola Reed Knouse puts it: "From the beginning of the Unitas Fratrum in the middle of the fifteenth century... music has greatly enhanced the Moravians' ability to worship with the heart as well as the mind, to express and teach their faith to each other, to strengthen their communities, and to go around the world in mission and service."[189] A visitor to a Moravian service in Yorkshire confessed that the singing "made a deeper impression upon his Heart than the Preaching."[190] This commitment to hymn-singing as an integral part of mission was famously taken up in Methodism.

A stress on hymn-singing did not mean that evangelistic preaching was neglected, either among Moravians or Methodists. Peter Böhler pressed upon John Wesley the importance of the evangelistic task. On 6 March 1738, Wesley relates how "I began preaching the new doctrine, though my soul started back from the work." The "new doctrine" was "salvation by faith alone," as this had been outlined by Böhler. The first person to whom Wesley "offered

---

[185] Noll, *The Rise of Evangelicalism*, 194.
[186] Podmore, "The Anglicans and the Brethren," 628-9.
[187] Stead, "Moravian Spirituality and its Propagation," 253-5.
[188] Mason, *The Moravian Church*, 21. The book was D. Cranz, *The History of Greenland* (London, 1767).
[189] Nola Reed Knouse, ed., *The Music of the Moravian Church in America* (Rochester, NY: University of Rochester Press, 2008), 1.
[190] Podmore, *The Moravian Church in England*, 149.

salvation by faith," was a prisoner in Oxford under sentence of death, a man by the name of Clifford. Peter Böhler had, Wesley commented, "many times desired me to speak to him before," but Wesley had been reluctant, thinking that death-bed repentance was not possible.[191] On a subsequent occasion, later in March, Wesley again spoke to "the condemned man." and this time Wesley was able to report a dramatic change in the man's experience: "After a space he rose up, and eagerly said, 'I am now ready to die. I know Christ has taken away my sins; and there is no condemnation for me.'"[192] After his return from Herrnhut, Wesley began to engage in wider mission. He wrote on 17 September: "I began to declare in my own country the glad tidings of salvation."[193]

In examining the mission of the Moravians and its influence on Methodism, Colin Podmore has argued that in the period under consideration here the Moravians were not engaged in intentional missionary work in England. Podmore comments: "The Moravians did not seek people out, and they neither preached nor formed any group in London. This had not been their intention."[194] Podmore argues that Towlson "misunderstands their purpose completely, for it is clear that the Moravians sought fellowship with those who were already children of God; they wanted to tell of God's deeds to people whose eyes were already opened."[195] It is true, as Herbert McGonigle comments, that "proselytising" was not what the Moravians wanted to do in England.[196] However, it seems to me that Podmore overstates the case when he seems to suggest that the Moravians sought fellowship only with "those who were already children of God." Rather, Böhler was intent on talking to John and Charles Wesley in such a way as to "impress upon their minds the Gospel," so that they in turn would actively preach it.

Conclusion

"Evangelicalism" as Bebbington notes, "learned much from the Moravians."[197] In this study I have investigated some of the ways in which this can been seen in the early development of John Wesley's evangelical spirituality. Later Wesley became critical of a number of aspects of Moravian life. This is explored in detail by Towlson, who suggests that the "high-water mark of Methodist and Moravian fellowship" was a love feast on 1 January 1739.[198] John Wesley's journal records that he was with about sixty friends, including Charles, George Whitefield, and other prominent Methodist leaders, for a

---

[191] J. Wesley, journal entry for 6 March 1738 in *Works [BE]*, 18:228.

[192] J. Wesley, journal entry for 27 March 1738 in *Works [BE]*, 18:232-3.

[193] J. Wesley, journal entry for 17 September 1738 in *Works [BE]*, vol. 19, Reginald Ward and Richard Heitzenrater, eds. (Nashville, Tennessee: Abingdon Press, 1990), 12.

[194] Podmore, *The Moravian Church in England*, 22.

[195] Podmore, *The Moravian Church in England*, 9.

[196] McGonigle, *John Wesley and the Moravians*, 6.

[197] Bebbington, *Evangelicalism in Modern Britain*, 40.

[198] Towlson, *Moravian and Methodist*, 77.

love feast in Fetter Lane, London, and that "the Power of God came mightily upon us, insomuch that many cried out for exceeding joy, and many fell to the ground. As soon as we were recovered a little from that awe and amazement at the presence of his Majesty, we broke out with one voice, 'We praise thee, O God; we acknowledge thee to be the Lord.'"[199] Wesley would eventually distance himself from the teachings of some Moravians, for example regarding the necessity of full assurance for justification by faith. As Herbert McGonigle says, Wesley was to develop his understanding of justification and sanctification "in ways increasingly more Anglican and less Moravian."[200] Although Wesley would express grave doubts about the leadership of Zinzendorf, nonetheless he continued a friendly correspondence with Böhler up until the latter's death in 1775. Wesley also remembered the words of counsel that Zinzendorf gave him in his period in Georgia. Writing in 1771 to Joseph Benson, a Methodist preacher in his early twenties who was later to become president of the Methodist Conference, Wesley quoted the words (in Latin) from Zinzendorf. For Wesley, despite his break with the Moravians over certain theological matters, when it came to organizational leadership and spiritual formation, it was still the case that "the Count speaks."[201] Moravianism had an important and lasting influence on Methodist organization and spirituality.

---

[199] J. Wesley, journal entry for 1 January 1739 in *Works [BE]*, 19:29.
[200] McGonigle, *Sufficient Saving Grace*, 110.
[201] J. Wesley, Letter to Joseph Benson from 9 March 1771, *Letters*, 5:228.

Part II

Missional

Chapter 4

The Future of Wesleyan Missional Theology: Reconciliation and the Eucharist

By David Rainey

Introduction

In 1998 Clark Pinnock asserted an idea that has become common in the theology of missions. Pinnock stated, "The time is surely ripe for theological advance in the context of world missions."[202] He added, "The question is – will we grasp this opportunity for evangelical and Wesleyan theology?" Pinnock also claimed that "The identity of an evangelical theologian is defined more sociologically than precisely theologically."[203] It is legitimate to add that often missions has become a sociological study rather than a theological study and this has created added problems for the church's understanding of missions. The proposal offered in this essay is that John Wesley's understanding of the practice of mission was grounded in an ecclesiological theology of mission.

---

[202] Clark Pinnock, "Evangelical Theologians Facing the Future: An Ancient and Future Paradigm" in *Wesleyan Theological Journal*, vol. 33 no. 2 (1998): 7.
[203] Clark Pinnock, "Evangelical Theologians," 8.

Preliminary Overview

In 2004 William Abraham addressed the Wesleyan Theological Society with an essay titled, "The End of Wesleyan Theology."[204] He began, "Wesleyan theology is slowly being laid to rest,"[205] and then lamented, "There are as many Wesleys as there are scholars."[206] He continued:

> They have migrated to Evangelicalism, to Feminism, to Narrative Theology, to Liberation Theology, to Process Theology, to Paul Tillich, to Karl Barth, to John Howard Yoder, to Michel Foucault, to Rosemary Ruether, to Ellen Charry, to anything and to everyone under the sun.[207]

However, the problem is not that Wesley cannot be integrated to other appropriate theological traditions; it is that, for some, Wesley has been lost in the migration and one can no longer find Wesley. To put this in another, more caustic manner: Wesley and Wesleyan theology can no longer stand on its own, if Wesleyan theology must migrate to other forms in order to maintain any integrity. To recover Wesley, it's imperative that Wesleyan sources be brought forward in the conversation.

Consider the following example. Michael Zbaraschuk explains in an essay from the *Wesleyan Theological Journal* that, "As Wesleyan thinkers continue to refine their approaches to the theological world, both process thought and open theism are making the case to be conceptual theological options."[208] The essay was designed to offer theological directions for Wesleyan Christology but the difficulty with the essay appears when John Wesley made no contribution to the Christological discussion. To make Wesleyan theology more amenable to post-modern strategies and methodologies, some have ignored the historical-theological John Wesley and, in other cases, some have attempted to re-invent John Wesley altogether, not unlike Albert Schweitzer's, *Quest of the Historical Jesus*.

Perhaps the future of Wesleyan theology will enter a new invigoration.[209] The current essay builds on my recently published article, "The Established Church and Evangelical Theology: John Wesley's Ecclesiology."[210] William Abraham's concern that Wesley's "fervent sacramentalism" has been sidelined in the church's mission ought to be heeded. This essay seeks to recover a Wesleyan ecclesial theology by considering Wesley's own sacramental theology,

---

[204] William Abraham, "The End of Wesleyan Theology" in *Wesleyan Theological Journal*, vol. 40 no. 1 (Spring, 2005), p. 7-25.
[205] Abraham, "The End of Wesleyan Theology," 7.
[206] Abraham, "The End of Wesleyan Theology," 13.
[207] Abraham, "The End of Wesleyan Theology," 15.
[208] Michael Zbaraschuk, "Process Theology Resources for Open and Relational Christology" in *Wesleyan Theological Journal*, vol. 44 no. 2 (Spring, 2009): 154.
[209] See Tom Noble's 2010 address to the Wesleyan Theological Society, "To Serve the Present Age: Authentic Wesleyan Theology Today."
[210] David Rainey, "The Established Church and Evangelical Theology: John Wesley's Ecclesiology" in *International Journal of Systematic Theology*, vol. 12 no. 4, (October, 2010): 420-434.

which has been overlooked with respect to the question of missional theology.

Some further comments will be helpful to place the idea of a reassessment of the future of Wesleyan theology with a missional perspective in relation to the Eucharist. Over thirty years ago Albert Outler offered a useful assessment on John Wesley and why he had been ignored in the broader academic community. Outler wrote, "...we don't have many mass evangelists of record with anything like Wesley's immersion in classical culture, his eager openness to 'modern' science and social change, his awareness of the entire Christian tradition as a living resource – and even fewer with his ecclesial vision of a sacramental community as a nurturing environment of Christian experience."[211] It is the notion of "sacramental community" that should be recovered to develop not only a proposal for the future of Wesleyan theology but a proposal for the future of the Church's universal mission. What is needed is not simply a count of how many times the Eucharist is celebrated during the year but a continuation of Wesley's Eucharistic theology for the Church of the twenty first century. In light of this, it will be established that Wesley's Eucharistic theology and practice was integral to the eighteenth century revival.

John Wesley's Eucharistic Theology: Pre-1738

Recently, Geordan Hammond has continued his important research into the early years of John Wesley's ministry and theology.[212] His research confirmed that Wesley was influenced by the sacramental theology of the Non-Jurors and Daniel Brevint. Through these people Wesley accepted the concept of the mysterious presence of Christ at the Eucharist through the actual presence of the Holy Spirit. Wesley formulated this position before the beginning of the revival in 1738 yet Wesley never wavered on this point during the revival.[213] Thus, the bread and wine were effective channels of God's grace. This meant that the Eucharistic celebration was a key to the ongoing influence of the revival. As Geordan Hammond stated, "An important aspect of Brevint's theology (shared by the Wesleys) is that through celebrating the Eucharist, the faithful receive God's grace and are empowered for holy Living."[214] It is clearly evident in this sacramental theology that the communicant can be transformed by God's grace at the Eucharistic table. Hammond goes on to assert in his brief analysis of the 1745 publication *Hymns on the Lord's Supper*, "that the Wesleys led a revival that was (a) liturgical and evangelical."[215] For Wesley

---

[211] Albert Outler, "The Place of Wesley in the Christian Tradition" in *The Place of Wesley in the Christian Tradition*, Kenneth Rowe, ed. (New Jersey: The Scarecrow Press, 1976).
[212] Geordan Hammond, "The Wesleys' Sacramental Theology and Practice in Georgia" in *Proceeding of the Charles Wesley Society*, vol. 13 (2009): 53-73.
[213] Hammond, "The Wesleys' Sacramental Theology," 57.
[214] Hammond, "The Wesleys' Sacramental Theology," 64.
[215] Hammond, "The Wesleys' Sacramental Theology," 63.

it was the participation in the continually effective sacrifice of Christ on the cross expressed through the Lord's Supper that was so crucial. Our reconciliation to God transforms us into a "living sacrifice" and so the Lord's Supper applies the full effect of God's grace to the participant. This is partially affirmed in Kyle Tau's comment, "It is the church's union with Christ through the partaking of the sacrament that procures for us reconciliation with the Father."[216]

Geordan Hammond insisted, "John Wesley's high regard for the Eucharist was a constant and unwavering aspect of his life and ministry."[217] He is not alone in insisting that the Eucharist is an important key to understanding the eighteenth century revival. Albert Outler confirmed this in his editorial comment regarding Wesley's sermon, "The Duty of Constant Communion." The Sermon had been developed from John Nelson's writings. John Wesley wrote an extract of the 17th-18th century Non-Juror's sacramental theology in 1732. The sermon, though, was published in the June 1787 *Arminian Magazine* and Outler added, "What may be most noteworthy about this sermon is that it represents Wesley's fullest and most explicit statement of his Eucharistic doctrine and praxis..."[218] The point is that the future of Wesleyan theology can get its bearings directly from John Wesley in order to understand an authentic mission of the Church. Still, we need to recognize how his Eucharistic theology created mission. Wesley's Eucharistic theology is a theology of reconciliation; he also described this as holiness, i.e., love of God and neighbour. With this in mind he expected Methodists to attend the Eucharistic service each week. For Wesley this was integral to the holiness and mission of the church. It is then important to recognize that the Lord's Table was the place to experience reconciliation.

John Wesley's Eucharistic Theology: Post-1738

But it is important to note some alterations in Wesley's Eucharistic practice from the Georgian ministry to the outbreak of the revival in 1738 and in the following years. During his brief time in Georgia he followed a strict Non-Juror approach and, consequently, one might think that Wesley's method was invasive in investigating people's spiritual disciplines. After 1738 there is a discernable shift to a more open table without the priestly investigation into people's behaviour. Two illustrations will suffice to make this point. First, Wesley clearly made a break from his earlier "fencing" of the Table in his post-1738 disagreements with the "stillness" understanding of the London Moravians at Fetter Lane by identifying his openness in Eucharistic theology.

---

[216] Kyle Tau, "A Wesleyan Analysis of the Nazarene Doctrinal Stance on the Lord's Supper" in *Wesleyan Theological Journal*, vol. 43 no. 2, (Spring, 2008): 107.

[217] Hammond, "The Wesleys' Sacramental Theology," 59.

[218] See Albert Outler's comments on Wesley's sermon, "The Duty of Constant Communion" from "Sermons," vol. 3 of *The Bicentennial Edition of the Works of John Wesley* (Nashville, Tennessee: Abingdon Press, 1986), 427-428. Hereafter referred to as *Works [BE]*.

In part he wrote, "I showed at large that the Lord's Supper was ordained by God to be a *means of conveying* to men either *preventing* or *justifying*, or *sanctifying grace* ... that no *fitness* is required at the time of communicating but a *sense of our state*, of our utter sinfulness and helplessness; every one who knows he is *fit for hell* being just *fit to come to Christ*..." [219] Now the mission of the church has been identified. At the Lord's Table all are invited and depending on a person's spiritual state, it is possible to experience the awareness of sin and the need of Christ (preventing grace), or, a conversion to Christ (justifying grace), or, growth in holiness (sanctifying grace). Secondly, that this became the norm is evident in his own journal accounts of the hundreds, perhaps thousands, who attended his Eucharistic services throughout Great Britain. J. Ernest Rattenbury conveniently gave us an account of Wesley's estimated numbers of participants during the last ten years of his life. I will quote Rattenbury at length if only to emphasize that missions and the Lord's Supper were integrally united by Wesley.

> LEEDS – "Easter Day, I preached in the church morning and evening, when we had about 800 communicants; "at the communion was such a sight as I am persuaded was never seen in Manchester before, 11 or 12,00 communicants at once"; LEEDS – "We were ten clergymen and 7 or 800 communicants"; "I found it work enough to read prayers and preach, and administer the Sacrament to several hundred people"; MACCLESFIELD – "We administered the Sacrament to about 13,00 persons"; MANCHESTER again – "Mr. Baily came very opportunely to assist me, it was supposed there were 13 or 14,00 communicants"; "Easter Day – near 1000 communicants"; LEEDS – "Having five clergymen to assist me, we administered the Lord's Supper to 16 or 17,00 persons"; BRISTOL – "It was supposed we had 1000 communicants, and I believe none went away empty"; MANCHESTER – "We had 12,00 communicants"; SHEFFIELD – "I read prayers, preached, and administered the Sacrament to above 500 communicants"; OLD CHURCH, LEEDS – "We have eighteen clergymen and about 1,100 communicants"; SHEFFIELD – "I read prayers, preached, and administered the Sacrament to 6 or 7,00"; BIRMINGHAM – "Mr. Heath read prayers and assisted in delivering the Sacrament to 7 or 8,00 communicants."[220]

This account shall end with Wesley's record of his ministry in Dublin, Ireland:

> I preached at the new room at 7, at 11 I went to the Cathedral, I desired those of our Society who did not go to parish Churches, would go with me to S. Patrick's. Many of them did so. It was said the number of communicants was about 500; more than went there in the whole year before Methodists were known in Ireland.[221]

---

[219] See J. Wesley's journal entry form June 28, 1740, in *Works [BE]*, vol. 19, Richard Heitzenrater, ed. (Nashville, Tennessee: Abingdon Press, 1990), 159.

[220] J. Ernest Rattenbury, *The Eucharistic Hymns of John and Charles Wesley*, (Akron, Ohio: OSL Publications 1996), 2-3.

[221] Rattenbury, *Eucharistic Hymns*, 3.

To emphasize the place of the Lord's Table in the life of the Church, and for Wesley, during the revival, may not have been particularly unusual.[222] But, perhaps, it is remarkable that Wesley could attract such large crowds at the Eucharistic celebration.

Wesley consistently maintained that he was a "High Churchman."[223] It meant his model for church renewal was the first three centuries, along with a high regard for the ecclesial institution of the Church of England, which he combined with his political conservatism. Yet his ecclesiology was not narrowly focussed and now there is evidence of his open Eucharistic approach. Further support for Wesley's open approach can be gleaned from his writings. As the Methodist movement developed Wesley adopted a mission in which he intended to include all people in the renewal of the nation. In different ways this was controversial yet Wesley was aware that he could not gain approval from everybody all the time. His 1749 "Letter to a Roman Catholic" is a helpful example.

In the letter he distinguished between doctrine and opinion and his doctrine was grounded in the scripturally based Nicene Creed; his ecclesiology of the universal church was based on the trinitarian relationship with the living and departed humanity. He began the letter recognizing the controversy of his reconciling theology. He wrote, "Many Protestants (so called) will be angry with me, too, for writing to you in this manner..."[224] Near the end of the Letter he continued his ecumenical mindset, "If a man sincerely believes thus much and practices accordingly, can any one possibly persuade you to think that such a man shall perish everlastingly?"[225] Then he concluded, "My dear friend consider: I am not persuading you to leave or change your religion, but to follow after that fear and love of God without which all religion is vain."[226] John Wesley ended with a call to peace and reconciliation between Protestant

---

[222] W.M. Jacob gave a brief account of the regularity of Eucharistic practice in England. The frequency of the Eucharistic celebration depended on the size of population. For instance, he stated, "London's large population meant clergy frequently celebrated Holy Communion." Then he added, "During the early eighteenth century the majority of village clergy celebrated communion three times a year but bishops clearly exhorted incumbents to provide an additional celebration, usually on the Sunday nearest Michaelmas," *The Clerical Profession in the Long Eighteenth Century, 1680-1840* (Oxford: Oxford University press, 2007), 184, 185.

[223] This was not a term that can be easily defined in the eighteenth century. William Gibson's work on the early eighteenth century Bishop William Talbot indicated the looseness of categories such as "High Church" and "Low Church." Gibson concluded, "In short there was no clearly delineated doctrines that so easily differentiated High and Low Churchmen." See "William Talbot and Church Parties 1688-1730" in *Journal of Ecclesiastical History*, vol. 38 no. 1 (January, 2007): 48.

[224] J. Wesley, "Letter to a Roman Catholic" in *John Wesley*, ed. Albert Outler, (Oxford: Oxford University Press, 1964), 493.

[225] J. Wesley, "Letter to a Roman Catholic," 496.

[226] J. Wesley, "Letter to a Roman Catholic," 496.

and Roman Catholics.²²⁷ Although the Roman Catholic Church exercized no influence on the rise of eighteenth century Methodism, Wesley's attempt at reconciliation was quite remarkable.

Again, it can be repeated that Wesley consistently called himself a "High Churchman" so it is accurate to say that Wesley constructed his theology within the boundaries of the Church of England, based in Richard Hooker, and to that were added the Anglican interpretations of the first three centuries of the Christian church. But into the Methodist movement came many Dissenters. These were the people who opposed the established Church of England. Wesley knew the Dissenting ecclesiologies since both Wesley's father and his mother came from the Dissenting tradition but they left the Dissenters and moved into the Church of England. Wesley, during the revival, acknowledged that the Dissenters gave him genuine problems, yet he never opposed their involvement in Methodism.

Wesley's Further Reconciling Intentions

Wesley took the problems created by the Dissenters to the annual Conference meetings because he correctly claimed that they deliberately tried to move Methodism out of the Church of England, thus, for Wesley, they were a cause of disunity.²²⁸ If there is evidence of Wesley attempting reconciliation with Roman Catholics (at least he meant to end hostilities between the two traditions), then the Dissenting movement, as an acknowledged cause of disunity for the established Church and thus within Methodism, still required Wesley to portray Methodism as an inclusive reconciling movement and, therefore, no one could be excluded. Thus the Dissenters were allowed to remain, though Wesley disagreed with their intentions. At the same time Wesley had tried, at an early date in the revival, to maintain peace with the Methodists of the Calvinist theology, both within the Church of England and those opposing the Church of England.²²⁹ This open generosity is confirmed in his 1755 sermon, "Catholic Spirit." For the sake of Christian unity and reconciliation he wrote, "I inquire not, 'Do you receive the Supper of the Lord in the same posture and manner that I do?'"²³⁰ The formal practice of the Eucharist service of his early years had been replaced by an open visible Eucharistic Table of reconciliation during the revival.

---

²²⁷ J. Wesley, "Letter to a Roman Catholic," 498-499. For Wesley's more critical approach to Roman Catholicism, see David Rainey, "The Established Church and Evangelical Theology: John Wesley's Ecclesiology" in *International Journal of Systematic Theology*, vol. 12 no. 4 (October, 2010): 428.

²²⁸ J. Wesley, "Farther Thoughts on Separation from the Church," in vol. 9, *Works [BE]*, ed. Rupert E. Davies (Nashville, Tennessee: Abingdon Press, 1989), 539.

²²⁹ See Richard P. Heitzenrater, *Wesley and the People Called Methodists* (Nashville: Abingdon Press, 1995), 171-172. Heitzenrater gives a brief account of the attempt at reconciliation which was not entirely successful.

²³⁰ J. Wesley, "Catholic Spirit" in *Works [BE]*, 2:87.

The sermon, "The Means of Grace," made it clear that John Wesley knew that many Methodists disregarded the importance of the sacraments and for these Methodists a wedge divided spirituality and sacramental practice. Wesley rejected this; for him the sacraments were not an option but were vital for the Christian life. The sacraments effectively conveyed God's grace to the participant, thus the revival could not afford to downplay sacramental life. Yet, Wesley was also aware of the abuse attributed to sacramental practice; he commented, "all these means, when separate from the end, are less than nothing and vanity; that if they do not actually conduce to the knowledge and love of God they are not acceptable in his sight..."[231] Though he recognized the possible misdirection in the sacramental act he did not reject sacramental practice but endeavored to place it in its proper theological place. Wesley believed there was nothing "automatic" in the sacraments, i.e., the sacraments did not contain grace in themselves; it is God who works through these appointed channels of grace. He continually asserted that the means of grace which included the sacraments, transforms the participant. In the sermon he wrote his familiar phrase, "By the 'means of grace' I understand outward signs, words, or actions ordained by God, and appointed for this end – to be the *ordinary* channels whereby he might convey to men preventing, justifying, or sanctifying grace."[232] He implied that in like manner to the sacraments, prayer or the reading of scripture can become abusive but one does not abandon the practice because of misuse.

It is in this sermon, "The Means of Grace," that we find Wesley's emphasis on the Lord's Supper as a converting ordinance and should not be abandoned in opposition to the ill conceived "waiting on God" model of the London Moravians. He stated, "use all the means which God has ordained. For who knows in which God will meet thee with the grace that bringeth salvation?"[233] To this he would then add at the end of the sermon the spiritual value of the means of grace, "not for their own sake, but in order to the renewal of your soul in righteousness and true holiness."[234] As stated earlier, it is possible to discern the implication that the Lord's Supper is to be a constant activity for the unconverted and the believer in the development of the spiritual life.

It is worth noting that Charles Wesley was completely in line with this way of theological thought. From *Hymns on the Lord's Supper* is Hymn #165:

> How happy are Thy servants, Lord,
> Who, thus remember Thee!
> What tongue can tell our sweet accord,
> Our perfect harmony.

---

[231] J. Wesley, "The Means of Grace" in *Works [BE]*, 1:381.
[232] J. Wesley, "The Means of Grace" in *Works [BE]*, 1:381.
[233] J. Wesley, "The Means of Grace" in *Works [BE]*, 1:395.
[234] J. Wesley, "The Means of Grace" in *Works [BE]*, 1:396-397.

> Who Thy mystery supper share,
> Here at Thy table fed,
> Many, and yet but One we are,
> One undivided bread.
>
> One with the living Bread Divine,
> Which now by faith we eat,
> Our hearts and minds, and spirits join,
> And all in Jesus meet.
>
> So dear the tie where souls agree
> In Jesu's dying love:
> Then only can it closer be,
> When all are join'd above.[235]

Reconciliation as Inclusiveness

A slight change in direction will add to the depth of the analysis of Wesley's missional agenda and his critical assessment of renewal in the church. In his remarkable but small treatise, "Thoughts Upon a Late Phenomenon" (1788), Wesley offered a critical assessment of renewal movements throughout history. His assessment stated that revival movements had only a short duration; thirty years was the norm before a renewal movement lost its original effectiveness.[236] He brought this analysis into his own life by describing the beginning of Methodism and the immediate attempt by some to separate from the established Church. This, for Wesley, was a disastrous move and had been rejected by repeated Conferences.[237] Wesley added a note that has often been ignored: "they will not be a distinct body."[238] Here he meant that Methodism would not separate from the Church of England and therefore would not become a distinct body. Years earlier in 1742 he had used a similar approach.[239] Wesley followed a basic Nicene theology interpreted through the sixteenth century Reformation to define Methodism in general terms:

> A Methodist is one who has the love of God shed abroad in his heart by the Holy Ghost given unto him; one who loves the Lord his God with all his heart, and with all his soul, and with all his mind, and with all his strength. God is the joy of all his heart and the desire of his soul...[240]

In these quotes Wesley refused to be drawn into a narrow definition of exclusion. His attempt was to include all people from all the Christian traditions. Once the revival began in 1738 Wesley displayed this generosity of God's love in his Eucharistic practice and theology.

---

[235] J. Ernest Rattenbury, *Eucharistic Hymns*, 202.
[236] J. Wesley, "Thoughts Upon a Late Phenomenon" in *Works [BE]*, 9:535.
[237] J. Wesley, "Thoughts Upon a Late Phenomenon" in *Works [BE]*, 9:536.
[238] J. Wesley, "Thoughts Upon a Late Phenomenon" in *Works [BE]*, 9:536.
[239] J. Wesley, "The Character of a Methodist" in *Works [BE]*, 9:32-46.
[240] J. Wesley, "The Character of a Methodist" in *Works [BE]*, 9:35.

The Current Situation

Howard Snyder's contribution in the edited work, *Evangelical Ecclesiology: Reality or Illusion?* is an important chapter on the dynamic understanding of the church.[241] Though I disagree with his overly critical use of the word "institution," Howard Snyder provided a useful way to see the bigger picture of the church.[242] As a dialogue partner with Howard Snyder's essay let me add a much earlier work, T.W. Manson's, *The Church's Ministry* (1948). Manson's basic agenda was to establish that the essential ministry of the church is the "continuation of the Incarnation." All other ministries are derivative from Christ. Manson made some significant statements on the ministry of the church; one such statement deals with the Church as a living organism: "Again because the Church is a living organism we cannot simply go back to the New Testament times and say that whatever we find there must be binding for ever, and that anything in the Church's life and organisation that cannot be shown to have existed in the Apostolic Age has no right to exist at all."[243] That seems to resonate with John Wesley's ecclesial methodology and formation. John Wesley never implied a debate between "organic" versus "institutional;" he held both ideas together in evangelical tension and it is a key in understanding Wesley's missional ecclesiology. And so, in combining Howard Snyder's contribution, T.W. Manson's book, and John Wesley's "High Churchmanship" with Eucharistic theology we discover an inclusive ecclesiology effective for the Church's missional agenda.

A Current Eucharistic Practice

In liturgical practice the Liturgy of the Table begins with the "passing of the peace." This act was not in the 18th century Eucharistic service, it was introduced in the 20th century. The "passing of the peace" made explicit what was implicit in the liturgy. This act is not a welcoming to the service, or the church, or the Table; it is an act of reconciliation. The priest states, "The peace of the Lord be always with you." The congregation responds, "And also with you." Then the instruction is given, "Let us offer one another the sign of peace." When properly done, the service is a direct statement that the church

---

[241] Howard Snyder, "The Marks of Evangelical Ecclesiology" in *Evangelical Ecclesiology: Illusion or Reality?* John G. Stackhouse, Jr., ed. (Grand Rapids: Baker Academic, 2003), 77-103.

[242] Howard Snyder's work appears to assert a more functional level of ecclesiology. He questioned the adequacy of the four traditional marks, "one, holy, catholic, and apostolic church," with the comment, "I suggest two inherent limitations: the ambiguity of the traditional marks and, more seriously, their inadequate biblical grounding." See "The Marks of Evangelical Ecclesiology," 84. I would question both assumptions. The four traditional marks are biblically based and were always open-ended, not restrictive, and they should be read in that manner.

[243] T.W. Manson, *The Church's Ministry* (London: Hodder & Stoughton Limited, 1948), 85-86.

is the place of reconciliation. The "passing of the peace" is a visible sign that God's people are a people of reconciliation and it is this visibility that conveys mission to the world. Anthony Thiselton repeated this idea by stating, "To share the peace in the Eucharist or the Lord's Supper is to learn the habit of living in a state of reconciliation with others, and of sharing collaboratively in a common mission and commitment."[244]

For the Eucharist to be viable the Christian community is not to be understood as a group of individuals gathered in worship; it is a group of people united at the Table of the Lord living in the grace of the Holy Spirit. Since the Eucharist is a thanksgiving celebration of Christ's sacrifice, the letter to the Ephesians becomes important. There we read, "For he is our peace; for in his flesh he has made both groups into one and has broken down the dividing wall, that is, the hostility between us...and might reconcile both groups to God in one body through the cross, thus putting to death that hostility through it" (Eph. 2: 14, 16). This is confirmed in Paul's second letter to the Corinthians, "So we are ambassadors for Christ, since God is making his appeal through us; we entreat you on behalf of Christ, be reconciled to God" (II Cor. 5: 20). Consequently, being, "a living sacrifice" (Rom 12:1) is a sacramental act and is a continuation of Christ's finished sacrifice which carries with it the enormous potential for missions in the theology of reconciliation through the incarnation. Sarah Whittle connected the community meal (Eucharist) in I Cor. 10-11 with Rom. 12:1. Concerning I Cor. 10-11 she stated, "This may be more than an interesting digression because it is on this very basis, says Paul, that the covenant meal we eat together-the cup we share and the bread we break-is participation in the body of Christ (I Cor. 10:16)." Then she concluded, "This corporate sacrifice is one of consecration and communion, an offering of peace and reconciliation with God and one another."[245]

Conclusion

If the explicit reconciliation theology is missing then the Eucharist becomes a ritual of habit rather than the declaration of the visible reconciled community known as the church. It is visible reconciliation through Christ's work and in the power of the Holy Spirit that creates the "marks of the church." Regardless of how many marks are authentic to the church's identity it is only in reconciliation that the church's identity becomes authentic. The Eucharistic practice of reconciliation among the participants in the service should be required in all Eucharistic liturgy. Such an act of reconciliation would then be applied to the world and all of creation. No doubt there are powerful eschatological implications in this. Just as Wesley excluded no one from the Table so all of God's creation should be in focus at the Eucharist. As Mary

---

[244] Anthony Thiselton, *The Hermeneutics of Doctrine* (Grand Rapids, Michigan: Eerdmans, 2007), 88.

[245] Sarah Whittle, "Bodies Given for the Body: Covenant, Community and Consecration in Romans 12:1" in *Wesleyan Theological Journal*, vol. 48 no. 1, (Spring, 2011): 101-102, 105.

Elizabeth Mullins Moore indicated, "The self-giving of God and humanity are critical to New Creation, and it is clearly glimpsed in the sacraments and in Jesus' giving of his own life for his friends (John 15:13)."

Chapter 5

The DNA of Mission-Shaped Discipleship

By Philip R Meadows

Introduction

There has been a number of unfolding and overlapping shifts in missiological thinking over recent years. First, the dominant understanding of mission as sending people overseas to pre-Christian cultures has been overshadowed by the need for missionary activity in our emerging post-Christian context. The "Gospel and Our Culture" movement, for example, has helped the church understand the Western world as a mission field, to which all the principles of cross-cultural mission can be applied.[246]

The second shift has been to liberate the whole idea of mission from bondage to the institutional structures of the church. It is not that the church of God has a mission, but that the mission of God has a church; or, in other words, missiology precedes ecclesiology. The "Missional Church" movement has sought to address the challenge of domestic mission by letting the principles of cross-cultural engagement shape the implementation of culturally relevant structures and activities.[247] The danger of this approach lies in settling for new kinds of nominally Christian community, being different in form, but equally languishing in spirit.

---

[246] This movement is rooted in the work of Lesslie Newbigin, whose corpus includes, *Foolishness to the Greeks: The Gospel and Western Culture* (London: SPCK, 1986).

[247] The seminal text for this movement is Darrell Guder, *Missional Church* (Grand Rapids, MI: Eerdmans, 1998).

A third shift, which is presently gaining momentum, attempts to refocus our attention from missional ecclesiology to mission spirituality,[248] and making authentic discipleship the starting point of missional thinking. It is "people" not "churches" that participate in the mission of God. The world is not evangelized by structures, but by people who love God and neighbor. Truly missional churches are communities of disciples who gather to help one another abide deeply with God, and live evangelistically in the world. In short, spirituality and discipleship is the link between missiology and ecclesiology.

It can be argued that the logic of these shifts was already anticipated in the missionary thrust of early Methodism. Although the movement emerges within a strongly Christendom culture, it related to the established church as an institution in need of renewal, and to the general population as "pagans" in need of evangelizing. Notwithstanding Wesley's claim that the people called Methodists could faithfully inhabit the structures of the established church, the missional impulse would often justify modes of organization and activity that directly challenged them.

Neither Wesley, nor the early Methodist preachers, use the language of "mission" as such, but they do speak about "the work of God" and being co-workers with God. This biblical language, however, perfectly captures the essence of the *missio Dei* as the activity of God in the world, and our participation in it. The "work of God" is fundamentally what God does to lead humanity through the whole way of salvation; by setting us free from sin, filling us with the divine life, and renewing us in holy love. On the one hand, we are co-workers with God as recipients of the *missio Dei*, to the extent that we are filled and transformed with the love of God and neighbor. The grace of God works in us so that we can "work out our own salvation" with fear and trembling.[249] On the other hand, we become co-workers with God as participants in the *missio Dei*, to the extent that the love and grace of God overflows our lives, and reaches out to others, in witness and service. In short, mission is ultimately a discipleship issue.

It is not surprising, therefore, that Wesley concludes "the grand stumbling-block" to the spread of the gospel is "the lives of Christians."[250] The generality of those who call themselves disciples are not actually living proof of the gospel. The real problem is when Christians lack the "power of religion" in their hearts, and fail to embody the beauty of holiness in their lives. Although God does save the multitudes in times of revival, Wesley notes that "in general, it seems, the kingdom of God... will silently increase, wherever it

---

[248] A disparate group of thinkers, including Susan Hope, *Mission-Shaped Spirituality* (London: Church House Publishing: 2010); Roger Helland and Leonard Hjalmarson, *Missional Spirituality* (Leicester: IVP, 2011).

[249] Cf. J. Wesley, Sermon 85, "On Working Out Our Own Salvation" in *The Bicentennial Edition of the Works of John Wesley*, vol. 3 (Nashville: Abingdon Press, 1976–). Hereafter, *Works [BE]*.

[250] J. Wesley, "The General Spread of the Gospel" in *Works [BE]*, 2:495.

is set up, and spread from heart to heart, from house to house, from town to town."[251]

Mission-shaped disciples are those who "live the gospel" in word and deed, through the ordinary flow of everyday life. The gospel is not just a message, but a life lived: "the medium is the message." In his hymn, "God of All Power, and Truth, and Grace," Charles Wesley taught the Methodists to pray, "That I thy mercy may proclaim, / That all mankind thy truth may see, / Hallow thy great and glorious name, / And perfect holiness in me." We have a gospel of holy love, and it takes a holy people to communicate that message effectively. God's chosen medium is the witness of ordinary people whose lives are made extraordinary by the holy love of God and neighbour.

This chapter explores what it means to develop the spiritual life of mission-shaped discipleship for the contemporary church. Using the biological metaphor of DNA, the nature of mission spirituality is described by identifying four central themes, or genes, of Wesleyan theology and spirituality.[252] Having mapped this genome, it becomes possible to discern how the contemporary church may have repressed these genes, and how renewal can come through re-expressing them. Finally, some implications for adapting church leadership to this process of "gene therapy" are explored.[253]

Mapping the Genome of a Disciple-Making Movement

The "inherited church" of mainline denominationalism continues to struggle through a time of considerable decline, and has not adapted well to its changing environments. This has prompted some to search for ecclesial DNA rooted in Scripture alone, unsullied by the genetic defects of competing historic traditions and fossilized institutions. While such an approach may get at the ecumenical heart of the "primitive" church, it also places Methodist denominations, along with other historic traditions, on the horns of a dilemma.

On the one hand, if the search for ecclesial DNA means bypassing the tradition altogether, then we are no longer the "People called Methodists" in any meaningful sense. On the other hand, if it means depending on the current state of the denomination, then we seem to be stuck with a defective gene pool. Behind this dilemma is an identity crisis about what it means to be Methodist at all: whether we are actually committed to identifying the distin-

---

[251] J. Wesley, "The General Spread of the Gospel" in *Works [BE]*, 2:493. Wesley also develops this argument in "Scriptural Christianity" in *Works [BE]*, 1: 159-180.

[252] I have developed this genome further in: Philip Meadows, *The Wesleyan DNA of Discipleship* (Cambridge: Grove Books, 2013).

[253] The fourfold genetic code of Wesleyan mission spirituality, outlined here, forms the "way of life" embodied in the Inspire movement (inspiremovement.org). Much of the theological reflection in this chapter has arisen from the author's involvement in this movement, to introduce mission spirituality within the Wesleyan and Methodist families, and beyond.

guishing traits of this Christian family, in order to pursue fresh expressions of the charisms that gave birth to the tradition.

Methodism is an interesting case study because it started out as a movement of mission and renewal within the Church of England during the eighteenth century. John Wesley's primary concern was not to "do church differently," but renewing "scriptural Christianity" in order to help its members live as "real Christians." The Wesleyan tradition reminds us that church is first and foremost a community of disciples, and the revitalization of our churches will depend upon the renewal of authentic discipleship. The first task is to identify those traits by mapping the genome of the movement, passed on by John Wesley as founder and spiritual parent.

Gene 1: Seeking Holiness

Why do the "People called Methodists" matter? What is it that makes them distinctive enough to be worth preserving? First, John Wesley claimed that God had risen up the Methodist movement "to reform the nation, particularly the church, and to spread scriptural holiness over the land."[254] Second, he believed that the doctrine of Christian perfection was "the grand *depositum* which God has lodged with the people called Methodists; and for the sake of propagating this chiefly He appeared to have raised it up."[255] In short, God had set them apart, and sent them out, to invite all people into a journey of faith, marked by holiness of heart and life, with the goal of perfect love. For William Sangster, this is Methodism's "unfinished task," and for which it must be "born again."[256]

Historically speaking, the wider church has done much to make holiness appear either unattractive or unattainable. It has praised spiritual élitism. It has fostered moral and spiritual legalism, which has led to numerous instances of hypocrisy. The idea of "perfection" can be less than enticing. On the one hand, it is typically thought of in absolute moral terms, as something reserved for the angels, or as possible for God alone. On the other hand, our technical culture has predisposed us to think of perfection in terms of flawless performance. Both divine perfection and technical perfection are quite beyond human attainment. Far from inspiring a life of virtue and excellence, such expectations of perfection are more likely to engender disillusionment, despondency, and despair. Proclaiming a gospel of perfection hardly seems like offering good news to humanity.

---

[254] J. Wesley, "Minutes of Several Occasions" in *The Works of John Wesley*, vol. 8, Thomas Jackson, ed. (London, 1872) edn, AGES digital CD-ROM (Rio, WI: 2002), 326. Hereafter, *Works*.

[255] J. Wesley, Letter to Robert Carr Brackenbury, September 1790, in *The Letters of John Wesley*, vol. 8, John Telford, ed. (London: Epworth Press, 1931), 238.

[256] William Sangster, *Methodism: Her Unfinished Task* (London: Epworth, 1947); and, *Methodism Can Be Born Again* (London: Hodder & Stoughton, 1938).

It is right to be wary of striving for perfection, but Wesley himself disavowed any such "perfectionism."[257] His language of holiness and perfection was really a way of speaking about the spiritual maturity we are called towards throughout scripture.[258] From the Pietists he learned that holiness was a heart fully devoted to God, expressed in a life of loving obedience. From the Mystics he learned that holiness was the fruit of an intimate and conscious communion with God that takes flesh in costly service to others. From the Evangelicals he learned that the pursuit of holiness is by faith and grace alone, begun in the experience of new birth and the personal assurance of forgiveness. The gospel of early Methodism was the invitation to embark on an "experimental" way of salvation, in which the promise of evangelical conversion was a necessary step towards being saved to the uttermost. Wesley summarizes "scripture perfection" as "pure love filling the heart and governing all our words and actions."[259]

It can be argued that the simple aim of Wesley's teaching on perfection was to captivate the imagination with a scripturally-rooted vision of Jesus-shaped and Spirit-filled discipleship, when lived to the full.[260] This vision (goal or *telos*) of "perfect love" was pursued as both a command and a promise—a life worth seeking, because it was something that God longs to give. Wesley argues that a Methodist is not one who has necessarily arrived at the goal, but one who hungers for it, and strives after it; that is, "any who sincerely follow after what they know they have not yet attained."[261]

Discipleship is a pursuit of holiness in which one is transformed into the likeness of Jesus, through the power of the Spirit, while living for the gift of perfect love. From the perspective of mission spirituality, this pursuit is driven by a longing for life made beautiful by the indwelling presence and power of God. The "beauty of holiness" is seen in the life of Jesus, and discipleship is about becoming more like him in all our thinking, feeling, speaking and doing. When Christians truly grow in the likeness of Christ, Wesley claims that non-believers will "begin to give attention to their words" and "will surely be led to consider and embrace their doctrine." When those who live without God come into contact with a people whose lives are radiant with divine beauty, the truth of the gospel is not only credible but attractive and compelling. Wesley concludes that "the holy lives of the Christians will be an argument they will not know how to resist."[262]

---

[257] See Wesley's opening disclaimers in Sermon 40, "Christian Perfection" in *Works [BE]*, 2:99-124

[258] Wesley adopts the language of perfection from the Latin, *perfectio*, which translates the Greek terms, *telos* and *teleios*, meaning "end" or goal or maturity.

[259] J. Wesley, "A Plain Account of Christian Perfection" in *Works* 11:469.

[260] For example, Wesley's tract on "The Character of a Methodist" was meant to inspire the movement with a desire for lives that are filled, transformed and overflowing with holy love of God and neighbour (*Works* 8:376f).

[261] J. Wesley, "The Character of a Methodist" in *Works* 8:384. Both this tract and Sermon 40, "Christian Perfection" adopt the now-and-not-yet language of Phil 3:12.

[262] J. Wesley, Sermon 63, "The General Spread of the Gospel" in *Works [BE]*, 2:496.

Gene 2: Spiritual Discipline

Once captivated by the promises of scriptural holiness, Wesley encouraged the early Methodists to strive for evangelical conversion and perfection in love through the spiritual disciplines, or "means of grace."[263]

By these means, we become recipients of what Wesley calls the two "grand branches" of salvation. On the one hand, grace is everything that God has done for us in Christ to forgive our sins and bring us into right relationship with the Father (i.e. justifying grace). On the other hand, grace is everything that God does in us through the Spirit, to give us new birth, set us free from the power of sin, and conform our lives to the likeness of Christ (i.e. sanctifying grace). If it is by grace that God reaches out to embrace us, then it is by faith that one enters into that embrace. Conversion may be understood as attaining a conscious union with God; discipleship as a deepening communion with God in daily life; and mission as the extension of God's love through us to embrace others.[264]

The spiritual disciplines are "means of grace" through which this life-transforming communion with God is entered, deepened and extended. These include "works of piety": such as prayer, searching the Scriptures, participating in the Lord's Supper, and fasting or abstinence. Wesley also includes "works of mercy" as means of grace: both in terms of caring for the body, such as feeding the hungry, clothing the naked, visiting the sick and imprisoned; and caring for the soul, such as "awakening sinners" and "[contributing] in any manner to the saving of souls."[265] In this way, Wesley encourages us to think of mission and evangelism as works of mercy. These means of grace are also called "good works" insofar as they enable us to live as co-workers with God. First, we become co-workers with God by "working out our own salvation" through repentance, faith and holy living. Second, we are called to be co-workers with God by working for the salvation of others. When our works of piety lead to works of mercy, we are caught up in a movement of divine grace that fills, transforms and overflows our own hearts and lives. Discipleship shaped by the means of grace is how we become recipients of, and participants in, the missional flow of God's love.

In one sense, it might be said that the love of God is cultivated primarily through works of piety, and love of neighbor is expressed primarily through works of mercy. In another sense, however, they are inseparable because cultivating intimacy with God will inevitably send us out to meet the needs of others, because God's heart is to heal the sick and save the lost. Wesley warns that we cannot make serving God in works of piety an excuse for neglecting our neighbour in works of mercy. If it comes to a choice, we must be ready to leave the sanctuaries of private devotion or public worship "at charity's al-

---

[263] Cf. J. Wesley, Sermon 16, "The Means of Grace" in *Works [BE]*, 1:378-397.

[264] This theology is expanded further in Philip Meadows, "Entering the Divine Embrace: Towards an Ancient-Future Wesleyan Theology of Evangelism" in *Wesley and Methodist Studies*, vol. 3 (2011): 3-30.

[265] J. Wesley, Sermon 43, "The Scripture Way of Salvation" in *Works [BE]*, 2:166.

mighty call."²⁶⁶ This relationship between devotion and mission is perfectly embodied in the life of Jesus; in whom zeal for works of mercy was the immediate overflow of his intimate relationship with God, in the power of the Spirit.

Gene 3: Sharing Fellowship

Seeking holiness means striving for a God-centered life through the spiritual disciplines. It takes deep spiritual friendships of mutual accountability and spiritual direction, however, to keep us attentive to God, and intentional about the pursuit of perfect love. Wesley said that "as the sun is the centre of the solar system, so…God is the centre of spirits;" but warns that "we are encompassed on all sides with persons and things that tend to draw us from our centre."²⁶⁷ He understood how the rigors of daily life cause us to become "uncentered" or "unhinged from God," and "habitually inattentive" to his presence and leading. The life of discipleship requires a posture of continual "watchfulness."

It is for this reason that Wesley taught the early Methodists that there was no such thing as "solitary Christianity" because they could not become holy on their own.²⁶⁸ The core purpose of Methodist society was "to watch over one another in love" (cf. Heb 13:17), so they might "help each other to work out their salvation" (cf. Phil 2:12). Wesley lamented over the poverty of Christian fellowship in most parish churches of his time:

> Who watched over them in love? Who marked their growth in grace? Who advised and exhorted them from time to time? Who prayed with them and for them, as they had need? This, and this alone is Christian fellowship: But, alas! Where is it to be found?... We introduce Christian fellowship where it was utterly destroyed. And the fruits of it have been peace, joy, love, and zeal for every good word and work.²⁶⁹

Wesley was convinced that the pursuit of holiness would fail apart from the support of spiritual friends who shared the journey of discipleship together.

Contemporary Methodism can be intentional about worship and pastoral care, while completely neglecting the need for mutual accountability (sharing life deeply with one another) and spiritual direction (helping one another discern the presence and leading of God). Yet this was the essence of early Methodist fellowship. The societies were subdivided into small groups of up to twelve people, called "class meetings,"²⁷⁰ who held one another accountable to three simple rules: (1) Do no harm; (2) Do all the good one can (works of mercy); and (3) Attend to the ordinances of God (works of piety). These groups had a "class leader" who would be the first to share, and then take the

---

[266] J. Wesley, Sermon 92, "On Zeal" in *Works [BE]*, 3: §II:9, BCE 3.
[267] Cf. J. Wesley, Sermon 79, "On Dissipation" in *Works [BE]*, 3:314.
[268] J. Wesley, Preface to "Hymns and Sacred Poems" (1739), *Works* 14:437.
[269] J. Wesley, "A Plain Account of the People Called Methodists" in *Works* 8:267.
[270] J. Wesley, "A Plain Account of the People Called Methodists" in *Works* 8:269f.

opportunity to "advise, reprove, comfort or exhort, as the occasion required."[271] The class meeting is reminiscent of the way Jesus gathered and apprenticed the twelve disciples.

Those who hungered for greater spiritual maturity were also gathered into even smaller groups of four or more, called "bands," arranged by age and sex.[272] This enabled a "closer union" by which they could have more open confession and penetrating conversation. The aim was to help one another grow in grace through the most besetting challenges, and to wrestle with God for the promise of perfect love. This is reminiscent of the way Jesus chose to invest in a "band" of three from among the twelve disciples (Peter, James and John) to share the deepest moments of his own life.

The Wesleyan emphasis on accountability may seem like a curse to those who are content with their own private spirituality, or who expect little from the Christian life. People are right to be wary of accountability, however, if it is associated with forms of evaluation, reward and punishment, rather than sharing, healing and growth. The small groups in early Methodism practiced mutual accountability in the context of spiritual direction, with the goal of helping one another become more attentive to the presence of God, and more responsive to the leading of the Spirit. The challenge of deep spiritual friendship was grasped as a blessing, albeit with "fear and trembling," by those who long to abide more deeply in God's grace and live more fully into his purpose for their lives.

Gene 4: Everyday Mission

As we have seen, seeking holiness, spiritual discipline, and sharing fellowship all contribute to a life that is missional by nature. From a Wesleyan perspective, mission is best understood as the character of a holy people who are set apart for God and sent out into the world, to live and work for his praise and glory. Wesley affirms that "the root of religion lies in the heart, in the inmost soul" and that this is "the union of the soul with God, the life of God in the soul of man." This is the heart of missional spirituality. But "if this root be really in the heart, it cannot but put forth branches" through our lives and into the world.[273]

First, the ethos of everyday mission is embodied in what Wesley calls "social holiness." By this, he does not mean engagement in social activism or working for social justice, but simply that every Christian life is shaped by a nexus of personal relationships through which the life, love and grace of God may be revealed and spread to others. It means living as the "salt of the earth" and as the "light of the world" (cf Matt 5:13-16). As salt, Wesley says, "It is your very nature to season whatever is round about you... This is the great

---

[271] J. Wesley, "The Nature, Design and Rules of the United Societies" (1739) in *Works* 8:287f.

[272] J. Wesley, "A Plain Account of the People Called Methodists" in *Works* 8:274f.

[273] J. Wesley, Sermon 24, "Upon Our Lord's Sermon on the Mount: Discourse 4" in *Works [BE]*, 1:541.

reason why the providence of God has so mingled you together with other men, that whatever grace you have received of God may be communicated to others."[274]

As light of the world, Wesley claims that "the heart which is renewed after the image of God, cannot but strike every eye which God hath opened" and others will "perceive how desirable a thing it is to be thus transformed into the likeness of him that created us." He continues, "Let your words be the genuine picture of your heart...that all may see the grace of God which is in you" and some "will take knowledge that ye have been with Jesus." Moreover, "let it shine more eminently in your actions, in your doing all possible good to all men" and "let it be your sole aim, that all who see your good works may 'glorify your Father which is in heaven'."[275] Social holiness is the kind of incarnational life found in Jesus. It is grace made visible, holy love made flesh.

Second, the spirit of everyday mission is encapsulated in Wesley's principle of "good stewardship,"[276] and being fully surrendered to God's purposes. A good steward is one who knows that life is not given for us to do as we please, but to do what pleases God, so that his Kingdom purposes may be fulfilled through us. Life is a gift from God, not to be owned and possessed, but to be enjoyed in the process of giving it back to God, by serving others in word and deed. All of our intellectual powers, bodily capacities, material wealth, time and talents are to be surrendered into God's hands, moment by moment, as each occasion demands.

Only a good steward can commit every past achievement, every present opportunity, and every future aspiration into the hands of God. It requires a sense of good stewardship, and a missionary heart, to say the annual covenant prayer, "I renounce my own wisdom, and do here take thee for my only guide. I renounce my own will, and take thy will for my law."[277] Wesley taught the early Methodists to pray every week, "To thee, O God... I give up myself entirely: May I no longer serve myself, but thee, all the days of my life... Be thou the sole disposer and governor of myself and all; be thou my portion and my all."[278] And this is what it means to serve others by denying self, taking up our cross daily, and following Jesus as mission-shaped disciples.[279]

For Wesley, good stewardship and prayerful surrender are embodied in a life of social holiness, as God "sends" us to serve our families, friends, neighbours and strangers. Perhaps the most strategic method commended by Wesley was visiting the sick and needy. Although there is no formula for this

---

[274] J. Wesley, Sermon 24, "Upon Our Lord's Sermon on the Mount: Discourse 4" in *Works [BE]*, 1:537.

[275] J. Wesley, Sermon 24, "Upon Our Lord's Sermon on the Mount: Discourse 4" in *Works [BE]*, 1:547-548.

[276] Cf. J. Wesley, Sermon 51, "The Good Steward" in *Works [BE]*, 2:282-298.

[277] J. Wesley, *Directions for Renewing Our Covenant With God*, 2nd ed. (London: The Foundry, 1781), 21.

[278] J. Wesley, "A Collection of Forms of Prayer for Every Day of the Week" in *Works* 8:262f.

[279] Cf. J. Wesley, Sermon 48, "Self Denial" in *Works [BE]*, 2:247-248.

practice, he says "it may not be amiss, usually, to begin with inquiring into their outward condition" and bodily needs. Yet, he urges,

> these little labours of love will pave your way to things of greater importance... While you are as eyes to the blind, and feet to the lame, a husband to the widow, and a father to the fatherless, see that you still keep a higher end in view, even the saving of souls from death, and that your labour to make all you say and do subservient to that great end.[280]

The general implication of Wesley's thinking, however, is that God "brings" others into our realm of influence, on a daily basis, often in unexpected ways. We are never short of opportunities to serve others in works of mercy; the only question is whether we will surrender to the impulses of the Spirit when they arise.

Gene Therapy for Disciple-Making Churches

John Wesley left the Methodist movement with a cautionary prognosis about its future. He said, "I am not afraid that the people called Methodists should ever cease to exist either in Europe or America. But I am afraid lest they should only exist as a dead sect, having the form of religion without the power. And this will undoubtedly will be the case unless they hold fast both the doctrine, spirit, and discipline with which they first set out."[281] Mapping the Wesleyan genome has been an exercise in holding out these charisms. Insofar as Wesley's prognosis may offer a useful diagnosis of the contemporary church, this map can help to identify ways in which that genome has been repressed. It can also suggest some ways in which re-expressing these genes might correct (or reverse) the effects of harmful mutations.

In general, it may be observed that many Christian communities are languishing because they have invested more in the form of religion than the power of godliness. To put it more bluntly, highly institutionalized mainline denominations have been more concerned about running (and growing) churches than making (and growing) disciples. Reflecting on the purpose of church structure, Wesley asked, "What is the end of all ecclesiastical order? Is it not to bring souls from the power of Satan to God, and to build them up in His fear and love. Order, then, is so far valuable as it answers these ends; and if it answers them not, it is worth nothing."[282] There is an inseparable connection between the form and power of religion, insofar as the form becomes a means for seeking the power, and the power has an opportunity to be expressed in relevant forms. Nevertheless, Wesley says, "I would observe every punctilio of order, except where the salvation of souls is at stake."[283]

---

[280] J. Wesley, Sermon 98, "On Visiting the Sick" in *Works [BE]*, 3:390-391, 393.
[281] J. Wesley, "Thoughts Upon Methodism" in *Works* 13:258.
[282] John Telford, ed. *The Letters of the Rev. John Wesley* (London: Epworth Press, 1931), 2:76. Hereafter abbreviated *Letters*.
[283] J. Wesley, "Letter to the Rev Mr D_" in *Letters* 4:146.

There is a widespread conviction that Methodism needs to recover its character as a movement, and that local churches need greater spiritual vitality.[284] The logic of a missional movement dictates that seeking the power of godliness must precede investing in the form of religion. The way we "do church" is valuable only insofar as it functions as a means of grace, through which we become co-workers with God in making disciples. Contrary to this, however, is the conventional wisdom that revising the structures will lead to the renewal of discipleship and the revitalization of congregations. The argument here, however, is that re-expressing the Wesleyan genome will involve a reversal of this logic. The pioneers of early Methodism did not set out to plant churches that could make disciples, but to "plant the gospel" and make disciples who needed (and longed for) empowering community. A commitment to revitalising discipleship will more naturally lead to the renewal of the church, and the creative revision of its structures. If we invest disproportionately in the form of religion, we end up with power failure. If we invest extravagantly in the power of godliness, however, we are more likely to end up with mission-shaped disciples who renew the church.

Expression 1: Seek Holy Living in order to Become Healthy Churches

The Wesleyan gene of seeking holiness can be repressed by a preoccupation with restructuring the church.[285] Viewed positively, the motivation for restructuring lies in negotiating the tension between a fear of diminishing resources and the hope for promoting renewal and mission activity. This leads to the development of mission statements, priorities, and core values to guide "new ways of working," and the provision of standardised training. New structures also means new leadership, committees and work teams to manage the new future.

Renewal easily gets confused with implementing some new vision of "doing church," and discipleship is reduced to serving the structures, all in the name of mission. If we start with discipleship, however, we are driven by a different question: What kind of people do we want to be? The gene of seeking holiness shapes a vision of becoming people who delight in the gospel of God's holy love, and who seek the fullness of a Spirit-filled life. People must

---

[284] This is reflected in the work of George Hunter, *The Recovery of a Contagious Methodist Movement* (Nashville, Tennessee: Abingdon, 2011), and Gil Rendle, *Back to Zero: The Search to Rediscover the Methodist Movement* (Nashville, Tennessee: Abingdon, 2011). Both these, however, tend to approach the question from the perspective of systems and structures.

[285] In British Methodism, for example, a Connexion-wide mantra of "restructuring for mission" has driven a range of organisational changes across districts, circuits, and local churches. United Methodism in America (and elsewhere) has committed itself to producing "vital congregations," largely through structural renovations.

desire to glorify God with their whole selves, and see his kingdom come in their daily routines.

One expression of this gene in early Methodism was the love feast, in which hungry disciples would gather to share testimony about their spiritual aspirations as well as attainments.[286] In Wesley's journal, and those of the early Methodist preachers, love feasts became regular occasions in which the presence of God was felt, and the power of the Spirit ran from heart to heart. They were opportunities for re-envisioning the true end of Christian life, and seeking the power to attain it. This wisdom warns us that changing structures without the goal of changed lives will not lead to healthy churches. But those who long for more of God also long for structures that can help them become more faithful disciples. Adapt to meet that need, and people will seek the spiritual life through which the church can be renewed.

Expression 2: Practice Spiritual Discipline in order to Experience Authentic Worship

The Wesleyan gene of spiritual discipline can be repressed by a preoccupation with worship services. In most congregations, the Sunday service defines what the church does primarily. Discipleship amounts to attendance at worship, and mission is about attracting new church-goers to improve attendance records. The church strives to make its services more lively, creative and transforming; and a lot of time is spent arguing about musical style, how disorganized worship can be, and whether people are satisfied. Behind all this, there is an unspoken assumption that God is more real, present and active during one hour on a Sunday morning than in the flow of everyday life. People come to church for the sake of being inspired, revived, and to feel happier.

Unfortunately, if the church service defines what the church does primarily, we are likely to end up as consumers rather than disciples. If one binges on one good weekly meal, one will end up starving for the rest of the week. To begin with discipleship means asking a different question: What kind of worshippers do we want to be? The gene of spiritual discipline shapes a vision of becoming people who find God to be just as real, present and active on Wednesday afternoon as Sunday morning. People who practice the presence of God, pray without ceasing and give thanks in all circumstances, every day of the week.

Wesley asks, "What is it to worship God?... It is, to love him, delight in him, to desire him with all our heart, and mind, and soul, and strength; to imitate him we love... to go through outward work with hearts lifted up to him; to make our daily employment a sacrifice to God."[287] So, at the gathering of the society meetings, they could sing, "And are we yet alive, / And see each other's face? / Glory and thanks to Jesus give / For His almighty grace!"

---

[286] Cf. J. Wesley, "A Plain Account of the People Called Methodists" in *Works* 8:274.
[287] J. Wesley, Sermon 24, "Upon Our Lord's Sermon on the Mount: Discourse 4" in *Works [BE]*, 1:544.

This wisdom warns us that renovating church services without deepening our walk with God will not lead to authentic worship. For those who stay connected to grace, worship services are not the start of a God-less week, but the culmination of a God-filled week. Adapt to this, and corporate worship provides an opportunity to celebrate the reality of God's presence and goodness through the ups and downs of daily life.

Expression 3: Make Spiritual Friends in order to Develop Real Fellowship

The Wesleyan gene of sharing fellowship can be repressed by multiplying church meetings. Although Christian fellowship can be sustained in worshipping congregations, we have also discovered the benefit of small groups, which help us make deeper friendships and grow in love for one another. Indeed, these groups can be where we "do church" most meaningfully, especially when church politics and Sunday services leave us cold and weary. One life-giving feature of small groups is that they are organized around hearing, reading and studying the Scriptures. For a growing number of people, however, there is a suspicion that fellowship still makes little impact on everyday life. So, we try to increase the spiritual depth of our meetings by making them more creative, interactive and experiential. As a result, we may find ourselves better informed, and even convicted, but still not really changed.

Unfortunately, it seems as though we are caught on the horns of a dilemma. On the one hand, if we start with the need for friendship, we may end up with social circles rather than spiritual communities. On the other hand, by starting with the need to study we may become mere learners rather than real followers of Jesus. If we start with discipleship, however, we ask a different question: What kind of friends do we want to be? The gene of sharing fellowship shapes a vision of becoming people who hold each other accountable for our daily walk with God: People who help each other discern God's presence and follow God's lead in the flow of everyday life.

In the class meetings, the early Methodists "experienced that Christian fellowship of which they had not so much of an idea before." Wesley says, "they began to 'bear one another's burdens,' and naturally to 'care for one another.' As they had daily more intimate acquaintance with, so they had a more endeared affection for, each other. And 'speaking the truth in love, they grew up in Him in all things, who is the head, even Christ'."[288] In the bands, "they wanted to pour out their hearts without reserve" and "many were delivered from the temptations out of which, till then, they had no way to escape." So, "they were strengthened in love, and more effectually provoked to abound in every good work."[289] This wisdom warns us that multiplying small groups without deepening spiritual friendships will not lead to real fellowship. But those who invest in deep spiritual conversation will be most stretched in both

---

[288] J. Wesley, "A Plain Account of the People Called Methodists" in *Works* 8:269.
[289] J. Wesley, "A Plain Account of the People Called Methodists" in *Works* 8:274.

their love and service, as hearers and doers of the word. Adapt to this, and we will love one another, as well as live the gospel more faithfully.

Expression 4: Engage in Everyday Mission in order to have Effective Outreach

The Wesleyan gene of everyday mission can be repressed by running mission projects and programs. The process is familiar: Delegate a mission committee; then develop an outreach strategy; then design a program of events; and finally drum up volunteers to run them. Yet people are evangelized by building relationships, not running programs. Mission activity will be ineffective if we are not filled with the love of God, and overflowing with love of neighbor.

Unfortunately, when we start with mission strategy we usually end up running programs rather than sharing faith. If we start with discipleship, however, we ask a different question: What kind of witnesses do we want to be? The gene of everyday mission shapes a vision of becoming people who are alive to God and share God's heart for others. People who seize opportunities to love others in word and deed, one work of mercy at a time.

For Wesley, visiting the sick was a missional discipline incumbent upon all Christians and could not be fulfilled "by proxy."[290] On the one hand, it is only through direct personal relationship that we can be salt and light in the world. On the other hand, it is only through serving people face-to-face that works of mercy become means of grace, as we are transformed by the missional flow of God's love in and through us. Actually, Wesley warns us that failure to serve as the Spirit leads, causes the spiritual life to gradually wither and die.[291] Self-centeredness not only cheats our neighbour of what God intended, but it kills the very life of God in the soul. This wisdom warns us that developing mission strategies without making mission-shaped disciples will not lead to effective outreach. But those who are seeking to abide deeply in God and live missionally in the world will see programs as opportunities for building relationships. Adapt to this, and we will share the kind of faith that makes disciples and renews the church.

Genetic Adaptations for Disciple-Making Leaders

Leadership in mainline denominations is typically aimed at maintaining churches rather than making disciples.[292] On the one hand, the need to preserve denominational structures has made managerial competence an indispensable quality. Simply fulfilling all the demands of institutional bureau-

---

[290] J. Wesley, Sermon 98, "On Visiting the Sick" in *Works [BE]*, 3:389.

[291] J. Wesley, Sermon 98, "On Visiting the Sick" in *Works [BE]*, 3:394-395.

[292] The British Methodist Church is being called a "discipleship movement shaped for mission." As an ordained presbyter in the denomination, I generally observe this to be more of an aspiration than an actuality. Scott Kisker offers a useful analysis of the defects in American denominationalism in, *Mainline of Methodist* (Nashville, Tennessee: Discipleship Resources, 2008), ch.1.

cracy, at both the local and national levels, is experienced as an exhaustive task. On the other hand, the desire to preserve flagging membership has often turned pastoral ministry into a mixture of personal therapy and palliative care. Holy living has been traded for cheap grace, and concealed the radical demands of the gospel on daily life. Some have spiritually impoverished lives, with an anaemic sense of God's presence, and little expectation of his power to transform.

Even where churches have tried to be more missional, they can end up repeating the same mistakes in new ways. We manage outreach projects, relevant worship and fresh expressions without addressing the underlying nominalism that plagues ordinary Christian life. Or we run membership courses and discipleship programs as quick fixes for renewing the church and trying to increase our confidence in the gospel. If we begin with the Wesleyan genome, however, it becomes clear that the spirit of a movement only comes as a gift of the Spirit to those who hunger and thirst for righteousness; who seek God's grace in the midst of daily life; who know that they cannot be real disciples without deep spiritual friendships; and who long to be used by God to transform the lives of others.

Examining the origins of the early Methodist movement reminds us that this way of life grows when people gather together to help one another pursue God with all their heart, mind, soul and strength. And it spreads, as God proves himself faithful to the promises of the gospel, and grace abounds from heart to heart, home to home, and church to church.[293] The spirit of a movement calls for leaders who delight in opportunities to mentor others in the way of Jesus. This final section will touch upon some wisdom from the early Methodist preacher-pioneers to assist reflection on how the gene therapy outlined above can renew the church and its mission from the inside-out.[294]

Adaptation 1: Feeding the Flock's Hunger

One dominant image of church leadership has been the pastoral imperative to ensure that parishioners feel satisfied and happy. Leaders invest their resources in creating worship experiences to lift the spirit, or leading study groups to inspire the mind, or giving pastoral care to comfort the soul. When the church becomes satisfied with these activities as ends in themselves, however, they can actually inoculate people from sensing the need for deep and lasting spiritual growth. This is why it must be remembered that Jesus also said, "blessed are those who hunger and thirst for righteousness, for they will be filled" (Matt 5:6).

---

[293] Steve Addison discusses the connections between relationships and adaptive methods in *Movements that Change the World*, Revised (Downers Grove, IL: IVP, 2011).

[294] Thomas Jackson, ed. *The Lives of Early Methodist Preachers: Chiefly Written by Themselves*, 4th ed., 6 vols. (London: Wesleyan Conference Office, 1871). Hereafter, *EMP*.

Among the early Methodist preachers, John Nelson's antidote to apathy among the early Methodists was "to create such a hungering and thirsting in them after inward holiness, that they may pant as the hart panteth after the waterbrooks, till all that is in them be made holiness to the Lord."[295] In the midst of a powerful love-feast, John Furz recalls how some local leaders were "so filled with zeal for the glory of God, and the good of souls" that they "went into the country villages, sung and prayed, and exhorted people to turn to God."[296] George Shadford reflected that, "if we had more of God in our hearts, there would be more of him on our tongues, and shining in our lives; for out of the abundance of the heart the mouth speaketh."[297]

The Wesleyan gene of seeking holiness reminds us that we were made for an intimate and daily sense of God's presence; for a deep experience of God's acceptance and power to change our hearts and lives; and for surrender to God's will in all things. Making disciples who desire to grow means encouraging them to hunger for more of God in their own lives, and to hunger for the kingdom in the prospering of local communities. The spirit of a movement calls for leaders who long for the fullness of spiritual life in themselves, and are committed to sharing these desires with others. After the manner of love feasts, disciple-making leaders will inspire one another with real-life testimonies of personal transformation and everyday mission. Those who are hungry will feast on the promises of God, develop an expectation of spiritual growth, and delight in opportunities to spread the gospel of holy love.

Adaptation 2: Equipping People for Life

Church leaders spend much of their energy striving to help people encounter God on special occasions, at certain times of the week. They invest their resources in arranging prayer meetings, leading bible studies, and conducting pastoral visits. The problem comes when this perpetuates the idea of an "omnicompetent" leader that insulates people from the personal responsibility of discipleship and the challenge of everyday mission. Jesus did not merely pray for his disciples, he taught them how to find God for themselves in the flow of everyday life: "This, then, is how you should pray: 'Our Father... Give us this day...'" (Matt 6:9).

The early Methodist preachers understood that intimacy with God was the life of discipleship and mission. Thomas Walsh set the example of one who lived in "a momentary spirit of watchful prayer" whether "prostrate upon his face, kneeling, standing, walking, eating, in every posture, and in every place and condition." It was the challenge of mission that led Thomas Rankin to the need for "more earnest prayer, searching the Scriptures, and walking more closely with God."[298]

---

[295] *EMP* 1:152
[296] *EMP* 5:127
[297] *EMP* 6:176
[298] *EMP* 5:160.

The Wesleyan gene of spiritual discipline reminds us that we were made to hear God's still small voice of guidance in the messy details of life; to taste God's goodness in the ups and downs; to see God in a neighbor, and share his heart for the least and the lost. Making disciples who connect with God means teaching people how to pray and practice the presence of God in daily life. The spirit of a movement calls for leaders who long for God's transforming presence, and know how to help others stay connected with God's grace in all the spiritual disciplines. Disciple-making leaders will train people to explore the diversity of ways that God meets us, speaks to us, and empowers us for discipleship and mission day by day: through works of piety (prayer, searching the scriptures, fasting or abstinence) and works of mercy (serving the needy and sharing our faith).

Adaptation 3:
Don't Just Attract Crowds, Invest in People

Most church leaders have been trained to think that making a difference means attracting a crowd, and seeking to influence as many people as possible through high-impact meetings. Ministry by mass appeal has not only influenced our worship gatherings and outreach activities, but our discipleship strategies as well. We try to make disciples by delivering conferences, training events, courses and workshops. When leaders are turned into experts rather than spiritual guides, however, they are absolved of the need to be "real" examples and mentors. Although Jesus did attract crowds, his main strategy for changing the world was to invest in some for the sake of the many: "He appointed twelve that they might be with him and that he might send them out" (Mark 3:14). He invested in deep spiritual friendships with this small group of disciples, and an even smaller "band" of three (Peter, James and John). They experienced three years of intensive spiritual formation, in which Jesus shared his life with them, so they might become like him and continue his mission.

When Matthias Joyce became disillusioned with a lack of overt response to his preaching in the early Methodist societies, he found encouragement through regular meeting with the classes. He noted that "nothing has a greater tendency to lift up the hands that hang down, than to hear those who have sat under us relating the good they have received thereby."[299] After a similar experience, Thomas Rankin celebrated how "the whole economy of Methodism" (i.e. societies, classes and bands) worked together "to promote the great end for which they were designed, - the glory of God in the salvation of souls."[300] Taking on the responsibility for a class meeting was typically how leaders were raised up; and meeting in band was how they sustained themselves through the challenges of ministry. Wesley himself understood the importance of leaders meeting together for mutual support. In the same way

---

[299] *EMP* 4:265
[300] *EMP* 5:159-60.

that Jesus chose his closest disciples, Wesley formed "select bands" whom he could mentor by example, and with whom he hoped, "I might unbosom myself on all occasions, without reserve."[301] The ultimate goal, however, was to raise up those who would be "a pattern of love, of holiness, and of good works" for the movement.

The Wesleyan gene of sharing fellowship reminds us that disciples are made through sharing life deeply with others, in relationships of mutual accountability and spiritual direction. Making disciples who share the journey means going deeper than mass meetings and even house groups, by encouraging very small bands of disciples to long for more of God, to keep in step with the Spirit, and to become more like Jesus in heart and life. The spirit of a movement calls for leaders who long for God's guidance themselves, and know how to help others find it through deep spiritual conversation. Disciple-making leaders will do the work of spiritual guides by investing in a few at a time; and who, in turn, become capable of multiplying that investment in the lives of many others.

Adaptation 4: Moving beyond Strategic Development

Very often, church leaders think of engaging in mission in terms of ambitious, high risk, and creative activities. They engage in evangelistic events, door-to-door visitation, Alpha-style courses, seeker services, church plants and fresh expressions. Care must be taken, however, that commitment to this kind of activity does not blind us to the opportunities we have for sharing faith in the ordinary encounters of daily life. Jesus did not appear to have any discernible mission strategy other than touching and transforming the lives of all he met. He saw the people around him as those to whom God was reaching out with his love: "The Son... can do only what he sees his Father doing" (John 5:19).

As a young convert in the early Methodist movement, William Black recounted, "I felt a peculiar love to souls, and seldom passed a man, woman, or child without lifting up my heart to God on their account; or passed a house without praying for all in it... so that sometimes I was constrained to speak to them, though I met with rough treatment in return."[302] In his ministry among the early Methodists, the personal zeal of Thomas Walsh had the effect of "begetting in their souls a measure of the same zealous concern for the glory of God, and the salvation of sinners, which burned in his own breast."[303] His life was an example of stewardship and surrender, being resolved "to give himself up wholly to the dictates of the Holy Ghost, and to be ready to go what way soever the voice of heaven should call him."[304] Having "a heart al-

---

[301] J. Wesley, "A Plain Account of the People Called Methodists" in *Works* 8:277.
[302] *EMP* 5:257.
[303] *EMP* 3:121.
[304] *EMP* 3:85.

ways at leisure for God, attentive to His teaching, and obedient to His dictates, is the great thing; to which every design and pursuit must give place, if we mean to be truly great in the grace of God."[305]

The Wesleyan gene of everyday mission reminds us that we are made with the ability to discern the presence of God in those around us; to sense the impulses of the Spirit in the flow of daily life; and surrender to these opportunities for serving others, one work of mercy at a time. Making disciples who seize the moments means opening people's eyes to see God's providence at work among those who come into their path. The spirit of a movement calls for leaders who long to see God at work through their own lives to help others become fully surrendered co-workers in the kingdom. Again, John Pawson pleaded with a new generation of Methodist leaders, to "labour with all your might in maintaining the life and power of godliness, both in your own souls and those who hear you."[306]

Conclusion

This chapter has sought to make a contribution to the emerging conversations about mission spirituality and mission-shaped discipleship. Put simply, the role of the church in mission cannot be rightly understood apart from developing the spiritual life of mission-shaped disciples. Central to this argument is a right understanding of the relationship between the "form and the power of religion," or the outward practice and inward character of the Christian life. These are inseparable, insofar as the forms are means of grace, for seeking and cultivating the life-transforming presence and power of God (Gene 1). On the one hand, works of piety and mercy keep us connected to the grace of God in the flow of daily life (Gene 2). On the other hand, the mutual accountability and spiritual direction of Christian fellowship keeps us intentional about seeking God's presence and attentive to his leading (Gene 3). Through these means, discipleship becomes missional by nature, in the overflow of God's love and grace, from the inside-out (Gene 4).

In his sermon, *On Zeal*, Wesley sets out this dynamic pattern as the "entire, connected system of Christianity."[307] He defines zeal as a fervent and godly passion shaped by the "the flame of love" for God and neighbor. The different aspects (or Genes) of discipleship rightly demand our zeal but to different degrees, and Wesley uses the model of concentric circles as an illustration. The inner core of discipleship is the love of God and neighbor, rooted in the heart. Next to this are the inner desires and motivations, which are shaped by this holy love. Surrounding these character traits are the works of mercy, which are expressions of our love for neighbour; and then the works of piety through which the love of God is cultivated. Finally, the whole is encom-

---

[305] *EMP* 3:132.
[306] *EMP* 2:152.
[307] J. Wesley, Sermon 92, "On Zeal" in *Works [BE]*, 3:314.

passed by the fellowship of the church, which is both a means of grace and a visible witness to social holiness in the world.

Wesley is clear that the degrees of zeal with which we approach these different aspects of discipleship must increase from the outside. We must be zealous for the church and its structures, and that it should grow in both number and influence. But if that zeal is not directed by a zeal for the life and love of God in the soul, then church will become and end in itself instead of provoking its members to abound in love and good works. So, we must be more zealous for works of piety and mercy than the forms of church life. But if we become preoccupied with these means as ends in themselves, they can also become counterproductive. So, we must be more zealous still for the character that they are meant to form, and yet more zealous for the holy love that nourishes the whole. For Wesley, this order of priority is meant to ensure that the life and love of God can expand from the inside: from the heart, through our inward character, shaped by the means of grace, disciplined by Christian fellowship and church worship, and out into the world as the visible witness of holy lives. From a Wesleyan perspective, therefore, spirituality precedes ecclesiology in missional thinking. Investing in mission-shaped discipleship is the key to being (or becoming) authentically missional communities.

Chapter 6

John Wesley's Mission of Evangelism

By Ron Benefiel

Introduction

There was a remarkable revival in eighteenth century England. Much of the leadership of that revival would eventually become associated with the Wesley brothers and the Methodists. John Wesley in particular is now remembered as founder of a worldwide movement. He is remembered for his practical theology, his care for the poor and his organizational genius. But at times his passion for evangelism is overlooked. In this essay, I intend to explore the evangelistic mission of John Wesley.

I am particularly interested in the ethos and spirit of the Wesleyan revival, especially in the early years (1740s). Apparently, in the early years of the Methodist revival, the Wesleys requested new converts to write out their testimonies in the form of letters to John or Charles. The letters were delivered to the Wesleys and read in society meetings. To resource this project I will be drawing from a dozen of these testimony letters addressed to Charles Wesley. The letters I will be referring to were written mostly in London in 1740 and 1741.[308] I recognize that this is only a limited sampling (there are 150 such letters on file in the John Rylands library), and that there are limits to the generalization of the letters to the larger Methodist revival given that the letters are quite narrow in scope as they were written mostly in one city and limited to a two year time span. I am hopeful that these letters will effectively serve to illustrate the particular experiences of new converts that will add a dimension to our understanding of the people the Wesleys were reaching as well as the spirit of the overall revival.

Finally, I am interested in exploring the Wesleyan revival with an eye toward understanding Wesley's theological assumptions regarding evangelism.

---

[308] Rather than footnoting each of the references to the unpublished letters, clear reference will be mentioned in the text of the essay indicating the name of the author. Transcriptions of the letters may be found in the appendix.

While there may be ample evidence for the construction of a theology of mission in the Wesleyan tradition, and while Wesley's commitment to evangelism certainly fits well with his theological presuppositions (e.g. his emphasis on prevenient grace and Arminian theology), Wesley, of course, does not lay out a systematic theology of evangelism. Once again we are reminded that Wesley's theology is a practical theology. With this in mind, most of our understanding of Wesley's thinking on evangelism must be constructed from his preaching, his letters, Methodist hymns, and the practices of the early Methodists. In examining these, I am hopeful of discovering key theological concepts related to evangelism which may be useful in constructing a Wesleyan theology of mission.

Wesley's Passion for Evangelism

John Wesley was an evangelist. There were undoubtedly a number of influences in Wesley's life that helped to shape his thinking about evangelism and his calling as an evangelist. Some of these influences are exemplified early on in Wesley's decision to turn down the offer to follow in his father's footsteps in Epworth in favor of going to Georgia to evangelize the Indians. For Wesley, going to Georgia to evangelize the Indians was much more than a noble enterprise; it was grounded in a theological vision. His reasons for going were tied to his hope that out of his work there might emerge a new community that would re-capture the essence of primitive (New Testament) Christianity. He had idealized understandings of the Native Americans as people who were culturally and theologically innocent and untarnished by the fallen state of the world he lived in. He hoped this would be the opportunity to create a new community that truly exemplified primitive Christianity.[309]

His motivation as an evangelist was also related to "working out his own salvation." In his early years, the combination of his hopes for restoring or recreating a true primitive Christian community in which he and other believers would experience Christian perfection along with his own sometimes desperate fear of death and hell were powerful motivations. As Martin Schmidt states, "Wesley's call arises directly from his dialectic of life. His striving for sanctification as a return to primitive Christianity, his will in the primitive Christian conception of the indivisible oneness of the Body of Christ are the strongest motive forces."[310] Even though, by all rights, Wesley failed in his noble venture in Georgia, this experience both represents his missional thinking at the time and serves to further shape his thinking in preparation for the Methodist revival still to come.

For Wesley, evangelism was never just a theological premise; it was a passion and vocation. Skevington Wood writes, "Wesley was first and foremost an evangelist, and as such he was aware that his commission was to preach

---

[309] Martin Schmidt, *The Young Wesley* (London: Epworth Press, 1958), 22-23.
[310] Schmidt, *The Young Wesley*, 25.

the gospel."[311] In Wesley's own words, "A dispensation of the gospel is committed to me, and woe is me if I preach not the Gospel wherever I am in the habitable world."[312] And further, Wesley said he had but "...one point of view—to promote, so far as I am able, vital, practical religion; and by the grace of God to beget, preserve, and increase the life of God in the souls of men."[313] Wesley was decidedly pragmatic in his approach to his work. The urgency with which he sensed the need to preach the gospel to all who would hear superseded in his mind many other considerations. The means were important primarily as they were effective in accomplishing the ends. For example, the mission of calling sinners to repentance was such a compelling imperative for Wesley that established ecclesial boundaries and ecclesiastical authorities were relatively incidental in comparison. As Coleman states, Wesley was "...utterly pragmatic in planning strategy and establishing policy. Whether his approach was approved by church tradition or his ecclesiastical peers was not of great concern. The question was: Does it work?"[314]

Wesley wrote to a friend, "What is the end of all ecclesiastical order? Is it not to bring souls from the power of Satan to God, and to build them up in His fear and love? Order, then, is so far valuable as it answers these ends; and if it answers them not, it is nothing worth."[315] From this, it is not difficult to understand how Wesley came to disregard parish boundaries with the declaration that the "world is my parish." Henry Rack summarizes:

> He (Wesley) wrote to an unnamed friend... who had advised him to return to college or to sit still and not to interfere with souls in other people's parishes as this was contrary to "Catholic principles." Wesley responded that "scriptural principles" alone weighed with him and *they* commanded him to "instruct the ignorant, reform the wicked and confirm the virtuous." Since he was unlikely ever to have a parish, forbidding him to work in others' parishes meant not doing this work at all. And so to: "I look upon all the world as my parish... This is the work I know God has called me to."[316]

Wesley's passion for evangelism extended to his expectations and instructions to his Methodist preachers. The Methodist movement was to be an evangelis-

---

[311] A. Skevington Wood, *The Burning Heart* (Minneapolis: Bethany House, 1978), 147.

[312] Nehemiah Curnock, ed. *The Journal of Rev. John Wesley*, 8 vols. (London: Epworth Press, 1909-16), 2:257. Hereafter referred to as *Journal*.

[313] John Telford, ed. *The Letters of John Wesley*, 8 vols. (London: Epworth Press, 1931), 3:192. Hereafter referred to as *Letters*.

[314] Robert Coleman, *"Nothing to Do But to Save Souls"* (Grand Rapids, MI: Francis Asbury Press, 1990), 33.

[315] *Letters*, 2:77-78. See also Frank Baker, ed. *The Bicentennial Edition of the Works of John Wesley*, vol. 26 (Oxford: Oxford Press, 1982), 205, to "John Smith", June 25, 1746. Hereafter, this edition of Wesley's works will be referred to as *Works [BE]*.

[316] Henry Rack, *Reasonable Enthusiast* (Nashville, Tennessee: Abingdon Press), 189. See J. Wesley, *Works [BE]*, 25:614-617.

tic movement. Above all else, they were to be concerned with preaching the gospel and the salvation of souls. Wesley writes to his preachers, "It is not your business to preach so many times, and to take care of this or that society; but to save as many souls as you can; to bring as many sinners as you possibly can to repentance, and with all your power to build them up in that holiness without which they cannot see the Lord."[317]

John Wesley was apparently not especially animated in his preaching. The convicting influence on his listeners were the words themselves, "quickened by the Spirit" in the hearts and minds of his listeners. Typically, the content of his preaching was bold and to the point. He did not shy away from warning people to "flee the wrath to come" and clearly declaring the effects and results of sin, the judgment of God, and the reality of hell, along with, of course, the love of God and the promise of salvation. Witness these words of Wesley at the end of a message preached in St. Paul's Church in Bedford in 1758:

> O, who can stand before the face of the great God, even our Saviour Jesus Christ! See! See! He cometh! He maketh the clouds His chariots! He rideth upon the wings of the wind! A devouring fire goeth before Him, and after Him a flame burneth! See! He sitteth upon His throne, clothed with light as with a garment, arrayed with majesty and honour! Behold, His eyes are as a flame of fire, His voice as the sound of many waters! ... Hear the Lord, the Judge! "Come, ye blessed of my Father, inherit the kingdom prepared for you from the foundation of the world." Joyful sound! How widely different than that voice which echoes through he expanse of heaven, "Depart, ye cursed into everlasting fire, prepared for the devil and his angels!" And who is he that can prevent or retard the full execution of either sentence?... Hath he not bought you with His own blood, that ye might not perish, but have everlasting life? O make proof of his mercy, rather than His justice; of His love, rather than the thunder of His power![318]

The Social Context

A number of biographers (including Heitzenrater[319] and Rack[320]) have been careful to point out that the Methodist revival of the eighteenth century must be understood as part of a much larger revival that included not only England, but Wales, Germany and America, not only the eighteenth century, but from the seventeenth well into the nineteenth, and not only Methodists,

---

[317] Coleman, *Save Souls*, 16. (Wesley: included in the Minutes of Several Conversations Between the Rev. Thomas Coke. LL.D., the Rev. Francis Asbury, and Others, at a Conference Begun in Baltimore... in the year 1784, Composing a Form of Discipline for the Minister, Preacher, and Other Members of the Methodist Episcopal Church in America (Philadelphia: Charles Cist, 1785), 12.

[318] J. Wesley, "The Great Assize" in Albert Outler, ed. "Sermons," 4 vols. *Works [BE]*, 1:373-375.

[319] Richard Heitzenrater, *Wesley and the People Called Methodists* (Nashville, Tennessee: Abingdon Press, 1995), 97.

[320] Rack, *Reasonable Enthusiast*, 161.

but also Pietists, Puritans and Calvinists. This, of course, raises additional interest in the broad social contexts of these times and places. What characterized the social contexts of that day that provided such fertile ground for revival?

Specifically for our consideration here, what was the social context like in 18th century England? Popular thought has often attributed revival movements to times of significant social and economic instability. Certainly there were significant changes occurring related to the industrial revolution in 18th Century England with substantial movement from agricultural occupations to manufacturing and the trade guilds. This, in turn, contributed to increases in the urban population.

Henry Rack, however, points out that the economic conditions were reasonably stable in the earlier decades of the century.[321] He suggests an interesting alternative description of the social context that may have contributed to the openness to revival. According to Rack, the Church of England in Wesley's day had become relatively ineffective and lacked vitality leaving the common people without a meaningful religious or spiritual alternative. Methodism, along with other revival movements, stepped into the void. In fact, the Methodist revival tended to be stronger where the Church of England was weak, and weaker where the Church of England was relatively strong.[322] This weakness in the established church he attributes to the development of a civil religion that robbed the Church of England of its vitality. He writes:

> The seventeenth century... left a legacy of civil and religious strife, yet without destroying the sense that religion was a major source of social cement and stability if rightly understood and organized... The political stability achieved by one-party rule after 1714 needed to be accompanied by (if possible) a one-party church... In religious terms this also meant a more comprehensive, less dogmatic creed... with a major emphasis on practical morality in which all good men could agree. The result, for Anglicans at least, has been aptly described as a 'civil religion'... it was designed to appeal to the lukewarm multitude, and it enlisted their lukewarm support...[323]

Wesley's goal as a (relatively) loyal Anglican priest, of course, was not to lead people out of the established Church, but, in fact, to revive the Church. His hope was that the Methodists could become an *ecclesiolae* within the *ecclesia*. To the question in the *Larger Minutes*, "What may we measurably believe to be God's design in raising up the preachers called Methodists?" Wesley answered, "Not to form any new sect; but to reform the nation, particularly the church; and to spread Scriptural holiness over the land."[324] However, if Rack is correct, it means that the great majority of the common people may have

---

[321] Rack, *Reasonable Enthusiast*, 173.
[322] Rack, *Reasonable Enthusiast*, 172.
[323] Rack, *Reasonable Enthusiast*, 178.
[324] J. Wesley, "Remarks on a Defence of Aspasio Vindicated" in Thomas Jackson, ed. *The Works of Rev. John Wesley*, 14 vols. reprinted (Grand Rapids, Michigan: Baker Book House, 1980), 10:351. Hereafter referred to as *Works*.

typically had a reasonably strong religious background,[325] but the Church often did not offer much in the way of a vital faith. For example, consider these statements taken from testimonies of early Methodist converts:

> Thought myself a Christian but I found my self mistaken when it pleased God to reveal his dear son in me and to show me the way of salvation as for the articles of our church the doctrine of the spirit of God of regeneration and of justification by faith I was a stranger to them all nor do I remember to have heard any of them preachd or ixplaind by our clergy indeed I went to church and said my prayers and had a form of profession but --- nothing of the power I had no oyl in my lamp no inward principal of holiness in my heart what was I but a whited sepulcher
>
> Sarah Middleton, 1740

> With sorrow do I speak it I being of the Church of England I was att a grate loss to find a spiritual friend that could give me any spiritual comfort what minister I liked in the Church I found their lives was contrary to their doctrine that Satan would have often tempted me to believe that all religion was witchcraft often times he tempted me to deny the being of a god and att other times he would tell me if there was a god he need not concern his self with me
>
> Samuel Hewit, 1741

The religious background of the common people combined with common beliefs regarding the afterlife may also have contributed to their receptivity to the message of the evangelists. Themes of judgment, hell-fire, and eternal damnation were prevalent and strongly held. Rack notes: "What is common to them all is often a strong sense of hell, and this seems to be induced less by hell-fire preaching than by the subjects' own innate belief and conscience which appear to have required little to arouse them. They created their own hell."[326]

Here again, examples from testimonies of Methodist converts in the early years of the revival illustrate this quite well. Sarah Middleton writes to Charles Wesley, "I felt my self so vile that I thought hell was ready to swallow me up". Nathaniel Hurst writes: "...sometimes as I was standing I used to think that the ground whereon I stood was hot under me which made me almost to tremble and to think if the ground should open and swallow me up I should perish forever." And these words from Samuel Hewit:

> I was all of a sudden struck to all appearance with sudden death, O who can tell, but them that has felt the same the horror and confusion that I was in, death I thought lit hovering upon my cold lips and hell open and ready to receive me. The terror of the Lord was in array against me and in the agony I lay for some time. I said the Lord's prayer, I prayed earnestly for Christ's sake that I might not die...
>
> Samuel Hewit, 1741

---

[325] Rack, *Reasonable Enthusiast*, 173.
[326] Rack, *Reasonable Enthusiast*, 197.

The reality of hell was combined with a sense of sinfulness that brought a deep sense of conviction that was all consuming and frequently lasted for years. Their sense of sinfulness often was related not so much to flagrant violations of morality, but more frequently to sins of pride, often using the language of being "pharisaical." In fact, the testimonies typically state that they did not even know that they were such perverse sinners until they heard the preaching of Whitefield or the Wesleys! Maria Price writes to Charles in May of 1740:

> Dear Sir, my heart longs for words to tell how good my dear Saviour is to save such a dark dead stony hearted damned unbelieving Pharisee as I. I did often repent for one sin and did not know I had any more. But I had no sooner repented of it but I commited it again and was two-fold more a child of hell than before. Thus was I mourning and sinning and wondering that I could not overcome it myself.

Mary Ramsay writes that she is so miserable in her sins that she is unable to sing even at home. She writes to Charles, "And so I went on mourning that I could not mourn more and about a fortnight after you were come I fell into such mourning that my heart was ready to break. I came on Monday morning to speak with you but when I came I could not speak." And Elisabeth Hinson writes, "Satan came in and told me I had lost Christ and I mite as well hang myself. But god him is rich in mercy tords all delivered me from the evil of this temptation."

Perhaps in direct proportion to the penitents' sense of despair while under conviction was their sense of freedom and power they reported in their experiences of conversion. Consider the following testimonies:

> The Thursday following being Ascension day I had so much joy when you was preaching that I thought my soul seemed as if it was ascending into heaven. Indeed the joy began in the morning while Mr. Harris was preaching -- and it so increased in the evening while you was preaching that Methought I saw my Saviour in glory -- My soul seemed as though it was out of my body
>
> Mary Ramsay, 1740

> Hearing John Wesley preach to a Society in Bair Yard near Claremarket, I felt my heart open within me and like a fountain of water run from it and in that moment I felt such love, peace and joy passed all expression. We sang a hymn. I thought I was out of the body with the angels in heaven for I was so full of joy I could not express my belief.
>
> T. Cowper, 1741

> After two years deep convictions God rebuked the stormy wind and tempest and their was a great calm—I tasted that peace of God which Paseth all understanding of the natural man
>
> Samuel Hewit, 1741

The Incarnational Movement of Wesley's Ministry

The question arises at this point as to the general social description of the early Methodists. While it is true that there were people of influence in the movement including a few Anglican clergy and people of some status and wealth, most of the early Methodists appear to have been commoners, especially from the working classes. Henry Rack notes that Methodists were drawn especially from the ranks of the common workers, especially craftsmen, industrial workers, miners and fishermen. These mostly "industrial immigrants" found their "disorientation healed by Methodist fellowship."[327] Rupert Davies adds that members of religious societies had belonged mostly to the spiritual elite in previous years. But the Methodists were "open to all and sundry, and were to be found in places and among groups of people where spiritual growth had never been expected or found before."[328]

We have this descriptive account of the Methodist people from the *Memoirs* of James Hutton:

> [They] were composed of every description of persons, who, without the slightest attempt at order, assembled, crying "Hurrah!" with one breath, and with the next bellowing and bursting into tears on account of their sins; some poking each other's ribs, and others shouting "Hallelujah." It was a jumble of extremes of good and evil... Here thieves, prostitutes, fools, people of every class, several men of distinction, a few of the learned, merchants, and numbers of poor people, who had never entered a place of worship, assembled in crowds and became godly.[329]

These early Methodists were commoners, blue collar types, lots of people who would today be classified as "working poor." It must be obvious that Wesley's ministry was outside of his own social class. I would like to suggest that it was both kenotic (self-emptying) and incarnational (full participation and identification with those to whom he was ministering) in ways that are reminiscent of the life and ministry of Jesus. The whole Wesleyan movement, whether in ministries of mercy, justice, or evangelism, was toward the common people, especially toward the poor and those who were in physical, material or spiritual need.

As the incarnational movement of the Wesleyan revival gravitated toward those in need, it in turn enfolded new converts in ways that were both redemptive and empowering. Those who were used to being disempowered outsiders, frequently discovered a new identity and sense of belonging. Rupert Davies comments, "...Methodists were offered a double and interrelated citizenship of both earth and heaven, not one without the other. This was the 'exaltation of the humble and meek', and this was the breach in the class barrier through which the Methodists poured when they heard the 'pure word of

---

[327] Rack, *Reasonable Enthusiast*, 173.
[328] Rupert Davies, ed. "The Methodist Societies: History, Nature, and Design," *Works [BE]*, 9:14.
[329] James Hutton, in Wood, *The Burning Heart*, 137.

general grace.'"[330] Davies goes on to note that this had significant sociological implications for Methodist converts as well as for the movement as a whole.

> Wesley, by preaching a salvation available to all – and by meaning those words quite literally – struck right across this class structure both in its original and in its modified form. The landowners were not much moved by such a gospel, though they were often alarmed by it. The squirearchy and its clerical supporters saw its dangerous possibilities and resisted it by all means in their power. The people to whom its appeal went home were the scarcely educated tradespeople and artisans and superior farm-workers in the first place – people until then deemed to be capable of grasping only the elementary principles of Christianity, those usually identified with the Ten Commandments – and through them to the wholly illiterate peasants and urban "labouring classes" – people thought to be capable of nothing more than blind obedience to their masters. All these people, women no less than men, were now offered the status of children of God, heirs of all God's promises and responsible members of a community that granted both their natural rights as human beings and their supernatural rights as aspirants by the help of the Holy Spirit to Christian perfection. And they knew that if they entered that community they would have the further chance, if they were not too shy or too ill-equipped to take it, of leading classes, preaching from pulpits, and receiving a hitherto undreamed-of measure of education in the fulfillment of their office.[331]

Another dynamic frequently associated with revival movements among the common people, of course, is ecstatic manifestations or "enthusiasm." And "enthusiasm" was a characteristic mark of the Wesleyan revival. Wesley was sympathetic toward demonstrative manifestations while at the same time being committed to reason and rationality, a combination which led Henry Rack to label him a "reasonable enthusiast".[332] Wesley was living in an environment that was alive with spiritual energy and power. For the most part, he associated the ecstatic manifestations frequenting the Methodist meetings as indications of the moving of the Spirit similar to what had occurred in the book of Acts.[333] Henry Rack summarizes some of the manifestations that occurred in one brief period:

> On 17 April 1739 Wesley visited the Baldwin Street society in Bristol and while expounding Acts 4 'called upon God to confirm his word. Immediately one that stood by (to our no small surprise) cried out aloud, with the utmost vehemence, as in the agonies of death. But we continued in prayer till 'a new song was put in her mouth'. Then two people of good reputation were 'seized with strong pain' and 'roared' with disquiet of heart. A few days later people dropped to the ground as if 'thunderstruck'. Many others followed, most notably John Haydon, a man of 'regular life and conversation' who regularly attended church and sacrament and was a strong churchman and hostile to Dissent. He saw the convulsions as delusions of the devil, but then himself fell 'raving mad' after reading Wesley's sermon on 'Salvation by Faith'. He showed

---

[330] *Works [BE]*, 9:27.
[331] *Works [BE]*, 9:25-26.
[332] Rack, *Reasonable Enthusiast*, 173.
[333] Rack, *Reasonable Enthusiast*, 187.

symptoms of demon-possession, cursing the devil, but was relieved by prayer.[334]

Similarly, in the testimonies or early Methodist converts we find examples not only of "out of body" ecstatic experiences, but also of healings, convulsions, and fainting. Consider a few of the manifestations mentioned in our sampling of testimonies:

> my lord him loves sinner still carried on his work and brought all my sins to my remembrance and there I trembled and should have fell down but the popel heald me up and I was out of my senses but the lord awakened me with peace be unto you your sins are forgiving you
>
> Elisabeth Hinson, 1740

> .... soon after yu expounded at Fetterlane and then I was at that time and ever since filled with joy and peace in believing I received the forgiveness of sins and the witness of the Spirit and a dominion over sin at that very time. I trembled so with joy and cried that I did not know how to bear myself. You asked me if I found that peace that passed understanding. -- I said, "Yes, indeed I have."
>
> Maria Price, 1740

> The light of God shown on me once more and my soul was filled with love. Then I could lift up my heart again to the Lord and one day as I was at my work my soul was overpowered with the love of God that I knew not whether I was in the Body or out of the Body.
>
> Nathaniel Hurst, 1741

> I was at the same time restord to my bodily health as well as ever I was in my life
>
> Sarah Middleton, 1740

Field Preaching

Perhaps along with the Methodist commitment to ministry to and among the poor through works of mercy, the incarnational nature of the Wesleyan revival was well illustrated through field preaching. Rather than waiting for people to find their way into the church, field preaching moved the preaching of the gospel out to where the people were. It was a movement out of the cathedral and into the marketplace and out of established sacred spaces into unconventional public spaces. This had the effect of catching attention, of meeting people in their home turf. It was missional in the sense that it took the gospel to the people.

John Wesley, of course, didn't necessarily like the idea of field preaching. Whitefield had started preaching in the open air with remarkable success, and it was at Whitefield's urging that John Wesley reluctantly agreed to give it a try. He wrote in his *Journal*, "I could scarce reconcile myself at first to this strange way of preaching in the fields; having been all my life (till very lately)

---

[334] Rack, *Reasonable Enthusiast*, 194. (See *Journal*, 2:180-186, 189f.)

so tenacious of every point relating to order, that I should have thought the saving of souls almost a sin if it had not been done in church."[335] And in another entry we find these words, "What marvel the devil does not love field preaching! Neither do I; I love a commodious room, a soft cushion, a handsome pulpit. But where is my zeal, if I do not trample all these underfoot in order to save one more soul?"[336]

Wesley found the crowds that showed up for open air preaching far exceeded his expectations. The response was so overwhelming that he had to consider field preaching as a means of reaching the people. In his first day of preaching out in the open (April 2, 1739) in the brickfield near Bristol, he estimated the crowd that gathered to hear him preach to be around 3000 people. He had a similar response a few days later in Kingswood.[337] This was something he simply could not dismiss. Whether he liked field preaching was not the issue, it was an effective means of reaching the people. In his first month, he estimated that he had preached to about 47,500 people with an average showing of about 3000.[338] In the meantime, the numbers showing up to hear Whitefield preach were estimated at 15,000 to 30,000! Even if these figures are inflated, the point was that there were huge crowds of people turning up to hear these evangelists preach from tombstones in cemeteries, in the market square, under trees and in the rock quarries.[339] Perhaps true to his nature and often the reality check to John's zeal, Charles remained skeptical, especially with regard to the numbers that John was reporting. But on June 24, he decided to try it for himself and found that an estimated 10,000 people gathered to hear him preach![340]

Not only was the field preaching successful in drawing large crowds, people were being moved by hearing the Word preached. Apparently, especially early on, the first contact that many of the Methodist converts had with the movement was hearing Whitefield and the Wesleys preaching in the open. Many were deeply affected by the preaching they heard which frequently led them to attend other preaching services to hear these evangelists preach. Here again, they report being deeply moved, convicted of their sins, and confronted with the Truth of the gospel in ways that they had not heard or known previously. But all of this does not fully capture the impact of the evangelists' preaching on their listeners, not only John and Charles Wesley, but perhaps even more the preaching of George Whitefield. Consider some of the testimonies of those who were moved by the preaching of these evangelists:

---

[335] Reginald Ward and Richard Heitzenrater, eds. "Journals and Diaries," vols. 18-24, *Works [BE]*, (Nashville, Tennessee: Abingdon Press, 1988-2003), 19:46.
[336] *Works [BE]*, 23:203.
[337] Rack. *Reasonable Enthusiast*, 194.
[338] Heitzenrater, *People Called Methodists*, 100.
[339] Heitzenrater, *People Called Methodists*, 99.
[340] Heitzenrater, *People Called Methodists*, 99.

I went to hear Mr. John Westly his words was sharper to me then a two edged sword and I cannot but always honour him as an instrument in God's hands of shewing me the true way of salvation by Jesus Christ.

Sarah Middleton, 1740

Your sermon on the threefold state which I often heard with tears showed me I was one of those that was seeking god but as yet had not found him...

Martha Jones, 1740

Then the Lord was pleased to let me hear Mr. John Wesley one night at Fetter Lane -- the Lord spoke peace to my soul. He let me know my sins were blotted out by his Blood.

Nathaniel Hurst, 1741

...how I did rejoice when Mr. Whitefield came about to preach and how was that spark blown up that was just a dying away

Samuel Hewit, 1741

Their I heard Mr. John Wesley such a minister I never heard before.

T. Cowper, 1741

Then on a time when the Lord saw fit to let me see myself was by Mr. John at Wapping. He was explaining the sin of the holy Ghost there I was struck though Satan had not power to make me believe -- I had committed that sin – the Fryday following I heard you, sir, and there – I plainly saw my Saviour bleeding on the cross and the soldiers piecing his precious side... then I heard Mr. Whitefield att Besdey on the indwelling of the Holy Spirit and there I saw I was really half a beast and half a devil.

Awakened by the Reverend Mr. Whitefield:

Convicted by the Reverend Mr. Jn Wesley:

Converted by the Reverend Mr. Charles:

Margerit Austen, 1740

The street preachers obviously had their share of critics. Wesley replied to one such naysayer: "It were better for me to die than not to preach the gospel of Christ; yea and in the fields, either where I may not preach in the church or where the church will not contain the congregation."[341] Wesley also encouraged his preachers to preach in the open air. He wrote to one of his preachers who needed some encouragement, "Preach abroad... It is the cooping yourselves up in rooms that has damped the work of God, which never was and never will be carried out to any purpose without going out into the highways and hedges and compelling poor sinners to come in."[342] So Wesley was an evangelist on a mission to preach the gospel to the common people. Field

---

[341] *Letters*, 2:77f.,(25 June, 1746).
[342] *Letters*, 5:23. (to James Rea, 21 July, 1766).

preaching was not what he preferred, but it was what worked when it came to fulfilling his call.

Societies, Class Meetings and Bands

Wesley's approach to evangelism was not limited to calling people to justifying faith alone, but rather, as Albert Outler points out, his understanding of evangelism always included calling people to holiness of heart and life.[343] Wesley was not preaching justification alone, but his call was to Christian perfection. Outler writes:

> Another aspect of Wesley's newfound success was his firm conviction that conversion is never more than the bare threshold of authentic and comprehensive evangelism. Most of his hearers were already church members of one sort or another. What they needed was new depth and dimension in their nominal Christian professions... always, 'preaching Christ' was aimed beyond confession and conversion toward the fullness of faith and the endless maturing of life in grace... the evangelist accepted a continued responsibility for his converts' growth in grace; thus, sanctification became the goal and end of all valid evangelistic endeavor...[344] (21)

From this perspective, Wesley's approach to evangelism began in field preaching but also included enfolding earnest seekers into small accountability groups. Heitzenrater notes that even with the incredible success of field preaching, it was in Methodism's small groups where people were most likely to experience initial conversion and the assurance of forgiveness from sin.[345]

For Wesley, Christian holiness was necessarily social in nature, that is, it was essentially relational with regard to perfect love for God and neighbor. As such, it was necessary for the pursuit of holiness not to be a private matter, but rather it was lived out in Christian community. The cornerstone of this community in which people pursued and experienced Christian holiness was the small group. Small groups created the structure and accountability for believers to pursue holiness of heart and life.

The structure of the small groups is well known. To quickly review, the total membership in a given location was the society. Within the society there were class meetings and bands. In addition, for some periods and in some places there were also penitent groups and select societies. All members of the society also belonged to a weekly class meeting which was organized by geography and cut across age, gender and marital status. Newcomers typically were invited to class meetings before they were admitted to the society. For those who wanted a deeper level of accountability they could also belong to a band that also met weekly. The bands were organized with respect given to

---

[343] Albert C. Outler, *Evangelism and Theology in the Wesleyan Spirit* (Nashville, Tennessee: Discipleship Resources, 1996), 21.

[344] Outler, *Evangelism and Theology*, 21.

[345] Heitzenrater, *People Called Methodists*, 99.

gender, age and social class. Penitent groups were formed for those who had been active in the past but who had fallen away and wanted to return to the fold. Select societies consisted of leaders who not only held one another accountable but also served as a sounding board to the pastor (or specifically to the Wesleys). Bands might be considered to be something of an inner circle of the society, and the select society an inner circle of the bands.[346]

The accountability expected in the groups was quite rigorous. Regular accountability of members in class meetings regarding the serious pursuit of the holy life determined whether or not individuals remained in good standing. Those in good standing received tickets which were required for entrance into the meetings of the society. Probing questions were asked every week in the class meetings regarding their Christian walk and their pursuit of holiness. (See Appendix A). The accountability in the bands were even more demanding. Before believers joined a band they were asked searching questions about their desire to be fully transparent with others in the group in order to be accountable for their spiritual growth in Christian love. (See Appendix A). Once admitted, members of the bands met for an hour together once a week in which these five questions were asked of every member:

1. What known sins have you committed since our last meeting?
2. What temptations have you met with?
3. How was you delivered?
4. What have you thoughts, said, or done, or which you doubt whether it be sin or not?
5. Have you nothing you desire to keep secret?[347]

Underlying all this was Wesley's understanding that we are called not only to be saved from our sins, but we are called to love God with our whole beings and our neighbors as ourselves. While it is the work of the Spirit which accomplishes this, the Spirit of God works in us through means of grace. Members of class bands and class meetings held each other accountable for works of piety (attending worship, partaking of the sacrament, prayer, Bible study, etc.) and works of mercy (caring for the poor, visiting the sick) which were understood to be means of grace in the lives of earnest seekers and believers. The small accountability groups were also means of grace for those who were sincere enough in their Christian commitment to want to be held accountable for the way they lived. David Lowes Watson writes:

> Perhaps the most significant word throughout these guidelines is that Wesley described all of the disciplines as *works*: works of mercy and works of piety. The implication is profound. By *doing* these things, we open ourselves to grace. This is not to say that we can earn God's grace. That would be a contradiction in terms. But it is to say that we can so order our lives that we are more recep-

---

[346] *Works [BE]*, 9:13.
[347] *Works [BE]*, 9:78.

tive to grace, more open to grace; that there are means, or channels, through which we can receive grace more abundantly.[348]

While the complex structure of the accountability groups was not sustained over time, the part they played in providing structures for evangelism, assimilation, discipleship, and leadership development is incalculable. While Whitefield is generally considered to have been the stronger preacher, the small group structures of the Wesleys conserved, sustained and nurtured the work of the revival in ways that proved to be far more beneficial in the long run.

Conclusion

In conclusion, John Wesley was an evangelist for whom matters of mission had priority over propriety. Even though he was a loyal Anglican, he was less concerned about winning the favor of established authorities than he was about winning the lost. His passion for evangelism especially applied to the common people. Even though most were in some sense churched, many were not being challenged by the Church with a vital Christian faith. Wesley's intent was to create an ecclesiolae within the ecclesia, a movement of vital primitive Christianity within the established Church that would not only serve to reach the lost, but also to revive the Church.

Wesley's movement to the common people, to those in need, was kenotic and incarnational. That is, it was a movement from places of power and privilege to the margins. It was a movement that resembled the movement of Jesus and the Kingdom of God. Wesley's pragmatism in combination with this incarnational/kenotic movement resulted in the development of creative and unorthodox programmatic methods of evangelism such as field preaching and small accountability groups for seekers and converts. While the methods he used were decidedly pragmatic, they were always at the service of the mission of the Methodist movement which was grounded theologically in his doctrine of Christian perfection. For Wesley, the mission of evangelism was not limited to calling people to forgiveness, but extended to calling them on to Christian perfection. Field preaching, class meetings and bands all worked together as part of Wesley's overall strategy of evangelism.

The letters of testimony available to us for this study, though limited in time and place, illustrate to some degree the dramatic experiential impact of the Methodist revival in the lives of ordinary people. It is apparent from reading the letters that the converts were taken mostly from the ranks of the less educated and less influential. It is also apparent, that these early Methodist converts had come to understand themselves to be sinners in need of God's grace in a way that they had not understood in their participation in the established Church. Frequently they made reference to previously believing that they were morally respectable good Christians, but particularly under the preaching of the evangelists, they had come to realize their sinful state.

---

[348] David Lowes Watson, *Covenant Discipleship* (Nashville, Tennessee: Discipleship Resources, 1994), 48.

This new understanding of their sinful state was accompanied by a deep and overriding sense of conviction that left them miserable and afraid, sometimes for years. Images of death and hell were very real. All this combined to strongly motivate them to seek God. The preaching and counsel of the evangelists promised the hope and assurance of salvation. Their deep sense of conviction and contrition was matched, in due time, with an equally powerful sense of forgiveness and freedom from sin when they received, often unexpectedly, the grace of God for salvation. The reports of their experiences were typically quite dramatic and often accompanied by unusual manifestations of trembling, fainting as well as reports of physical lightness and healing. The language they used of their involvement was not limited to their initial conversion experiences, but typically extended to the pursuit of Christian perfection and holy living. The gratitude in their letters was not limited to God, but readily extended to the evangelists. The nature of their reports illustrates, at least in this limited perspective, that the influence of the Methodist revival was nothing short of life changing for them. They had been desperately lost in their sins and now they had come to know the power of the love and grace of God which not only gave them assurance of salvation, but motivated them to pursue a life of perfect love.

Finally, the incarnational/kenotic nature of Wesley's mission combined with Wesley's understanding of holiness might be especially helpful in constructing a Wesleyan theology of evangelism. Wesley's theology is grounded in the holiness of God and manifested, by the grace of God and the power of the Holy Spirit, in the people of God. The holy character of God becomes descriptive of the character of the people of God restored in God's image. God's character of holy love becomes the source of love for the people of God in mission. The incarnational movement of God in Christ Jesus into the world, then, is the basis for the incarnational engagement of the church in evangelism as well as ministries of mercy and justice. Stanley Rankin weaves this together with these words:

> As love for God grows, so does love for neighbor, because God's own Spirit instills this love in the believer. Since neighbor love is a reflection of God's image in the believer, and since full restoration of the image of God is the goal of Christian perfection, love necessarily motivates one toward service, because it reflects God's own relational nature as well as God's determination to reclaim what has been lost... the closer one draws to Christ and the more one loves God, the closer one is drawn to the neighbor and the more one feels the compassion of Christ for the lost and lonely, the estranged and afflicted.[349]

John Wesley was an evangelist. For those of us in the Wesleyan holiness tradition, this is a central dimension of our heritage as well as our reason for being. Ultimately, of course, our commitment to evangelism is not based on our own sense of urgency, or our commitment to historical traditions. Rather, out of the heart of God has come a mission of redemption in the world. As

---

[349] Stanley Rankin, "A Perfect Church: Toward a Wesleyan Missional Ecclesiology" in *Wesleyan Theological Journal*, vol. 38, no. 1 (Spring 2003): 89-90.

people restored in the image of God, the priorities and passions of God become our own. We are compelled to preach the gospel in the world because we are God's people and we share His redemptive incarnational mission.

> To save what was lost, from heaven he came;
> Come, sinners, and trust in Jesus's name;
> He offers you pardon, he bids you be free:
> If sin be your burden, O come unto me![350]

---

[350] Franz Hildebrandt and Oliver Beckerlegge, eds. "A Collection of Hymns for the Use of the People Called Methodists," *Works [BE]*, (Nashville, Tennessee: Abingdon, 1983), 7:85-86.

Appendix A

Requirements for Entrance into a Class-Meeting[351]

From: ***The Nature, Design, and General Rules, of the United Societies* (1743)**

"There is only one condition previously required in those who desire admission into these societies, 'a desire to flee from the wrath to come, to be saved from their sins.' But wherever this is really fixed in the soul it will be shown by its fruits. It is therefore expected of all who continue therein that they should continue to evidence their desire of salvation,

First, By doing no harm, by avoiding evil in every kind [examples: taking the name of God in vain, profaning the day of the Lord by doing ordinary work or buying and selling, drunkenness, buying or selling liquor or drinking them unless in cases of extreme necessity, fighting, going to law with a brother, giving or taking things on usury, uncharitable conversation, especially speaking evil of ministers or those in authority, the putting on of gold or costly apparel (including enormous bonnets), taking such diversions as cannot be used in the name of the Lord, singing songs or reading books which do not tend to the knowledge or love of God, self indulgence, laying up treasures on earth, etc.]

Secondly, By doing good, by being in every kind merciful after their power, as they have opportunity doing good of every possible sort and as far as is possible to all men;

To their bodies, of the ability which God giveth, by giving food to the hungry, by clothing the naked, by visiting or helping them that are sick, or in prison.

To their souls, by instructing, *reproving,* or exhorting all they have any intercourse with; trampling under foot that enthusiastic doctrine of devils, that 'we are not to do good unless *our heart be free to do it.*' [examples: doing good

---

[351] See *Works* [BE], 9:70-78.

especially to the household of faith, employing them preferably to others, buying one of another helping each other in business, diligence and frugality,

Thirdly, By attending upon all the ordinances of God. [Examples: public worship, ministry of the Word, The Supper of the Lord; Family and private prayer, searching the Scriptures, and fasting or abstinence." (70-73)

From: *Rules of the Band Societies* (1738)

Questions proposed to every one before *he* is admitted amongst us may be to this effect:

1) Have you the forgiveness of your sins?
2) Have you peace with God, through our Lord Jesus Christ?
3) Have you the witness of God's Spirit with your spirit that you are a child of God?
4) Is the love of God shed abroad in your heart?
5) Has no sin, inward or outward, dominion over you?
6) Do you desire to be told or your faults?
7) Do you desire to be told of all your faults, and that plain and home?
8) Do you desire that every one of us should tell you from time to time whatsoever is in his heart concerning you?
9) Consider! Do you desire we should tell you whatsoever we think, whatsoever we fear, whatsoever we hear, concerning you?
10) Do you desire that in doing this we should come as close as possible, that we should cut to the quick, and search your heart to the bottom?
11) Is it your desire and design to be on this and all other occasions entirely open, so as to speak everything that is in your heart, without deception, without disguise, and without reserve?

Appendix B

Letters to Charles Wesley, 1740-1741[352]

Maria Price, 18 May 1740

My dear father in God I now declare unto you with a joyful heart as well as I can remember how the Lord worked in my soul by you my own father. I came to you about the beginning of last March was a year by the desire of a friend as dead as myself.

I had been a partaker of the bread and wine for some months but not of the body and blood of my loving Saviour.

Dear Sir, my heart longs for words to tell how good my dear Saviour is to save such a dark dead stony hearted damned unbelieving Pharisee as I. I did often repent for one sin and did not know I had any more. But I had no sooner repented of it but I commited it again and was two-fold more a child of hell than before. Thus was I mourning and sinning and wondering that I could not overcome it myself. That one sin was passion.

Your discourse and your prayer gave me so much comfort that when I came home I said to the same purpose (person?) "This is the day of salvation". You bid me read the 7th to the Romans. You said that was my state and I did read it and found much comfort insomuch that I began at the first Chapter in order to read them through to see what was in them. But as I was a reading, I think it was the sixth Chapter, I was forced to lift my eyes off the book and look about me like a person that was born blind and that moment recieved light (sight?).

---

[352] These are partial transcripts from the John Rylands Library, Manchester, England.

.... soon after you expounded at Fetterlane and then I was at that time and ever since filled with joy and peace in believing I received the forgiveness of sins and the witness of the Spirit and a dominion over sin at that very time.

I trembled so with joy and cried that I did not know how to bear myself. You asked me if I found that peace that passed understanding. -- I said, "Yes, indeed I have."

Dear Sir, I am your own daughter in God.

Maria Price

Nathaniel Hurst, 1741

When first the lord sent Mr. Whitefield out into the fields I went to hear him in Moorfields. I liked what he said very well I said I would go again accordingly I went on the next Sunday and ever since I have followed the Lord in his appointed ways. I had a form of godliness for some time but knew but little of the power.

Then the Lord was pleased to let me hear Mr. John Wesley one night at Fetter Lane -- the Lord spoke peace to my soul. He let me know my sins were blotted out by his Blood. This was in the Christmas week -- this Christmas two years.

My master one night forced me to stay at home which caused us to have words. Then anger broke out of me.

Sometimes as I was standing I used to think that the ground whereon I stood was hot under me which made me almost to tremble and to think if the ground should open and swallow me up I should perish forever.

The light of God shown on me once more and my soul was filled with love. Then I could lift up my heart again to the Lord and one day as I was at my work my soul was overpowered with the love of God that I knew not whether I was in the Body or out of the Body.

Mary Ramsay, 4 June 1740

The first time I heard Mr. Whitefield was the 2nd of June last. His text was out of the gospel of St. John, the 17th Chapter the 3rd Verse.

I liked the discourse exceeding well but applied it to myself so well that I scold at a young gentleman that was a scoffer. He called somebody that was by him Whitefield's disciple and laughed and scoffed and I told him he was the devil's disciple.

I went on as usual to church every Sunday to the sacrament every month preparing myself the whole week before. -- So I came with a whole week's righteousness, or rather a whole week's Pharisaical hypocrisy.
(Again to hear Whitefield July 21 -- Sat pm -- at Kinsington. Subject was Gen 3:15. -- "Showed us our sinful nature". Went the next day. John 7:37-39)

...That time I heard little of his sermon being full of the devil but knew it not for there was a fine gentleman and his spouse in the place where I stood that mocked every word he said and much interrupted those that stood by them.

I scolded them and called them infidels. I would go home in a great hurry with a great deal of the sermon in my heart so that I could repeat half or sometimes three quarters of the discourse.

When Mr. Whitefield told us we was by nature half beast and half devil there was something in that heart of mine that showed it was very true.

John W. came to town Sept. 4 at Dowgate (?) Hill (text -- John 16:16)

Trial was coming on for before that as soon as my neighbors and acquaintances knew that I went to hear the field preachers they began to persecute and took their chilfren from me and put them to other schools.

I continued to go to the Foundery Sundays and Thursdays and to the Society in Brick Lane and there was great division in the Society that grieved me very much and I knew not what to do. I was very loathe to leave them and staying with them there was disputes and animosities. I came away from them and at last the Lord sent you, Reverend Sir. I can admire ye wisdom of God in seeing how he sends out the Labourer -- one after another. That what one has planted the other waters and the Almighty gives the increase.

And so I went on mourning that I could not mourn more and about a fortnight after you were come I fell into such mourning that my heart was ready to break. I came on Monday morning to speak with you but when I came I could not speak.

The Thursday following being Ascension day I had so much joy when you was preaching that I thought my soul seemed as if it was ascending into heaven. Indeed the joy began in the morning while Mr. Harris was preaching -

- and it so increased in the evening while you was preaching that Methought I saw my Saviour in glory -- My soul seemed as though it was out of my body.

Margerit Austen, 19 May 1740

And there again I was much affected with the word, finding myself to be the very person: and so continued to follow him wherever I could and indeed the Lord by his ministry did awaken me. And I saw myself to be a lost undone sinner: Then on a time when the Lord saw fit to let me see myself was by Mr. John at Wapping. He was explaining the sin of the holy Ghost there I was struck though Satan had not power to make me believe -- I had committed that sin - the Fryday following I heard you, sir, and there - I plainly saw my Saviour bleeding on the cross and the soldiers piecing his precious side... then I heard Mr. Whitefield at Besdey on the indwelling of the Holy Spirit and there I saw I was really half a beast and half a devil.

For the truth of whole doctrine in the strength of the Lord I am ready to lay down my life.

Elisabeth Hinson 25 May 1740

I was a Pharisee but god was plest to convince me by hearing Mr. Witfeals sermon that I may know him and the power of his resurrection but know further it plesed god to send your dear brother to come I am bound in duty to pray for so long as I live it pleased god that I went to Mr. pearkens and he was upon the 13 chap of Corinthians and thear I knew myself a damd sinner. I came home and I thought I was then sinking into hell... your brother expounded the 12 chapter of sant John and the lord work mytilly in me and I felt a strong conviction and wold have hid it but my lord him loves sinner still carried on his work and brought all my sins to my remembrance and there I trembled and should have fell down but the popel heald me up and I was out of my senses but the lord awakened me with peace be unto you your sins are forgiving you I went home full of joye note knowing ware to --- myself so I continued all next day and then my joys left me Satan came in and told me I had lost Christ and I mite as well hang myself. But god him is rich in mercy tords all delivered me from the evil of this temptation. I was in darkness and know not god It pleased god to send your dear brother I whent to hear him his text was --- not that I said unto the --- you must be born again he polde down what I had bilt up he said a person will go on forty years for a graddual sanctification.

T. Cowper, 1741

By the providence of the Almighty, my friend heard of a religious society in Aldersgate Street, I think in the month of August, 1738. We went there and one night the Lord brought you and Mr. James Hutton. You began to preach on justification by faith alone and told them they must feel their sins forgiven them in this life or they never would in the life to come. I remember they YOUSED you ill and some were for putting you out of the room. But at last they suffered you to read a homily upon faith. I thought It comfortable doctrine but strange doctrine to me for I heard such before. The Lord did not suffer me to speak against it but he let me to see they were not right by their behavior toward you.

Then I heard of the SA--OR Society. Their I heard Mr. John Wesley such a minister I never heard before.

This was the first of October, 1738 in the beginning of the 28 years of my age.

Hearing John Wesley preach to a Society in Bair Yard near Claremarket, I felt my heart open within me and like a fountain of water run from it and in that moment I felt such love, peace and joy passed all expression. We sang a hymn. I thought I was out of the body with the angels in heaven for I was so full of joy I could not express my belief.

Sometimes I begin to think I have a new heart but the Lord is pleased to show me to the contrary that I have not yet but I have a hope in me that he will perfect his work in my soul before he takes me hence and gives me a clean heart.

Martha Jones, 1 June 1740

I should have been very glad if I had been excused from this task and was in hopes you would forget to ask me for it again. I knew it was my duty to obey you as my spiritual pastor. But in this I thought I could not indeed it was a secret pride in my heart which made me so unwilling... instead of the church the playhouse was my greatest delight...

I felt I was a damned sinner I strove all I could to stifle these convictions but neither company nor my beloved amusements seeing and reading plays would not do. The fire of god's wrath was kindled in my soul and I could not put it out...

I went on in this dead way upward of two years at last I heard of mr. Whitfeild a little before he went to Georgia I heard him preach four times but the account I had of his life had much more effect upon me then his sermons the piety of the young preacher made a deep impression and I had a glimpse how far I was from being a Christian

Your sermon on the threefold state which I often heard with tears showed me I was one of those that was seeking god but as yet had not found him...

Katharine Gilbert, 1740

Rev. Sir,

With humility I make bold to write these lines unto you, it being my grief of heart which is --- cause, upon ye account of your leaving us in this place of great work which ye Lord Jesus has done for me and in me thro: ye operations of ye Holy Spirit under your ministry I am constrained thro: love to acknowledge what ye Lord hath done for my soul, for I am pluckt as a firebrand out of ye fire. God as convinced me of sin, of righteousness and of judgment before ye Lord sent you and your worthy brother amongst us, I thought my self something but I can now see what I am by nature and deserved nothing but damnation. I knew nothing of faith alone in Christ nor of Operations of ye Holy Ghost nor what it was to be born of God and to become as a little child a new creature in Christ Jesus. I was ignorantly led and taught. My soul longeth to become more and more in purity of heart and to receive greater measure of ye love of God shed abroad in my heart. I humbly desire your prayers at ye throne of grace that God in Christ would perfect and compleat my salvation. I am not left without reproaches or threatenings by ye children of he world for ye words sake but I hope I am thro Christ overcoming this world I am not moved at their doings toward me as at ye contempt cast upon Gods word and children. May ye lord our God even Christ Jesus fill you more and more with his Spirit and crown your ministry wherever you go with thousands of souls in ye conversion of my guilty brethren. So continually prayeth your handmaid in ye Lord

Katharine Gilbert

Samuel Hewit, November 1741

I was all of a sudden struck to all appearance with sudden death, O who can tell, but them that has felt the same the horror and confusion that I was in, death I thought lit hovering upon my cold lips and hell open and ready to receive me. The terror of the Lord was in array against me and in the agony I lay for some time... I said the Lord's prayer, I prayed earnestly for Christ's sake that I might not die... I never would offend him in thought word deed any more All this I promised in my own strength so ignorant was I of the ways of God...

With sorrow do I speak it I being of the Church of England I was att a grate loss to find a spiritual friend that could give me any spiritual comfort what minister I liked in the Church I found their lives was contrary to their doctrine that Satan would have often tempted me to believe that all religion was witchcraft often times he tempted me to deny the being of a god and att other times he would tell me if there was a god he need not concern his self with me

After two years deep convictions God rebuked the stormy wind and tempest and their was a great calm – I tasted that peace of God which Paseth all understanding of the natural man

Satan told me I could not fall away -- though I know nothing of predestination doctrine the next thing I began to grow spiritually proud I despised others that had never gone through what I had . . . .

. . . I know by experience that spiritual pride is the foundation of predestination Many things is done away since I sit under your doctrine.

But God who began a good work would carry it on and how I did rejoice when Mr. Whitefield came about to preach and how was that spark blown up that was just a dying away but after all this I never saw the hundredth part of my own wicked deceitful heart till you and your dear brother....

Sarah Barber, May 1740

Reverend Sir:

Att your request: I here as far as the Lord gives me knowledge to see and to know my conversion which before I heard the Rev. Mr. Whitefield I was a publican living in the world as if there was no god but that I did not know it because I was not a notorious open offender. I therefore thought myself a very good person but the Lord was pleased to call me first by the ministry of Mr. Whitefield and by the ministry of Mr. John on a time when the Lord saw fit his subject was on the woman that stood behind our blessed Saviour when he was att meat at the Pharisee's house that she poured the box of ointment on him and att that time I went to sister Robinsons to get into the bands but could not be admitted then and told her my case but she told me I had no faith which indeed was true. --- Afterward I was admitted upon tryall and then I was most of the time in great doubts – then I hoped and found comfort and indeed the band was of great service to me for I never went away without some comforts. Then when the lord sent you to town I thought the Lord had something in store for me. --- But at night when we met again in your prayers the Lord was pleased to give me the second gift of faith to believe that Jesus was my Lord. There was several sisters had received the same gift

I beg leave – to subscribe myself your young babe in Christ,

Sarah Barber

Sarah Middleton, May 1740

Reverend Sir,

I write these lines to let you know what a Pharisee I was. I went to church and sacrament constantly and I thought I did very well for I was a strict Pharisee. I would not be in any ones company that said an hl word nor would I go a pleasureing as others did for fear of sin if I die at any time and mis my church. I thought some judgment would follow me so if any one had askd what hope I had of my salvation I would presently have said I never did any harm for I always did to others as I would they should do unto me and I thought I was very sincere so I did not fear but God would accept me that is the most account I could give of my self then but thanks be to God for his unspeakable mercy in bringing me by his free grace out of darkness I which I sat. Thought myself a Christian but I found my self mistaken when it pleased God to reveal his dear son in me and to show me the way of salvation as for the articles of our church the doctrine of the spirit of God of regeneration and of justification by faith I was a stranger to them all nor do I remember to have heard any of them preachd or ixplained by our clergy indeed I went to church and said my prayers and had a form of profession but --- nothing of the power I had no oyl in my lamp no inward principal of holiness in my heart what was I but a whited sepulchre the harlots and publicans would have entered into the kingdom of heaven before me how shall I sufficiently praise the Lord for first drawing me to hear Mr. Whitefeld but Satan would fain a kept me from hearing him but the Lord drawd me with the cords of his love so that I could not keep from hearing him where ever he went but when I have heard him say that every person born into this world deserves Gods damnation and tho' we went to church and did all the outward things we were but baptized heathens them words used to sink deep into my heart I had a great deal of sorrow under his preaching but when it pleased God to call him away I went to hear Mr. John Westly his words was sharper to me then a two edged sword and I cannot but always honour him as an instrument in God's hands of shewing me the true way of salvation by Jesus Christ. Sept. 10th 1739 I heard Mr. Westly take the 16 chapter of Acts verse 30 the words as flows what must I do to be saved then he explained the ten commandments which wounded me so much that I was hardly able to stand under him for I thought I had kept them as touching the law blamless from my youth up. But hearing them explain I felt I had broke all of them so that I could take no rest night nor day by reason of that load of sin which I felt within me for I felt a hell within me so that I often cryed out in the agony of my soul what must I do save for my souls was like the troubled sea so that it weight my body down so that my mother and others thought I should hardly overcomit that would had me taken many things but I know it was for sin so that I refused all outward comfort it used to press much upon me that the power of the lord was present to heal me so that I had hope against hope for I could plead with my dear saviour O Lord thou hast said come unto me all that are weary and heavy laden and I will give you rest. I felt my self so vile that I thought hell was ready to swallow me up but I found Christs everlasting arms was under me the 14 of Sepr. When I was in the greatest agony of soul I heard a voice say unto me daughter be of good cheer thy sins be forgiven thee at the same time I felt so much love in my heart that I could hardly contain my self for I wanted the whole world to feel what I did I was at the same time retord to my bodily health as well as ever I was in my life but I was much tempted to keep it to my self and not to tell Mr. Westly what the Lord had done for me but that saying of our lords pressed much upon me that there were ten cleansd but where are the nine there is none that is returned to give thanks save this stranger. So that gave me courage to go to him and let him know how gratius the lord had bien to me for I was catchd as a fire brand out of the fire I was full of pride and passion and every thing that was evil but did not no it for I never remember our teachers to speak against it for I was alive without the Law once but when it came in a spiritual meaning sin revived and I dyd but thanks be to God for his free grace for shewing mercy to the chief of sinners for it is not of him that willeth nor him that runneth but God that sheweth mercy Blest be the name that set me free the name that sure salvation brings the sun of righteousness as rose one me with healing in his wings blessed be God now I can say whom have I in heaven but thee and there is none upon earth that I desire besides thee thee I can love and thee alone with holy peace and inward bliss to find thou takest me for thy own O what a happiness is this glory be to the Lord I feel a continual peace and love springing up in my heart day by day I know I do not commit sin for my soul is always hungarying and thirsting after righteousness and I know I shall be feled I used to rest in going to church and sacrament but now I do not rest upon them but upon Christ Jesus my lord and my God but I find it a glorious liberty to use the means of grace and not abuse them glory be to thee O Christ. I find I gather strength daily for I usd to be afraid to speak to my carnal relations what God had done for my soul but now I find I am constraind to speak tho I know they will cast me out as a byword and a proberb or reproach when

I was of the world the world loved its own but now Christ has choose me out of the world therefore the world hates me but this I rejoice in for it only sets a mark upon me to show what master I belong to
I am
    Dear sir,

        Your affectionat but unworthy sister in Christ,

        Sarah Middleton

Part III

Biblical

Chapter 7

Holiness and Community in 1 John

By Kent E Brower

Introduction

The very brevity of the Johannine Epistles contributes to the fact that they do not make a significant contribution to most NT theologies.[353] They have, of course, been reasonably well served in commentary series,[354] but monographs concentrating on their theology are not abundant.[355] Interest in them within

---

[353] See Larry W Hurtado, *Lord Jesus Christ: Devotions to Jesus in Earliest Christianity* (Grand Rapids/Cambridge: Eerdmans, 2003), 208-226 may be an exception. He devotes a whole section to discussion of Johannine Christianity partially because his attention is directed to Christ devotion. The aberrant teaching (from John's perspective) of the schismatics alluded to in 1 John may have emerged through the interpretation of their *experiences*.

[354] See Rick Williamson, *1, 2 and 3 John: A Commentary in the Wesleyan Tradition* (NBBC; Kansas City: Beacon Hill, 2010), S. S. Smalley, *1, 2, 3 John* (WBC, rev. ed; Waco: Word, 2010), Robert W. Yarbrough, *1–3 John* (BECNT; Grand Rapids: Baker, 2008), John Painter, *1, 2 and 3 John* (SP 18; Collegeville: Liturgical Press, 2002), David K. Rensberger, *1 John, 2 John, 3 John* (ANTC; Nashville: Abingdon, 1997), G. Strecker, *The Johannine Epistles* (Hermeneia; Minneapolis: Fortress, 1996), Marianne Meye Thompson, *1 – 3 John* (IVPNT; Downers Grove: IVP, 1992), R. E. Brown, *The Epistles of John*, (AB 30; New York: Doubleday, 1982), I. H. Marshall, *The Epistles of John*, (NICNT; Grand Rapids: Eerdmans, 1978), F F Bruce, *The Epistles of John* (London: Pickering and Ingalls, 1970). Three classic commentaries are by B. F. Westcott *The Epistles of John: The Greek Text with Notes* (London: Macmillan, 1883), A. E. Brooke, *A Critical and Exegetical Commentary on the Johannine Epistles* (ICC; Edinburgh: T. & T. Clark, 1912), and C. H. Dodd, *The Epistle of John* (Moffatt; New York: Harper, 1946).

[355] See Edward Malatesta, *Interiority and Covenant: A Study of* einai en *and* menein en *in the First Letter of Saint John* (AnBib 69; Rome: Pontifical Biblical Institute, 1978), John Bogart, *Orthodox and Heretical Perfectionism* (SBLDS 33; Missoula: Scholars, 1977), J

the scholarly community is usually linked to a fuller discussion of the Johannine community and the Fourth Gospel.[356]

Any discussion of 1 John immediately is confronted with its text, form and style. It has several interesting textual points. It is written in deceptively simple language with a limited vocabulary; topics are frequently repeated; ideas are introduced then developed later. All this makes 1 John notoriously difficult to outline in linear form. That alone cannot account for apparent inconsistencies (see 1:8-10; 3:8-9). But it should alert us to the fact that its interpretation does not depend upon a logical flow from one verse to the next. Rather, a number of interlocking ideas are developed by repetition and elaboration from a variety of angles.

The content of 1 John owes much to its socio-historical context. Several scholars attempt to situate the Epistle more precisely in the early church. But hard evidence is limited and difficult to weigh.[357] Reconstruction cannot be done solely from the epistles – almost all scholars now think of some relationship between the Johannine Epistles and the Fourth Gospel. On the literary level, links between them have long been noted.[358] The Fourth Gospel is essential to understanding the Epistles whether one takes the view that 1 John responds to issues in an earlier edition of the Gospel or whether it is better explained as the last of the Johannine writings.[359] John[360] presupposes the narrative theology of the multi-layered Fourth Gospel. Few if any direct references to the Scriptures occur in the Epistle, but once again the intertex-

---

Lieu, *The Theology of the Johannine Epistles* (NTT; Cambridge: CUP, 1991), Stephen S. Smalley, "The Johannine Community and the Letters of John" in *A Vision for the Church: Studies in Early Christian Ecclesiology* (ed Markus Bockmuehl and Michael B Thompson; (Edinburgh: T & T Clark, 1977), 96-105. Most monographs that treat theological themes include the whole Johannine literature. See, for example, Gary M. Burge, *The Anointed Community: The Holy Spirit in the Johannine Tradition* (Grand Rapids: Eerdmans, 1987) and Rodney A. Whitacre, *Johannine Polemic: The Role of Tradition and Theology* (SBLDS 67; Chico: Scholars, 1982).

[356] See Oscar Cullmann, *The Johannine Circle: Its Place in Judaism, amongst the Disciples of Jesus and in Early Christianity* (London: SCM, 1976ET), R. E. Brown, *The Community of the Beloved Disciple: The Life, Loves and Hates of an Individual Church in New Testament Times* (New York: Paulist, 1979), D. Bruce Woll, *Johannine Christianity in Conflict: Authority, Rank, and Succession in the First Farewell Discourse*, (SBLDS 60; Chico: Scholars, 1981).

[357] See Brown, *Community* for the most widely known reconstruction but most commentators offer their own suggestions. See, for example, Painter, *1, 2 and 3 John*, 27-114 and Yarbrough, *1-3 John*, 5-21 for differing views.

[358] See Brooke, *Commentary on the Johannine Epistles*, i-x, Painter, 62-70.

[359] Most scholars see the Epistles as related in some way to the gospel rather than the Gospel responding to the Epistles. See Brown, *Epistles*, 14-35 for a full discussion on issues relating to authorship. See also Martin Hengel, *The Johannine Questions* (London: SCM, 1990ET). Stephen Smalley thinks Revelation is the earliest book in the Johannine literature with the fourth gospel preceding the epistles. Yarbrough, *1-3 John*, 5-16 is one of a minority of scholars positing John bar Zebedee as the author.

[360] John will be the designation given to the author of the Epistles and the Fourth Gospel without addressing the question of actual authorship.

tual relationship with the Fourth Gospel where the Scriptures are central is assumed.

While the precise context of this Epistle may be in dispute, some sort of schism has occurred (2:19). Few doubt that dysfunction in the community has arisen from theological distortion – and the theological deviations of John's opponents have cost them their spiritual life in community. Perhaps by the time 1 John is written, the community is in the advanced stages of disintegration. If so, John is trying to reassure his readers in their community life. To foster appropriate community life he reminds them of their core beliefs and experiences.

Theology and ethics are woven together in this Epistle because it is so intensely practical and pastoral. Language that may be more theologically loaded in the Pauline letters, for instance, is unconsciously used in this pastoral enterprise. That does not detract from its richness. Rather, it confirms the link between orthodoxy and orthopraxy. All of this makes reading and hearing this deceptively simple Epistle of immense and timeless practical value for believers who are seeking to live as God's holy people in community and mission.

Theological Ethics

Jesus is the Christ

A proper understanding of Jesus' identity as Messiah, his teaching, and his life should issue in fellowship amongst them and with the Father and his Son Jesus Christ (1:3). Conversely, the lack of fellowship demonstrated by the secessionists is thought by the writer to betray a distorted Christology; more specifically, their failure to understand the implications of the incarnation. This is clear right from the opening lines. John writes, *we declare to you what was from the beginning, what we have heard, what we have seen with our eyes, what we have looked at and touched with our hands, concerning the word of life* (1:1-2).[361] Three further passages (2:22-23; 4:2-3; 5:6) elaborate on this theme. John's whole discourse is to be read in the light of the reality of the incarnation, the constancy of the tradition they have received concerning it, and the indissoluble connection between the earthly Jesus and eternal life in God. The bare facts of the earthly Jesus are crucial but John's opponents have failed to grasp their significance for their shared life.

But what are the precise nuances of the theological deviation? The difficulty in identifying these is well known. One suggestion is that his opponents espouse a form of docetism that is developed more fully by Cerinthus (c. 100AD). But the problem in 1 John is not a denial that Jesus has lived in the flesh per se. It is almost inconceivable that *any* member of the Johannine

---

[361] *Word of life* could imply the proclamation of the gospel, but the echoes from John 1:4 *in him was life* are strongly in favour of thesis reading the phrase "word of life" as referring to Jesus. NIV thus capitalizes the term.

community, past or present, would deny Jesus' human existence. Furthermore, it is likely that all people in the Johannine community agree that Jesus is the Messiah, the Son of God (see John 20:31).

Brown thinks that the secessionists accept the facts about the life and death of Jesus but understand them in a way that "weakened the human content of the formulas, not the divine."[362] That seems correct as far as it goes and certainly fits well with some developments in the post-biblical period.[363] But the problem is not just a denial or even weakening of the humanity of Jesus. It is also the failure to understand the connection between the flesh-and-blood Jesus and God, and its formative place in their lives in community. John firmly connects the incarnate Jesus with God the Father; the flesh-and-blood Jesus is fully in the divine sphere as well as in the human. Thus according to the Fourth Gospel Jesus, the Word become flesh, does the works of the Father and expresses the will of the Father. He is also in an intimate and mutual relationship with the Father.

Crucially, the risen Christ bears our humanity, albeit a transformed humanity. On the one hand, in taking on our humanity in the Incarnation, he offered perfect obedience to the Father in that very humanity. On the other hand, our obedience to the Father is offered through the Spirit in the one perfectly obedience son of the Father. Our obedience to the Father is in and through the perfectly obedient son. Thus, the life, teaching and example as well as the death of the incarnate one are essential for the life of the holy community centered on him. For this group, however, somehow the new commandment of Jesus that they should love one another has become detached from their beliefs almost as if Jesus were not speaking for God. The intellectual knowledge that Jesus is the Messiah may be vital, but those who truly *know* the Son, that is, have an experiential relationship with him in community, also know the Father and like the Son, are obedient to the Father whose will is announced and exemplified in the life of the Son.

God is Father

While neither the Fourth Gospel nor the Epistle explicitly states that God is Father, this assumption is seen most clearly in the Father – Son relationship. First John uses "father" fourteen times directly connected to the Son. In his life with the disciples Jesus reveals the character of the Father to the community. Marshall notes that "the Christian doctrine of a personal, fatherly God is dependent upon the revelation of God given in Jesus . . . [and] acceptance of Jesus as Son automatically leads to personal communion with God as Father.[364] Without seeing Jesus, the Father remains obscure. The Epistle builds

---

[362] Brown, *Epistles*, 352.

[363] See Smalley "Community," 96. Underlying the polemical tone of 1 John, Smalley detects two main opposition groups. One group with Jewish roots finds it difficult to think of the man Jesus as divine; the other group thinks of him as little less than God.

[364] Marshall, *Epistles of John*, 159.

on the language of the Johannine Jesus: *Whoever has seen me has seen the Father* (John 14:9b). This is confirmed in 2:22-23 with its clear connection between the confession that Jesus is the Messiah and Jesus is the Son. Conversely, to acknowledge the Father is to acknowledge the Son, the one whom the Father has sent (see John 13:20).

In Johannine thought, Jesus Messiah is both the agent and revealer of God the Father because he is the unique Son and pre-existent Word who has become flesh (see John 1:14). In his incarnation he embodied God's good purposes for his created order. These are set out in terms of the command to love one another. Indeed, this is their identifying characteristic: *By this everyone will know that you are my disciples, if you have love for one another* (John 13:35). This is not an insular love, however. Jesus' followers are sent on mission: *As the Father has sent me, so I send you* (John 20:21). The fulfilment of this command and mission is predicated on the indwelling of the new community in the mutuality of the Father and the Son: *The glory that you have given me I have given them, so that they may be one, as we are one, I in them and you in me, that they may become completely one, so that the world may know that you have sent me and have loved them even as you have loved me* (John 17:22-23). The words of Jesus are the words of the Father; the commands of Jesus are the commands of the Father.

Of great importance to John is the fact that Jesus offers perfect obedience to the Father. And this obedience of the Son to the Father is carried out in the very real complexities and all the ambiguities of human existence. According to the Fourth Gospel, Jesus does not seek to do his own will but the will of the one who sent him (John 5:30) and this is tied to the work that Jesus is to do: *My food is to do the will of him who sent me and to complete his work* (John 4:34; see 6:38, 39). Jesus does the works of the Father, is obedient to the Father and knows the will of the Father. He and the Father are one. He himself is the Righteous One because he acts as the Father acts, does what the Father wills and remains in the dynamic perfect love of the Father. He provides a model of obedience for the disciples because he does the will of the Father. The obedience of the Son to the Father is not merely a good example to be emulated by his followers. Rather, the means of obedience is provided for those who are God's people in that they remain in Christ. If they are to be the holy people of God on his mission, they must be secure in their understanding of who Jesus is and the implications of that for their lives.

God is Light

Jesus also reveals that *God is light* (1:5). As if to reinforce this identity and to emphasize that this confession has content, John adds, *and in him there is no darkness at all*. Against the background of the Graeco-Romans deities with their mixture of follies and foibles, the purity of God stands in sharp contrast. There is no mixture in the quality of God's light – it is pure and unalloyed. Malatesta states that this highlights the perfection of God who is "the model and source of the holiness revealed in and communicated through

Christ to the Christian community."[365] But that is not the primary thrust this statement. It has immediate practical implications. "To say that God is light is to acknowledge the necessity of walking in the light. The light of God is the light of God's love, and to walk in the light is to walk in love."[366] This kind of love is impossible in human terms. Yarbrough notes that "the prospect of disparate peoples (early Christian churches were often multi-ethnic) upholding a true *koinonia* (κοινωνία, fellowship) of humanness across ethnic and cultural lines would have been exceedingly rare in the ancient world" and adds, in apparent understatement "and is still far from universal."[367] Conversely, walking in the darkness, is manifest in the fragmented life of the community. Those who no longer walk with them in fellowship are no longer walking in the light of God; they are in darkness. This is primarily the sin that requires confessing, forgiveness and cleansing. Only so can the love of God be manifest in the people of God. The confession that God is light carries ethical implications on a horizontal as well as a vertical trajectory.

Interestingly enough, the Fourth Gospel does not say that God is light, but repeatedly emphasizes that Jesus is the light of the world (see, for example, John 1:9; 3:19; 9:5). No consciousness of any incongruity between these claims is apparent. By setting out this metaphor right at the beginning of the Epistle, John gives an implicit reminder that when one sees Jesus as the light, this also reveals who God is. And this knowledge governs behavior. Those who walk in the light of God are those who emulate the life of Jesus and who participate in the fellowship of Father and Son, essentially in the love of the triune God. That love is the essence of mutual participation in the life of the triune God that occurs in the community of God's holy people.

God is Love: The Holy Trinity

NT scholars and theologians alike acknowledge that the Johannine literature provide key insights for later Trinitarian theology. The notion of mutuality in the triune God that can be seen in the Fourth Gospel is not developed in 1 John. Rather, it lies behind the bald statement that *God is love* (4:8b). The identity of God moves well beyond abstraction. The incarnation itself is a concrete revelation of the very being of the God of love. John explains it like this: *God's love was revealed among us in this way: God sent his only Son into the world so that we might live through him. In this is love, not that we loved God but that he loved us and sent his Son to be the atoning sacrifice for our sins* (4:7-10).

The revelation of God as love is to be read especially in the context of the Father-Son relationship. According to John 13 – 17, the relationship between Father and Son (the Spirit is woven into the whole discourse) forms the foundation for the community of believers. The community is to enjoy the intimacy of the Father-Son relationship (John 17:21-23).[368] Because God has

---

[365] Malatesta, *Interiority and Covenant*, 99; see also 104, 112.
[366] Painter, *1, 2 and 3 John*, 106.
[367] Yarbrough, *1-3 John*, 57.
[368] See K E Brower, *Holiness in the Gospels* (Kansas City: Beacon Hill, 2004), 63-81.

created people in his image, they are creatures created to be in relationship. People are not isolated individuals because "God is not solitary but a loving communion that is distinguished by overflowing life."[369] Jesus reveals the being-in-communion who is God. The revelation that God is love is not the picture of a lonely being looking for company but of a being that is relational in essence. Nor is it the picture of a trinitarian being somehow in process of completion or fulfilment needing relationship with the created order.

Thus, "to be in the image of God is to be called to a relatedness-in-otherness that echoes the eternal relatedness-in-otherness of Father, Son and Spirit."[370] It mirrors the mutual hospitality of the persons of the Trinity. And that revelation of who God is, is the essential pre-understanding of who his people are to be. Because God the Holy Trinity is "a community of love and mutuality,"[371] the essence of the relationship between God and his people and within the community of believers itself is centred entirely on love and lived in mutuality. Malatesta suggests that "the contemplation of oneself and of the community as loved by the Father should spontaneously lead the members likewise to love one another"[372] but this love is far more than an awareness that leads to response. It is rooted in the intimate and transformative relationship of God's people with the very being of God. This, in fact, is the relationship to which Jesus refers in his prayer: *Father, I desire that those also, whom you have given me, may be with me where I am, to see my glory, which you have given me because you loved me before the foundation of the world* (John 17:24).[373] This love is to characterise God's people because they are abiding in the very life of God. Their very existence as the people of God is possible only because they share in the life of God.

In the Fourth Gospel, the love of God is expressed extensively in terms of sending (see John 3:16-17). According to John 1:19, Jesus is the lamb of God who takes away the sin of the world. The Epistle has Jesus as the offering for sin. According to Brown, John makes this point explicitly against his opponents who see the death of Jesus as a stage on Jesus' journey but not salvifically important.[374] They thereby miss the mission of God. John "interpreted the giving and sending to include the whole career of Jesus, including his atoning death for sins."[375] The revelation of the love and glory of God the Father comes to its clearest expression in the death of the Son (see John 12:27-28). But the death of Jesus is redemptive as well as revelatory.[376] Through the

---

[369] Clark D Pinnock, *The Flame of Love* (Downers Grove: IVP, 1998) 31.

[370] Colin E Gunton, *Christ and Creation* (The 1990 Didsbury Lectures; Carlisle: Paternoster, 1992), 101.

[371] Pinnock, *Flame of Love*, 29.

[372] Malatesta, *Interiority and Covenant*, 300.

[373] See Kallistos Ware, *The Orthodox Way* (London: Mowbray, 1979), 33. Ware writes that the essence of this relationality is "an unceasing movement of mutual love."

[374] See Brown, *Community*, 113.

[375] Brown, *Epistles*, 552. The following section develops the work of Whitacre, 124-133.

[376] Smalley, *Epistles*, 244.

death of the Son the Father's love and forgiveness are made known. God is love and because it is an outward-going love, it is a saving love. His redemptive purposes are all accomplished, John tells us, through the death of Jesus.

As far as John is concerned, God sent his Son to be the *savior of the world* (2:2; 4:19). John has an inclusive view of the breadth of God's salvation. At first, this seems somewhat surprising because John is uncompromising about those who are outside the community. But that does not limit the atoning significance of Jesus' death. "John rules out the thought that the death of Jesus is of limited efficacy: the possibility of forgiveness is cosmic and universal."[377] In principle, it could include the secessionists even if in practice repentance is improbable (see 5:16). Despite the thraldom of the world to the evil one, God loves the world and sent his Son into the world so that all might live (4:9).

The inclusive redemption offered in Christ is described as *the atoning sacrifice for our sins*.[378] The word ἱλασμός has been the subject of intense debate.[379] Should it have the sense of "expiation," that is, the covering or wiping clean of sins, or should it be "propitiation" in the sense that it is the removal of obstacles to relationship? According to 2:2, Jesus is both the advocate and the atoning sacrifice. "What he pleads on behalf of sinners is what he himself has done on their behalf."[380] But this should not be viewed in any sense as "presenting God as an unwilling judge from whom forgiveness has to be wrested by the advocate for sinners"[381] since God himself is the one who gave Jesus his Son. God is faithful and forgives *because* "while remaining righteous in being and action (δίκαιος), he has made it possible for us to become righteous."[382] This, then, is forgiveness granted, guilt assuaged and change effected in the context of unfathomably costly love. This is redemptive love in which Jesus is "the sacrifice for all sin."[383]

This is not all that this notion of cleansing from all sin implies, however. John is not simply setting up an abstract doctrine of the atonement. Cleansing needs to be understood in the context of God's covenantal faithfulness and the human need for healing, restoration and reconciliation. Only so can they be part of God's reconciling mission. God is faithful and righteous to cleanse from all sin. God's seeking love is covenantal faithfulness. His purpose is to restore the world to life. This is restorative rather than punitive

---

[377] Marshall, *Epistles*, 119.

[378] καὶ αὐτὸς ἱλασμός ἐστιν περὶ τῶν ἁμαρτιῶν ἡμῶν, οὐ περὶ τῶν ἡμετέρων δὲ μόνον ἀλλὰ καὶ περὶ ὅλου τοῦ κόσμου (2:2); καὶ ἀπέστειλεν τὸν υἱὸν αὐτοῦ ἱλασμὸν περὶ τῶν ἁμαρτιῶν ἡμῶν (4:10).

[379] See Marshall, *Epistles*, 118, for reference to key word studies. As Marshall himself points out, 119, note 29, "the word-group can have different nuances in different context, and in some cases it bears more the sense of expiation while in others it bears more the sense of propitiation."

[380] Marshall, *Epistles*, 119.

[381] Marshall, *Epistles*, 119.

[382] Smalley, *Epistles*, 31.

[383] Smalley, *Epistles*, 244.

righteousness, the righteousness that makes reconciliation between parties.[384] Unrighteousness mars relationships, whether it is an activity or hostility, seen most clearly in breach of covenant faithfulness to God through disobedience and played out in marred human relationships. If we remember the relational connotation of covenantal righteousness, then forgiveness in God's terms is far more than wiping the slate clean – it is restoring the relationship between God and his alienated beings. In John's context, impurity brings separation; cleansing removes the defilement that causes separation and brings the separated ones, the estranged parties, together again. The well-worn "at-one-ment" description of atonement more adequately captures the full significance of Jesus' sacrificial death than either the notion of covering our sins (expiation) or of the satisfaction of God's righteous wrath (propitiation). It gets to the heart of the manifestation of sin: breaches in relationships within the community that are completely antithetical to any claim to be walking in the light and to be born of God.

God's redemptive activity in Christ also destroys the power of the evil one. Lest his readers be anxious about the powers arrayed against them, John writes, *The Son of God was revealed for this purpose, to destroy the works of the devil* (3:8; see John 12:31). This idea expresses the language of John 16:33 where Jesus offers assurance to his beleaguered followers that they should take courage because he has conquered the world. Here John offers comfort to his readers in reminding them that they have in fact been overcomers because they have put their faith in the one who overcomes (2:13-14). Their strength comes from the fact that they are born of God, and *whatever is born of God conquers the world. And this is the victory that conquers the world, our faith. Who is it that conquers the world but the one who believes that Jesus is the Son of God?* (5:4; see 4:5). The victory of Christ is held along with the fact that *the whole world lies under the power of the evil one* (5:19). This is closely related to the heart of the problem – because the implication for John of the departure of the secessionists is that by leaving the community, they have aligned themselves with the world.

Fellowship with One Another

The identity of God as light in this epistle has implications for the life of Christian discipleship.[385] The holy community walks in the light. God is light and those walking in the light cannot simultaneously walk in darkness. That point has already been made explicitly in the Gospel. Now John reminds them that the life of the holy community is only possible through relationship, through knowing, abiding and remaining in Christ,[386] in *koinonia* with

---

[384] It is interesting that two of the commentators on this passage, Bruce and Marshall, both turn to Charles Wesley for poetic explanation. Bruce, *Epistles of John*, 50, cites "Arise, my soul, arise" while Marshall, *Epistles*, 119, cites "Father, whose everlasting love."

[385] Thompson, *1-3 John*, 40.

[386] See Andrew Brower Latz, "A Short Note toward a Theology of Abiding in John's Gospel" in *Journal of Theological Interpretation*, vol. 4 (2010), 161-168, Musa Kunene,

Christ and centered in the love of God. This fellowship, their mutual participation in Christ and with fellow believers, is far more than a natural affinity between people that may occur on a strictly human level. On the contrary, *koinonia* in the people of God is only possible through their mutual participation in the very being of the triune God of love. Although John's opponents claim to be in fellowship with God (1:6), they have put themselves in the category of outsiders – *they went out from us* (2:19) – those who walk in darkness.

Those who walk in the light live lives of obedience to God. This is not primarily to a set of rules. Nor is it a description of a state of being. John's choice of "walk" to describe the life of the community excludes any static notion. This is a dynamic life of relationship with the Father and Son which manifests itself in emulating the loving character of God and the obedience of the Son. It is not an obedience that is merely done for us on our behalf by Christ without any attendant obedience on the part of the followers. By abiding in him, we participate in his obedience and through grace (the Spirit indwelling the people of God) we are enabled to walk following him. John links the notions of walking, obedience, abiding and love in one statement: *By this we may be sure that we are in him: whoever says, "I abide in him," ought to walk just as he walked* (2:6-7). Obedience to the word – here almost certainly an allusion to the great commands to love God and neighbor – explains that bold claim in 2:5 – *whoever obeys his word, truly in this person the love of God has reached perfection.*[387]

To walk in the light, then, is parallel to abiding in God. Those who are born of God are his children and abide in him. In that life they mirror the love of God *in* the community and *for* the world. Those who claim to walk in the light cannot be impure. Hence, John reminds his readers that walking in the light involves purification: *And all who have this hope [in God] purify themselves, just as he is pure* (3:3). "In every way, then, the purity and holiness of the community is related to the purity and holiness of Jesus and 'remaining in Him' is the guarantee against sinning (3:3, 6,7)."[388]

But what about sin? Does John think Christians are a mixture of sinner and of saint or does he think that the phrase "sinning Christian" is an oxymoron? These are probably the most difficult questions to address in 1 John. On the one hand, the language of 1:8-10 labels those who claim to have no sin as liars; in 3:3-9 we read that those born of God cannot sin. Yarbrough thinks the first is a reference to the human condition: "God's eye beholds sin when he looks on humans."[389] But within the context of the debate between

---

"Communal Holiness in the Gospel of John: The Vine Metaphor as a Test Case with Elements of Comparative Ethnography and Implications for the Contemporary Church" (PhD thesis, The University of Manchester, 2010).

[387] See Kenneth G J Baker, "Perfection as Birthright: the Perspective on Christian Holiness in 1 John" (MA Dissertation, The University of Manchester, 1993), 50, "Christ purifies us from disobedience because he is obedient and from sin because he is sinless. Christ's life and death create the possibility of my freedom from sin."

[388] Baker, "Perfection as Birthright," 49.

[389] Yarbrough, *1-3 John*, 62.

John and the secessionists, this could well have been a logical consequence of the teaching that the blood of Jesus cleanses from all sin – therefore they are sinless now.[390] If this is so, the only way forward seems to be to read 1:8-10 along with 3:3-9 as language addressed to the community, rather than as conflicting passages to be isolated from the context of the problems facing the community.

John begins by tackling his opponents' main claims. There is a fundamental incoherence in their claim: *If we say that we have fellowship with him while we are walking in darkness, we lie.* And in his judgement they are indeed walking in darkness. The disruption of the fellowship is proof enough, so their claim to be walking in the light is manifestly false. To walk in the light means *we have fellowship with one another*, that is, the proof of the claim to be walking in God's light, to be abiding in him, is seen in community relationships, not in any exalted claims to individual spirituality. These people claimed to love God and be in fellowship with him. But, as John argues later, *Those who say, "I love God," and hate their brothers or sisters, are liars; for those who do not love a brother or sister whom they have seen, cannot love God whom they have not seen. The commandment we have from him is this: those who love God must love their brothers and sisters also* (4:20-21). Holiness can never be understood in strictly individual terms nor as self-possessed purity.[391] "It is not just the absence of sin which characterizes the true Christian; it is also the positive presence of love. Too often we think of Christian maturity in terms of freedom from sin. . . . But John wants us to see that spiritual life is characterized by positive acts of love, and that such love will be seen in the fellowship of the church as well as in our attitude to other people generally."[392]

The relationship with God and others is maintained through *the blood of Jesus his Son [that] cleanses us from all sin* (1:7). "The present tense [of cleanses] indicates an ongoing cleansing of those walking in the light as a basis for union with God."[393] This may well cohere with the statement to Peter by Jesus: *One who has bathed does not need to wash, except for the feet, but is entirely clean. And you are clean, though not all of you"* (John 13:10). The metaphor of walking, even for those in the light, implies the continual cleansing of the feet from the journey. It is both what God does for us and the basis of our ongoing relationship with God.[394] Conversely, the denial of any need for cleansing from sin is a rejection of confession and cuts believers off from the means of God's

---

[390] Painter, *1, 2, and 3 John*, 154.

[391] John Wesley's oft-misquoted statement reminds us of the social character of holy living. "Directly opposite to this [isolated mysticism] is the gospel of Christ. Solitary religion is not to be found there. 'Holy solitaries' is a phrase no more consistent with the gospel than holy adulterers. The gospel of Christ knows no religion, but social; no holiness but social holiness." *The Works of John Wesley*. Thomas Jackson, ed. vol. 14:321, Preface to Poetical Works.

[392] Marshall, *Epistles*, 133.

[393] Painter, *1, 2 and 3 John*, 145.

[394] Williamson, *1, 2 and 3 John*, 69.

grace. But *if we confess our sins, he who is faithful and just will forgive us our sins and cleanse us from all unrighteousness* (1:9).

Is there any distinction to be pressed between "forgive us our sins" and "cleanse us from all unrighteousness"? Marshall suggests that purification might "signal the removal not only of the guilt of sin but also of the power of sin in the human heart."³⁹⁵ In this passage and in 1:7, Smalley thinks that John assures his readers that God has made provision for their purity as well as actual sins. He writes, "in the death and resurrection of Jesus exists the possibility of purification from 'every' sin (πάσης ἁμαρτίας)."³⁹⁶ This conveys the breadth and scope of the redemption offered in Christ's death.³⁹⁷ But there may well be more. Unrighteousness, ἀδικία, may well have the connotation of injustice and specific evil deeds. Forgiveness of sins may therefore refer to the guilt of sin – the damaged relationship with God and humanity occasioned by our sins, while cleansing from unrighteousness is the "transformation that frees from wrongdoing via cleansing."³⁹⁸ Even here, John is writing to the community of believers, reminding them of the process of being cleansed and reconciled that will heal their community and enable them to walk in fellowship with God and each other.

Attempts to tease apart the singular "sin" in 1:7 from the plural "sins" in 1:9 are unconvincing. The point that John is making is at once simpler and more profound. Christ's atoning sacrifice is the sufficient remedy for all breaches of relationship and is continually efficacious as the community walks in the light of God. The cleansing occurs on the journey of the obedient followers of Jesus. The challenge for this interpretation, of course, comes from chapter three. After urging his readers to continue to abide in Christ, John writes, *See what love the Father has given us, that we should be called children of God; and that is what we are* (3:1). And just in case his flock didn't hear him correctly the first time, he repeats, *Beloved, we are God's children now* (3:2). The problem comes especially in 3:9-10 when John writes, *Those who have been born of God do not sin, because God's seed abides in them; they cannot sin, because they have been born of God. The children of God and the children of the devil are revealed in this way: all who do not do what is right are not from God, nor are those who do not love their brothers and sisters.* This is bold language indeed. How can John make such claims?

Those born of God do not sin. On the surface, this language could lead to a doctrine of sinless perfectionism. Indeed, taken in isolation, some of John's terms may lead to this distortion. Exactly what does John mean by "perfect love" and "love made perfect"³⁹⁹ in three key passages (see 2:5; 4:12, 17-18)?⁴⁰⁰

---

³⁹⁵ Marshall, *Epistles*, 114.

³⁹⁶ Smalley, *Johannine Community*, 24.

³⁹⁷ See John Wesley, *Explanatory Notes on the New Testament*. (London: Wesleyan-Methodist Book room, undated from a reprint by Peabody: Hendrickson, 1996), comments on 1 John 1:7 where he speaks of removing guilt and purifying.

³⁹⁸ Yarbrough, *1-3 John*, 65.

³⁹⁹Here we capture a glimpse of why this epistle has been so important to Wesleyan interpreters. See, for example, Mildred B Wynkoop, *A Theology of Love*

John is clear that the source of all love is God. God is love, and it is his love that is brought to its intended goal in people. God's love *has been perfected among us* (4:17) in that God's love achieves its purpose in us when it is "known/recognized and believed/accepted (4:16a). Thus belief is the basis for loving action because the acceptance of God's love involves love for one another. That is its goal."[401] As Williamson observes, "the true test of holiness occurs when God's love is manifest in the community's contacts with others."[402] God's love in us becomes the basis for all our activities; it is never a human achievement. "Love, like holiness, finds its source and definition in God. We cannot become truly holy or genuinely loving by our own striving."[403]

To what extent, then, is the community "perfect" because it has become part of the life of God? "Ontologically," Baker argues, "it is the very nature of those who have been born of God that they do not sin. [First John] 3:9 is not *prescriptive but descriptive!* The freedom from sin it describes is not just freedom from committing certain acts but of belonging to the sphere of activity where sin has no place."[404] There are dangers in this perspective, of course. Bogart argues that (what he calls) orthodox perfectionism arises out of the conviction that the believer is born from above.[405] So John claims purity for himself and his followers[406] but does so in contrast to the claims of the heretical perfectionists. They make a claim to *"intrinsic* human perfection, possessed by man as a *right*, not, as in the case of Christian perfection, *given* to repentant sinful man as a *gift* from a forgiving Father."[407] But Bogart's analysis needs to be nuanced slightly. John's opponents accept the gift character of their birth from above but understand perfection as a static possession that is theirs as a right and possession rather than utterly dependent upon an ongo-

---

(Kansas City: Beacon Hill, 1972). Equally the whole perfectionist problem may well be one of the reasons that this epistle is marginalized in New Testament theology. Biblical theologians typically, and perhaps unconsciously, construct their theology on a Pauline grid to the comparative neglect of the gospels and the general epistles. The result is an unbalanced concentration on the Pauline view of justification and sanctification without the further nuance brought by these other NT resources.

[400]ἀληθῶς ἐν τούτῳ ἡ ἀγάπη τοῦ θεοῦ τετελείωται (2:5); θεὸν οὐδεὶς πώποτε ἐθέαται. ἐὰν ἀγαπῶμεν ἀλλήλους, ὁ θεὸς ἐν ἡμῖν μένει καὶ ἡ ἀγάπη αὐτοῦ ἐν ἡμῖν τετελειωμένη ἐστίν (4:12); Ἐν τούτῳ τετελείωται ἡ ἀγάπη μεθ' ἡμῶν, ἵνα παρρησίαν ἔχωμεν ἐν τῇ ἡμέρᾳ τῆς κρίσεως, ὅτι καθὼς ἐκεῖνός ἐστιν καὶ ἡμεῖς ἐσμεν ἐν τῷ κόσμῳ τούτῳ. φόβος οὐκ ἔστιν ἐν τῇ ἀγάπῃ ἀλλ' ἡ τελεία ἀγάπη ἔξω βάλλει τὸν φόβον, ὅτι ὁ φόβος κόλασιν ἔχει, ὁ δὲ φοβούμενος οὐ τετελείωται ἐν τῇ ἀγάπῃ (4:17-18).

[401] Painter, *1, 2 and 3 John*, 281.
[402] Williamson, *1, 2 and 3 John*, 149.
[403] Williamson, *1, 2 and 3 John*, 151.
[404] Baker, "Perfection as Birthright," 28, his italics.
[405] Bogart, *Orthodox and Heretical Perfectionism*, 2.
[406] Bogart, *Orthodox and Heretical Perfectionism*, 38.
[407] Bogart, *Orthodox and Heretical Perfectionism*, 34, his italics.

ing relationship to the Holy One. Holiness movements at any time can succumb to this distorted perfectionism. It has its roots firmly in authentic Johannine soil but fails to take seriously the power and deceptiveness of sin as well as the relational character of Christian holiness. As Swanson notes, "those who think themselves most free from sin are those most at risk, and this is true of the community of faith as much as it is of the individual."[408]

But that still leaves us with the problem of human experience. Most commentators take the view that those who have been born of God do not sin, because God's seed abides in them; they cannot sin, because they have been born of God (3:9) refers to habitual sin.[409] True though that is, it weakens the force of the argument. John seems to be saying that sin in the children of God is unthinkable, however often it happens. This does not preclude sin occurring. If it does occur, the community should pray for forgiveness and restoration and God will give life to such a one-- to those whose sin is not mortal (5:16).[410] If anyone does sin, we have an advocate with the Father, Jesus Christ the righteous (2:1).

John's whole argument is set in the context of the apocalyptic turn of the ages: *Children, it is the last hour!* and *the Son of God was revealed for this purpose, to destroy the works of the devil* (5:18). Hence, the one born of God is outside the baleful control of the evil one. John acknowledges the eschatological tension within that statement. They are children of God now. But there is a "not yet" dimension as well – *what we will be has not yet been revealed. What we do know is this: when he is revealed, we will be like him, for we will see him as he is* (3:2).

Living in the Spirit

John's readers know the words of Jesus: *You must be born from above* (John 3:7). They therefore know that ethnicity no longer determines participation in the people of God. This new people has its origins in God through a new birth quite apart from human origin. They are born of the Spirit. The implications of this new birth are central to John's encouragement of his community and his castigation of the secessionists. If birth into the family is divine in origin,

---

[408] D Swanson, "Sin and Love in 1 John," *The Flame,* 70 (No. 1, 2004): 21.

[409] John Wesley, *Notes on the New Testament, loc. cit.,* stated that whoever committed sin (3:5) "transgressed the holy, just and good law of God, and so sets his authority at nought; for this is implied in the very nature of sin. But Christ came into the world 'to take away our sins' - to destroy them all, root and branch, and leave none remaining." His emphasis was focused upon abiding: only those who abide "in communion with him, by loving faith, does not sin - while he so abides." The same emphasis occurs in his explanation of 3:9. "Whosoever is born of God - By living faith, whereby God is continually breathing spiritual life into his soul, and his soul is continually breathing out love and prayer to God, doth not commit sin. For the divine seed of loving faith abideth in him; and, so long as it doth, he cannot sin, because he is born of God - Is inwardly and universally changed." For Wesley, inability to sin is possible but contingent upon continual abiding in Christ.

[410] For Wesley, "any sin but total apostasy from both the power and form of godliness" may be forgiven.

the knowledge that they are abiding in him is also of divine origin. "Abiding" is a central Johannine theme. In the Fourth Gospel the metaphor of abiding in the vine refers almost exclusively to the relationship of the community to its source in God.[411] Here John states, *By this we know that we abide in him and he in us, because he has given us of his Spirit* (4:13). "The presence of the Spirit is no "optional extra" but the identifying characteristic of every believer."[412]

But therein lies a problem. The secessionists are convinced that they have the Spirit's anointing on their lives. Larry Hurtado argues that they may well be claiming to have advanced so far in their close relationship with God that they are beyond sin, "perhaps even a certain divine-like freedom from the whole question of sin."[413] They claim that their innovations in theology come from the inspiration of the Spirit. That should not surprise us in a Johannine community where it is expected that the Spirit would lead into all truth (see John 14:25-26; 16:12-15).

The problem is not that their claim is based upon Spirit revelation. It is because the content is incompatible with the revelations they have already received from their own earlier endowment of the Spirit.[414] John tackles the problem first by dealing with his opponents. Not only is their theology wrong, their lack of love and seceding from the group shows that they were never believers from the beginning.[415] Essentially, they are antichrists. Here again the theme has to do with the community.[416] It is only within the community of believers that the reality of abiding in God may be assayed. Those abiding in him act and live in love with their siblings.[417] By contrast, those who do not demonstrate love for their spiritual siblings live in the sphere of the evil one. In characteristically blunt language, John writes *Whoever does not love abides in death. All who hate a brother or sister are murderers, and you know that murderers do not have eternal life abiding in them* (3:14). The world that is hostile to God accepts the secessionists and listens to them (4:5) but hates the people of God (3:13). For John, no clearer evidence is needed to demonstrate that the secessionists are no longer part of the people of God. It is a consequence of their failure to understand their true identity in Christ. Flawed beliefs have issued in wrong practices.

John reassures his flock. He writes, you have been anointed by the Holy One, and all of you have knowledge. I write to you, not because you do not

---

[411] See Kunene, who argues that the vine metaphor in John 15 is primarily communal.

[412] Baker, "Perfection as Birthright," 86.

[413] Hurtado, *Lord Jesus Christ*, 414.

[414] Hurtado, *Lord Jesus Christ*, 408-411.

[415] See Marshall, *Epistles*, 152, "A person who makes a genuine profession of faith can be expected to persevere in his faith," although elsewhere John warns his readers against the danger of failure to persevere.

[416] See Baker, "Perfection as Birthright," 87, "Holiness is first a matter for the church, and then for the solitary member."

[417] See Baker, "Perfection as Birthright," 28, "Those born of God are inevitably bound to those who share the same parentage (5:1, 2)."

know the truth, but because you know it, and you know that no lie comes from the truth (2:21).[418] This is no private or elitist matter. The spiritual elitism of John's opponents issues in schism not in the strengthening of the fellowship. And that disruption of fellowship completely invalidates their claim to be spiritually superior – in fact, it turns their claim of sinlessness and closeness to God completely on its head. John's flock need have no fear of the world because the one that is in you is greater than the one who is in the world (4:4). He warns them, however, not to love the things of the world – the desires of the flesh, the desire of the eyes and the pride in riches – because these do not come from God (2:16).

Conclusion

With the exception of the term *Holy One* (2:20), typical holiness terminology is absent from 1 John. Nevertheless, John gives a firm "Yes" to the whole notion of holy living. Those born of God, abiding in Christ and walking in the light and guided by the Spirit are to live the life of God's holy people. This is the life of God in which they participate, enabling them to be part of the mission of God. For those born of God, walking in the darkness of sin and alienation is unthinkable. Thus, no matter how often or how many Christians may fail to walk constantly in the light, sin is never the norm for the people of God. Second, John gives an equally firm "No" to any notion of sinless perfection as a possession or right of either the community or individuals within it. Holiness is not a thing or even an individual spiritual experience. It is only as we are walking in the light of God and in loving relationship with our brothers and sisters that we can talk about love made perfect and Christian holiness. This is the normal walk of the Christian life. Third, sin is anything that causes a breach between God and his people or between his people. This is not the normal state of the people of God. But the dangers of the world, of sin and the evil one still lurk for the people of God. Hence, the continual cleansing blood of Christ remains the only and all sufficient means of maintaining our relationship as God's holy people with the holy God as well as entering into that relationship. Fourth, in the context of abiding in him, in obedience to him, and in fellowship with one another, love is perfected. This is not a self-generated sense of good will towards others but a mutual loving participation in the life of the community, whose source of life is the God who is love. And the love of God enables and impels the mission of the holy people of God.

---

[418] See Baker, "Perfection as Birthright," 84, "The Spirit operates *through* doctrine, not to it, from it or independently of it."

Part IV

Practical

Chapter 8

Praedicare Verbum Dei: John Wesley's Theology of Preaching

By Joseph Wood

Introduction

Preaching has become a focal point in the area of Wesley and Methodist studies. Wesley's acceptance of the irregularity of preaching outdoors, the use of lay preaching, and the tension that arose as a result has painted a dramatic picture of the early Methodist movement. The large crowds that gathered to hear Whitefield and Wesley are a testament to the effectiveness of his preaching methods, and the societies subsequently established by Wesley exemplify his desire that preaching must be accompanied by discipline. The societies gathered for scriptural preaching and teaching with the expectation that members of the body of Christ would be built up in faith, love and holiness.[419] Paul Chilcote noted that the "proclamation of God's Word in corporate worship and the rediscovery of the 'living Word' among the early Methodist people was the life force of the movement."[420] As these societies grew in number, the need for preachers grew as well.

Two reasons for employing lay preachers were clearly expressed in Wesley's writings: 1) Methodist preachers were, "extraordinary messengers, raised up to provoke the ordinary ones to jealousy," and 2) the Methodist preachers addressed the growing need for preaching in the emerging societies.[421] Ac-

---

[419] J. Wesley, *Explanatory Notes Upon the New Testament* (London: The Epworth Press, 1952), 713. Hereafter noted *ENNT*.

[420] Paul Chilcote, "The Integral Nature of Worship and Evangelism" in *The Study of Evangelism: Exploring a Missional Practice of the Church*, Paul Chilcote and Laceye C. Warner, eds (Grand Rapids, Michigan: Eerdmans, 2008), 258.

[421] J. Wesley, "Prophets and Priests" in *The Bicentennial Edition of the Works of John Wesley* (Nashville: Abingdon Press, 1976-), 4:479. Further references to texts in this

cording to Kenneth J. Collins, "lacking suitable labourers to reap a burgeoning harvest, Wesley began to employ lay preachers, that is, unordained assistants whose ministries would be limited, for the most part, to the task of preaching."[422] Wesley's use of irregular preaching methods, as well as his use of lay preachers, was not widely accepted by the clergy. It was one thing for preaching to be held outdoors by clergymen like Wesley and Whitefield, but it was another for a lay-person to be found preaching anywhere. Consequently, lay preaching became a central issue of the tension between the Wesley and other ministers within the Church of England.

As Methodism grew, and as the tension grew between Methodists and the clergy of the Church of England, many society members, primarily dissenters, began to want more than preaching from the lay-preachers. A number of the clergy spoke out against the Methodists, which made many society members uncomfortable about receiving the sacrament at the hands of these Church of England clergy. As a result, they wished to receive the sacraments from their lay preachers. However, Wesley's theology of ministry did not allow for un-ordained sacramental administration. Wesley has been criticized by both his peers and subsequent interpreters for what appears to be an inconsistency. Why would he allow – and promote – lay preaching, but firmly reject lay sacramental administration? Much of what has been written on the issue of lay ministry has focussed on his pragmatic reasons for employing lay ministers, namely, that there was a growing need for preaching. However, few interpreters of Wesley have acknowledged that Wesley's theology played a significant role in the use of lay preachers. It was not simply a pragmatic decision; it stemmed from a deeply held theological position: Preaching and administration of the sacraments are two different practices, one of which required the authority conferred through ordination.

Because of the irregularity of Methodist lay ministry, preaching became a topic to which Wesley dedicated much time in writing. He defended his use of lay preachers to his critics and he wrote much to his own lay preachers about their role in Methodism and the Church in England. Two primary works of Wesley, *A Farther Appeal to Men of Reason and Religion* (1745) and *On Prophets and Priests* (1789), provide a framework upon which one may develop both Wesley's theology of preaching and his advocacy and intentions for lay preaching in the societies. Unlike previous studies which have focussed solely on the practice of preaching and the controversy surrounding lay ministry, this chapter will first develop Wesley's theology of preaching and second, its implication for Methodist lay preachers.[423]

---

edition will be given as *Works [BE]*, followed by volume number and page reference. See also Wesley, "Minutes," *Works [BE]*, 10:177.

[422] Kenneth J. Collins, *John Wesley: A Theological Journey* (Nashville, Tennessee: Abingdon Press, 2003), 108.

[423] See Richard Heitzenrater, *Mirror and Memory: Reflections on Early Methodism* (Nashville, Tennessee: Kingswood Books, 1989), 162-173; Adrian Burdon, *John Wesley and His Preachers* (Aldershot: Ashgate Publishing, 2005); Michael Pasquarello III, *John Wesley: A Preaching Life* (Nashville, Tennessee: Abingdon Press, 2010).

Wesley's Theology of Preaching

In order to develop Wesley's theology of preaching it is important to note the particular Anglican tradition from which it originates. The works of Richard Hooker (1554-1600) and Bishop Jeremy Taylor (1613-1667) will identify a theology of preaching as exemplary of a particular line of Anglican thought in the sixteenth and seventeenth centuries.[424] Hooker dedicated a significant amount of his *Lawes* to explaining the concept and practice of preaching. According to Hooker, there are two kinds of preaching: exhortation of the Scriptures and reading the Scriptures.[425] Exhortation of the scriptures includes the exegesis, analysis, explanation, and the opinion of a preacher given to the audience by way of speech or publication. In this form of preaching, a passage or verse is selected and, "the mysteries which lie hid therein" are "explained by lively voice, and applied to the people's use as the speaker in his wisdom thinketh meet."[426] Most modern readers would understand this form of preaching as the ordinary way by which the Word of God is proclaimed from the pulpit. Yet, Hooker was quick to point out that there is a difference between the Scriptures exhorted word for word and a sermon attempting to explain it. Hooker's context provoked his stance against the claim that the Scriptures were only valuable if exhorted, or preached, through sermons.[427] Whereas some Puritans claimed that hearing and responding to the Word of God required a sermon, Hooker appealed to the activity of the Holy Spirit in creating response. He referred to a second type of preaching: reading the Scriptures. According to Hooker, the "Church as a witness preacheth his mere revealed truth by reading publicly the sacred Scripture. So that a second

---

[424] For more on the particular line of thought, see John Munsey Turner, *Conflict and Reconciliation: Studies in Methodism and Ecumenism in England 1740-1982* (London: Epworth Press, 1985), 44-45; Eric Griffin, "Practical Catholicism: John Wesley's Theology of Bishops Reconsidered" in *Churchman*, vol. 112, no. 4 (1998): 324-338; Mark Chapman, *Anglican Theology* (London: T&T Clark, 2012), 103-125; 151-153.

[425] Richard Hooker, *The Works of that Learned and Judicious Divine Mr. Richard Hooker: With an Account of his Life and Death by Isaac Walton*, arranged by Rev. John Keble in 3 Volumes (Oxford: Clarendon Press, 1888), 5.19.1. Hereafter noted, Hooker, *LEP*, book, chapter, section. "Moses and the Prophets, Christ and his Apostles, were in their times all preachers of God's truth; some by word, some by writing, some by both. This they did partly as faithful witnesses, making mere relation what God himself had revealed unto them; and partly as careful expounders, teachers, persuaders thereof. The Church in like case preacheth still, first publishing by way of testimony or relation to the truth from which from them she hath received, written in the sacred volumes of Scripture; secondly by way of explication, discovering the mysteries which lie hid therein. The Church as a witness preaches his mere revealed truth by reading publicly the sacred Scripture. So that a second kind of preaching is the reading of the Holy Writ." See also, Stephen Sykes, John Booty, Jonathan Knight, eds. *The Study of Anglicanism*, revised ed. (London: SPCK, 1998), 14.

[426] Hooker, *LEP*, 5.19.1, 5.21.1.

[427] See Philip Secor, *Hooker: Prophet of Anglicanism* (Kent: Burns and Oates, 1999), 162-198. See also Alan Bartlett, *A Passionate Balance: The Anglican Tradition* (Maryknoll: Orbis Books, 2007), 106.

kind of preaching is the reading of Holy Writ."[428] Appealing to the commands and actions of the Old and New Testaments, Hooker resolved that the reading and hearing the Scriptures is the purest and most effectual form of receiving the truth about salvation in Christ. This does not mean explication had no value; rather, Hooker's argument was aimed specifically at what he saw as de-valuing the reading of the Scriptures by the Puritans.

According to Hooker, the Law of Moses required the Jewish people to have weekly readings of the Law, and the Apostle Paul promoted the regular reading of epistles in the churches.[429] To him, this practice had continued in the Church as the primary means of proclaiming the message of salvation to the world.[430] For Hooker, the reading of the Scriptures was the purest form of preaching because the reader and hearer relied solely on the work of the Spirit through inspiration and grace for understanding. "Wherefore when we read or recite the Scripture, we then deliver to the people properly the word of God," and, "Reading doth convey to the mind that truth without addition or diminution, which Scripture hath derived from the Holy Ghost."[431] According to Hooker, Spirit-led reading or hearing the Scriptures was the purest form of preaching. This is one of the reasons why the reading of the Scriptures aloud in worship remains integral to the Anglican liturgical tradition.[432]

Bishop Jeremy Taylor followed the theology and practice fostered by Hooker regarding preaching. In his book, *Holy Living*, a highly formative book for Wesley, Taylor explained that there are two types of preaching: reading/hearing the Scriptures or reading/hearing sermons on the Scriptures. Both practices qualify as edifying to the receiver only in and through the work of the Holy Spirit. He explained,

> For God preaches to us in the Scripture, and by his secret assistances and spiritual thoughts and holy motions: good men preach to us when they, by popular arguments and human arts and compliances, expound and press any of those doctrines which God hath preached unto us in his holy word. The Holy Ghost is certainly the best preacher in the world, and the words of Scripture the best sermons...Good sermons and good books are of excellent use; but yet they can serve no other end but that we practise the plain doctrines of Scripture.[433]

Taylor, like Hooker, understood that the Scriptures alone are the surest means by which God proclaims the message of salvation to the world by His Spirit. Good sermons and books are important, but they are to be carefully engaged in an effort to rightly divide the Word of God from human wisdom.

---

[428] Hooker, *LEP*, 5.19.1.

[429] Hooker, *LEP*, 5.19.1, 5.22.2. See Deuteronomy 31.11-13, Colossians 4.16, and 1 Thessalonians 5.27.

[430] Hooker, *LEP*, 5.21.3.

[431] Hooker, *LEP*, 5.22.10, 5.22.6.

[432] For more see Walter Howard Frere, *A New History of the Book of Common Prayer: With a Rationale of its Offices* (London: Macmillan & Co. LTD, 1965).

[433] Jeremy Taylor, *The Rules and Exercises of Holy Living, Together with Prayers Containing The Whole Duty of a Christian* (Chicago: M.A. Donohue & Co., 1900), 310-311.

Taylor advised that prayer must precede the reading of the scriptures or hearing them read aloud or exhorted in a sermon. The Holy Spirit must be invoked and active in the life of the reader/hearer if any benefit or grace is to be received. Taylor advised to "Beg of God, by prayer, that he would give you the spirit of obedience and profit, and that he would, by his Spirit, write the word in your heart, and that you describe it in your life."[434] Whether by reading/hearing the Scriptures or reading/hearing an sermon on the Scriptures, preaching, for both Taylor and Hooker, was an instrument by which the Holy Spirit actively inspires and convicts believers and non-believers. Preaching is proclaiming the message of salvation and bringing humanity closer to God in Christ Jesus.[435]

Unlike Hooker and Taylor, it is not as easy to ascertain a clear definition of preaching from the works of Wesley. However, an exploration of two significant publications gives an indication that his theology of preaching follows that proposed by Hooker and Taylor. In Part III of his *A Farther Appeal to Men of Reason and Religion*, Wesley produced a defence of lay preaching, which includes a brief but summative description of his theology of preaching. Wesley's preachers were criticized because they were neither ordained nor educated. In short, it was held that what the lay preachers were doing could not have been preaching, because they were not properly authorised or trained to preach. Wesley's response could be read as a simplified theology of preaching. "Perhaps it will be said, 'But this is not preaching.' Yes, but it is essentially such. For what is it to preach, but *praedicare verbum Dei*; 'to publish the word of God? And this laymen do all over England; particularly under the eye of every bishop in the nation.'"[436] For Wesley, as for Hooker and Taylor, preaching, in the broadest sense, should not be restricted to the clergy. Publishing the word of God happens when one makes public the Scriptures.

To make his case, he went further. "Nay, is it not done in the universities themselves? Who ordained that singing man at Christ Church? Who is likewise utterly qualified for the work, murdering every Lesson he reads? Not even endeavouring to read it as the Word of God, but as an old song? Such a layman as this meddling at all with the word of God, I grant is a scandal to the English nation."[437] Wesley was emphatic that singing and reading are acts of publishing the Word of God. Wesley gave another example describing his view of preaching as "making public" the Scriptures. At Oxford all of the students were required to read three public lectures in moral philosophy on whatever subject the student preferred. As a student, Wesley's subject was "the love of God." Following this theology of *praedicare verbum Dei*, Wesley said, "Now what was this but preaching?"[438] In this instance, he also believed

---

[434] Taylor, *Holy Living*, 313.
[435] Paul Avis, *Anglicanism and the Christian Church: Theological Resources in Historical Perspective* (London: T&T Clark, 2002), 115-116.
[436] J. Wesley, "A Farther Appeal to Men of Reason and Religion," *Works [BE]*, 11:298.
[437] J. Wesley, "A Farther Appeal," *Works [BE]*, 11:299.
[438] J. Wesley, "A Farther Appeal," *Works [BE]*, 11:299.

he was publishing the Word of God. Wesley's explanatory note on 1 Timothy 4:13 gives evidence of reading as preaching. It stated, "*Give thyself to reading* – Both publicly and privately. Enthusiasts observe this! Expect no end without the means."[439] By enthusiasts Wesley meant those who sought manifestations of the Spirit beyond the proper operations of the Spirit, in this instance, the reading of Scripture. As a means of grace, the reading of Scripture must be read aloud, publicly. Again, reading is publishing the Word of God, *praedicare verbum Dei*. It is clear that preaching, for Wesley, was understood broadly as publishing of the Word of God either by speech, song or in print, and any exhortation of that Word of God, either by speech, song or in print.

Wesley and Pneumatology in Preaching

Wesley's theology of preaching is best understood in light of his pneumatology. For Wesley, at no point is preaching true or valid, if the Holy Spirit is not active. Wesley was adamant on this point. "For what can be more undeniable than this, that our preaching is vain, unless it be attended with the power of that Spirit who alone pierceth the heart? and that your hearing is vain, unless the same power be present to heal your soul, and to give you a faith which 'standeth not in the wisdom of men, but in the power of God?'"[440] It is by the operation of the Holy Spirit that any preaching, whether done by reading or by hearing, is effective. Wesley's pneumatology regarding preaching was not developed in isolation from other sources. In the same *Appeal* Wesley found authority for his assertions within his own Church. Quoting *The Book of Common Prayer* and the *Homilies* of the Church of England, Wesley produced a litany of theological instruction on the operations of the Holy Spirit. He stated:

> In her Daily Service she teaches us all to beseech God "to grant us his Holy Spirit, that those things may please him which we do at this present, and that the rest of our life may be pure and holy;" "O Lord, from whom all good things do come, grant to us, thy humble servants, that by thy holy inspiration we may think those things that are good, and by thy merciful guidance may we perform the same;" "that it is [the Holy Ghost] which giveth eloquence and utterance in preaching the Gospel;" "In reading of God's word, he profiteth most that is most inspired with the Holy Ghost;" "Human and worldly wisdom is not needful to the understanding of Scripture, but the revelation of the Holy Ghost, who inspireth the true meaning unto them that with humility and diligence search for it." Every proposition, which I have anywhere advanced concerning those operations of the Holy Ghost, which, I believe, are common to all Christians in all ages, is here clearly maintained by our own Church.[441]

---

[439] J. Wesley, *ENNT*, 779.

[440] J. Wesley, "A Farther Appeal to Men of Reason and Religion," *Works [BE]*, 11:153.

[441] J. Wesley, "A Farther Appeal to Men of Reason and Religion," *Works [BE]*, 11:166-170.

Anyone who acknowledges the official liturgy and *Homilies* of the Church of England must acknowledge the vitality of the operation of the Holy Spirit in the life of the Church, particularly in the preaching of the Word. Wesley's pneumatology informed his understanding and practice of preaching. *Praedicare verbum Dei* is preaching done through the Spirit.

A further example of Wesley's pneumatological understanding of preaching is found in a response to an accusation received in 1747. Wesley's opponent proposed that any praise, prayers, or preaching "which man sets about in his own will, and at his own appointment, which can begin and end at pleasure, do or leave undone, as himself sees meet, are but superstitious, will-worship, and abominable idolatries."[442] To the contrary, Wesley proposed that true worship is the result of the operation of the Spirit.[443] Just as the human will must be inspired if our worship is to be spiritual worship, the will, apart from God's movements, cannot produce effective preaching. He stated:

> It is not my own will to preach at all. It is quite contrary to my will. Many a time have I cried out, "Lord, send by whom thou wilt send; only send not me!" But I am moved by the Spirit of God to preach: He clearly shows me it is his will I should; and that I should do it when and where the greatest number of poor sinners may be gathered together. Moved by Him, I give up my will, and appoint a time and place, when by his power I trust to speak in his name.[444]

For Wesley, preaching is pneumatological. It is a non-sacramental act in which the Word of God is made public by reading or singing the Scriptures aloud or in private, and where the Word of God is exhorted in the form of a sermon animated by the working of the Holy Spirit. Influenced by Richard Hooker and Bishop Jeremy Taylor, Wesley's theology of preaching as *praedicare verbum Dei* sheds light on why Wesley defended the practice of lay preaching.

"On Prophets and Priests" (1789)

Written on his last journey to Ireland, *On Priests and Prophets* was, like many other sermons written after 1784, intended to reiterate the nature and purpose of Methodism and to encourage the Methodists to continue their allegiance to the Church of England.[445] Wesley's purpose in Ireland was to settle the Methodists there who had been receiving reports of his actions in 1784 regarding the American Methodists. Adrian Burdon explained:

---

[442] J. Wesley, "A Letter to A Person Lately Joined with the People Called Quakers" in *The Works of the Rev John Wesley, MA*, edited by Thomas Jackson, 14 volumes (Kansas City: Beacon Hill Press, reprinted 1978), 10:180-181. Further references to texts in this edition will be given as *Works*, followed by volume number and page reference.

[443] Wesley recognized the unique practices of Quaker worship. His understanding and critique is more fully developed in the letter noted above.

[444] J. Wesley, "A Letter to a Person Lately Joined with the People Called Quakers," *Works*, 10:181.

[445] Burdon, *Authority and Order*, 72.

The sermon presented a resume of John Wesley's use of his preachers, in particular revealing the way in which they were subject to his authority. The kernel of the sermon was that the Methodist preachers were appointed, by John Wesley, to the work of preaching; they were not to take other work upon themselves, certainly not the administration of the sacraments, without further appointment by him.[446]

Throughout the sermon Wesley reminded his preachers of their calling in an effort to re-establish the nature and purpose of Methodism and Wesley's own authority as their scriptural *episcopos*.

Many scholars of Wesley and Methodism have mentioned this sermon, but few have recognised the value it contains for developing Wesley's theology of preaching and its relationship to ecclesiology.[447] Burdon provided a treatment of the sermon in order to support his thesis regarding Wesley's authority over his preachers. "The sermon was a demonstration of John Wesley, the scriptural *episcopos* of the Methodist people, revealing his will and exerting his authority."[448] Wesley's authority is one subject of the sermon, but the thrust of the work is concerned with the role of preaching in the Christian ministry, an issue that Burdon did not fully address. In a recent article, David Rainey pointed out the significance of this sermon for developing an understanding of Wesley's ecclesiology.[449] This sermon is significant for understanding the role of preaching in Wesley's ecclesiology.

Wesley's text was Hebrews 5:4, which reads: "No man taketh this honour unto himself but he that is called of God, as was Aaron." Albert Outler pointed out that this text was used for sermons by Thomas Bisse (1708), William Roberts (1709), and Edward Cobden (1753) prior to Wesley's sermon.[450] These sermons mentioned by Outler greatly differ from Wesley's interpretation however. For example, both Bisse and Roberts used the text to defend the divine right and necessity of the episcopacy in the Church. Bisse argued that the passage refers to God's ordaining the episcopacy as a tool used to perpetuate the unity and integrity of the Church. According to Bisse, "[He] alone, who is a God of order, founded this uniform and harmonious frame of government."[451] Likewise, Roberts illustrated that the passage suggests that

---

[446] Burdon, *Authority and Order*, 73.

[447] Albert Outler called this sermon an "interesting 'failure.'" See *Works [BE]*, 4:74. Gwang Seok Oh only mentioned the sermon in a footnote in *John Wesley's Ecclesiology* (Lanham: Scarecrow Press, 2008), 247. Frank Baker referred to the sermon as, "a piece of pious propaganda rather than a sermon" in *John Wesley and the Church of England* (London: The Epworth Press, 1970), 313. Henry Rack argued that the sermon was practical in nature, not theoretical or theological in *Reasonable Enthusiast: John Wesley and the Rise of Methodism* (London: The Epworth Press, 1992), 525.

[448] Burdon, *Authority and Order*, 75.

[449] David Rainey, "The Established Church and Evangelical Theology: John Wesley's Ecclesiology" in *International Journal of Systematic Theology*, vol. 12, no. 4 (October 2010): 428.

[450] J. Wesley, "Prophets and Priests," *Works [BE]*, 4:75.

[451] Thomas Bisse, *A Defense of the Episcopacy: A Sermon Preached before the University of Oxford At St. Mary's on Trinity Sunday 1708* (Oxford: The Theater, 1708), 19.

the episcopacy is necessary for the Gospel ministry to continue. His conclusion focused on the role of Aaron as being a type of ordained minister: "From hence it is evident, first, that he, who officiates in Divine matters, is to be set apart, and to have a distinct commission from the rest of mankind; and secondly, this commission must be derived from divine institution."[452] Both of these sermons used the same passage to defend the episcopacy as the only valid form of church government and ordination under the episcopacy as the only valid form of continuing the ministry of the Church. Wesley, however, took a different approach.

Instead of focusing on Aaron, who is mentioned in the passage, Wesley focused on Moses, who is not mentioned in the passage. To those who proposed that this passage provides scriptural evidence that only the ordained have authority to preach, Wesley argued otherwise. According to Roberts, "we may observe, that though our Saviour had many followers, yet none of them presumed to preach or baptize, or perform any other sacred office, 'till they were particularly commissioned by Him."[453] Roberts presumed that preaching and baptizing, or prophesying and sacramental administration, are particular tasks meant solely for the ordained. On the contrary, Wesley claimed that there was no definitive biblical evidence for this. Rather, to Wesley, "there is one grievous flaw in this argument, as often as it has been urged. 'Called of God, as was Aaron!' But Aaron did not preach at all: He was not called to it either by God or man. Aaron was called to minister in holy things; -- to offer up prayers and sacrifices; to execute the office of a Priest. But he was never called to be a Preacher."[454] According to Wesley, the roles of prophet and priest were entirely distinct from each other in the Old Testament; and they have existed "in every age" since. The example given of Aaron and Moses exemplifies the differences in the two roles. Aaron was called of God to be a priest, not a prophet. Moses also was called of God but to be a prophet, not a priest.

Prophets

What did Wesley mean by the term, "prophet"? In a pamphlet directed specifically towards the people called Methodists, Wesley cautioned his followers against false prophets. In this pamphlet Wesley defined a true prophet in the following way: "By prophets here (as in many other passages of Scripture, particularly in the New Testament) are meant, not those who foretell things to come, but those who speak in the Name of God: Those men who profess to

---

[452] William Roberts, *The Divine Institution of the Gospel Ministry, and the Necessity of Episcopal Ordination, Asserted by Proofs from Scripture, and the Practice of the Primitive and Purest Ages of the Christian Church*, 4th edition (London, 1709), 2.

[453] Roberts, *The Divine Institution of the Gospel Ministry*, 6. Italics mine.

[454] J. Wesley "Prophets and Priests," *Works [BE]*, 4:75.

be sent of God, to teach others the Way of Heaven."[455] He called later prophets "teachers sent of God."[456] According to Wesley, prophets are teachers who speak in the Name of God in an effort to bring those who listen to them nearer to God. Prophets publish the Word of God. A "true prophet," according to Wesley, is, "every teacher whom [God] has sent, [and] bringeth forth the good Fruit of Holiness."[457] Wesley understood the role of the prophet to be one of teaching, preaching, and producing good fruit. The role of priest, conversely, is to administer divine things like the sacraments.

After establishing the distinction between the role of prophet and priest, Wesley then described two types of prophet: ordinary and extraordinary. Ordinary prophets of the Old Testament, "were those who were educated in 'the schools of the prophets' (1 Samuel 19:18), those who were trained up to instruct the people, and were ordinary preachers in their synagogues. In the New Testament they are usually termed scribes, or *nomikoi*, 'expounders of the law.' But few, if any of them, were priests."[458] As Christianity was established, according to Wesley, the role of the prophet did not cease to exist, but it was redefined. The terms, "evangelist" and "teacher" took the place of prophet. The Apostle Paul speaks of God setting up apostles, prophets, and teachers in the Church (1 Corinthians 7:28). Wesley's note on this verse gives further insight into his understanding of the role of the prophet: "*Secondly prophets* – Who either foretell things to come, or speak by extraordinary inspiration, for the edification of the church."[459] In Wesley's note on Ephesians 4:11, he distinguishes between ordinary and extraordinary prophets.

> *And some prophets and some evangelists* – A prophet testifies of things to come; an evangelist, of things past: and that chiefly by preaching the gospel before or after any of the apostles. All these were extraordinary officers. The ordinary were: *Some pastors* – Watching over their several flocks. *And some teachers* – Whether of the same or a lower order, to assist them, as occasion might require.'[460]

According to Wesley, New Testament prophets were in one of two categories: ordinary were called to be pastors or shepherds, and extraordinary were called to be evangelists or prophets in the Old Testament sense identified by Wesley. Wesley further explained that extraordinary prophets are those "on whom the Holy Ghost came in an extraordinary manner."[461] Drawing a parallel between Aaron and Moses, he illustrated the difference between pastors and evangelists, or ordinary and extraordinary prophets.

---

[455] J. Wesley, *A Caution Against False Prophets, in a Sermon on Matt. vii. 15-20. Particularly Recommended to the People called Methodists* (Dublin: Printed by S. Powell in Crane-lane, 1750), 6.
[456] J. Wesley, *A Caution Against False Prophets*, 12.
[457] J. Wesley, *A Caution Against False Prophets*, 13.
[458] J. Wesley, "Prophets and Priests," *Works [BE]*, 4:77.
[459] J. Wesley, *ENNT*, 625.
[460] J. Wesley, *ENNT*, 713.
[461] J. Wesley, "Prophets and Priests," *Works [BE]*, 4:76.

But I do not find that ever the office of an evangelist was the same with that of a pastor, frequently called a bishop. He presided over the flock, and administered the sacraments: The former assisted him, and preached the Word, either in one or more congregations. I cannot prove from any author of the three first centuries, that the office of an evangelist gave any man a right to act as a pastor or bishop. I believe these offices were considered quite distinct from each other till the time of Constantine.[462]

Wesley argued that at the time of Constantine, these two offices merged into one, the priest acted as pastor and evangelist, priest as well as prophet. He further argued that this merging of the ordinary and extraordinary was an "evil" occurrence and one that must be overcome to be true to the primitive church. He explained that these two roles – the distinction between ordinary and extraordinary prophet – had become obscured in his own context: "Yet even at this day, although the same person usually discharges both those offices, yet the office of an evangelist or teacher does not imply that of a pastor, to whom peculiarly belongs the administration of the sacraments; neither among the Presbyterians, nor in the Church of England, nor even among the Roman Catholics."[463]

Wesley's bifurcation of the role of the priest as distinct from the role of extraordinary prophet in eighteenth century England caused tension.[464] This tension was fuelled by the clergy's argument that preaching required ordination. Collins noted Wesley's denial of this practice as legitimate: "In opposition to such a view, Wesley denied that the connection between the ministry of the Word and the ministry of the Sacraments was indissoluble. Instead he declared, lay people could exercise a prophetic office in the church through preaching."[465] Bishop Christopher Cocksworth emphasized Wesley's view that ministry guided by the Spirit ought not to be restricted to the ordained clergy.[466] Wesley claimed that already in the Church of England, there were those who preached without ordination.

> And it is never understood that this appointment to preach gives them any right to administer the sacraments. Likewise in our church, persons may be authorised to preach, yea, may be Doctors of Divinity, (as was Dr. Alwood at

---

[462] J. Wesley, "Prophets and Priests," *Works [BE]*, 4:77.

[463] J. Wesley, "Prophets and Priests," *Works [BE]*, 4:77-78.

[464] Priests in the Church of England were ordained to fulfil both requirements of prophet and priest, "public preaching" and "ministering the sacraments." See E.J. Bicknell, *A Theological Introduction to the Thirty-Nine Articles of the Church of England* (London: Longmans, Green and Co., 1944), 404-441.

[465] Kenneth J. Collins, "John Wesley's Concept of the Ministerial Office" in *Wesleyan Theological Journal*, vol. 23, no. 1 and 2 (Spring-Fall 1988): 108.

[466] Christopher Cocksworth, "Evangelical and Catholic in the Twenty-First Century" in *Methodist Sacramental Fellowship Bulletin*, no. 128 (Epiphany 2011), 19. "John Wesley was right to insist that it was wrong of the ordained ministry to gather to itself all the ministries of the Spirit."

Oxford, when I resided there,) who are not ordained at all, and consequently have no right to Administer the Lord's Supper.'[467]

Wesley argued that preaching should not be restricted to ordained clergy. According to Collins, Wesley's view although controversial was not original: "In fact, Wesley's polity seemed to be so new precisely because it was so old, reflective of primitive Christianity. Methodism was not the real innovator here, but rather the Church of England."[468] Rainey has argued this as well, based on his reading of Wesley's appropriation of the work of Richard Hooker.[469] Richard Hooker laid groundwork for Wesley's position nearly two centuries prior in *Ecclesiastical Politie*. Of prophets, Hooker said:

> Touching prophets, they were such men as having otherwise learned the Gospel had from above bestowed on them a special gift of expounding the Scriptures and of foreshadowing things to come. And we no where find Prophets to have been made by ordination, but all whom the Church did ordain were either to serve as presbyters or as deacons.[470]

Hooker affirmed that prophets teach or preach the Scriptures and do not require ordination, but they are forbidden to administer the sacraments. A peculiar calling of God by His Spirit, however, was necessary for prophecy. Bishop Jeremy Taylor published a work promoting religious toleration in 1646.[471] Taylor noted the significance of modern day prophets who are distinct from ordinary ministers, but are given the task of guiding the people of God to salvation. Taylor explained: "God has so set the prophets to guide us, that we also are to follow them by a voluntary assent by an act of choice and election."[472] Taylor and Hooker emphasized the importance of prophets in preaching and publishing the Word of God. Both writers acknowledged the difference between prophets and priests, and both pointed to the primary task of the prophet: preaching. These ideas influenced Wesley's theology of preaching, specifically in terms of the role of the prophet as justification for lay preaching.[473]

---

[467] J. Wesley, "Prophets and Priests," *Works [BE]*, 4:78.

[468] Collins, "John Wesley's Concept of the Ministerial Office," 118.

[469] Rainey, "The Established Church and Evangelical Theology," 428. "This view was based on the work of Richard Hooker, who had developed a very detailed account of lay leadership and of the clergy."

[470] Hooker, *LEP*, 5.78.6.

[471] J. Wesley, "A Plain Account of Christian Perfection," *Works*, 11:366.

[472] Jeremy Taylor, *A Discourse of the Liberty of Prophesying* (London: Luke Meredith, 1702), 226.

[473] Rainey, "Evangelical Theology and the Established Church," 428. According to Rainey, "Wesley made a clear distinction between the preacher and the priest."

Extraordinary Messengers and the Question of Authority

The primary task of the extraordinary prophet was preaching. To Wesley, preaching meant publishing the Word of God by speech, song or print animated by the operation of the Holy Spirit. There was still the tensious question of authority. If not by the authority of the Church, then by whose authority do extraordinary prophets preach? James Clark challenged Wesley on this matter in a letter from 1756. Clark referenced the Twenty-Third Article of Religion, which says:

> It is not lawful for any man to take upon him the office of preaching, or ministering the Sacraments in the congregation, before he be lawfully called, and sent to execute the same. And those we ought to judge lawfully called and sent, which be chosen and called to this work by men who have public authority given unto them in the congregation, to call and send ministers in to the Lord's vineyard.[474]

According to this article, it seems that Wesley had no grounds for accepting unordained persons to preach. Yet, his response was an appeal to the New Testament church, for, "In all cases, the Church is to be judged by the Scripture, not the Scripture by the Church."[475] According to Wesley:

> I believe several who are not episcopally ordained are nevertheless called of God to preach the Gospel. Yet I have no exception to the Twenty-third article, though I judge there are exempt cases. That the seven deacons were outwardly ordained to that low office cannot be denied; but when Paul and Barnabus were separated for the work to which they were called, this was not ordaining them. St Paul was ordained long before, and that not of man nor by men. It was inducting him into the province for which our Lord had appointed him from the beginning. For this end the prophets and teachers fasted and prayed and laid their hands upon them – a rite which was used, not in ordination only, but in blessing and many other occasions.[476]

It is important to note the hierarchy of authority: 1) Scripture, 2) the teachings of the first three centuries of the church, and 3) the Church of England. Wesley believed that the New Testament vision of the role of prophet differed from what had become common practice in his day, in which the role of prophet had merged with the role of priest. The activity Wesley describes in the excerpt above – that of the sending of Paul and Barnabus – was supplemented by further accounts from 1 Corinthians 12:28 and Ephesians 4:11-13. According to Wesley's note from 1 Corinthians 12:28: "*Secondly prophets –* Who either foretell things to come, or speak by the extraordinary inspiration,

---

[474] Bicknell, *A Theological Introduction to the Thirty-Nine Articles of the Church of England*, 404.

[475] J. Wesley, "Popery Calmly Considered" *Works*, 10:142.

[476] J. Wesley, "Letter to James Clark" 18 September 1756 in John Telford, editor, *The Letters of the Rev. John Wesley, A.M.*, 8 Volumes (London: The Epworth Press, 1931), 3:200.

for the edification of the church."⁴⁷⁷ Similarly, Wesley's note on Ephesians 4:11 says, "*And some prophets and some evangelists* – A prophet testifies of things to come; an evangelist, of things past: and that chiefly by preaching the gospel before or after any of the apostles. All these were extraordinary officers."⁴⁷⁸ According to Burdon, Wesley followed the tradition of ancient Christianity. He "distinguished the 'extraordinary' ministry of those who preached from the 'ordinary' ministry of those who maintained order and administered the sacraments."⁴⁷⁹ Wesley explained that, in "1744, all the Methodist preachers had their first conference. But none of them dreamed, that the being called to preach gave them any right to administer the sacraments. And when that question was proposed, 'In what light are we to consider ourselves?' it was answered, 'As extraordinary messengers, raised up to provoke the ordinary ones to jealously.'"⁴⁸⁰ This distinction between priesthood and extraordinary messengers or prophets served to govern the Methodist preachers throughout Wesley's life. At no point were the preachers ever to administer the sacraments for in doing so would be a "recantation of our connexion."⁴⁸¹ According to Burdon:

> John Wesley was very clear that the Assistants were to undertake a ministry of preaching only. They were not to undertake any further development. The Assistants were expressly forbidden to engage in any sacramental ministry. They were preachers first and last. The work was not to be undertaken lightly, but only in response to the call of God. He believed it to be the extraordinary gift of God that was to be exercised with a serious sense of responsibility by an exceptional group of people.⁴⁸²

As Burdon rightly noted, Wesley understood the call of his lay preachers as a call to preach. The purpose of their preaching was twofold: "To reform the nation, and in particular, the Church, to spread Scriptural holiness over the land."⁴⁸³ Wesley believed that many of the clergy of the Church of England were lacking in zeal; he also believed it was the calling and purpose of the Methodists to challenge and provoke them to live up to their office. This is evident in his *Address to the Clergy* in which he challenged his fellow clergymen to live up to their calling:

> I cannot compare you with Simon Magus: You are many degrees beneath him. He offered to give money for the Gift of God, the power of conferring the Holy Ghost. Hereby however he showed, that he set an higher value on the Gift than on the money which he would have parted with for it. But you do not: You set a higher value on the money than on the Gift; insomuch that you do not desire, you will not accept of the Gift, unless the money accompany it! The Bishop said, when you was ordained, "Receive thou the Holy Ghost." But that was

---

[477] J. Wesley, *ENNT*, 625.
[478] J. Wesley, *ENNT*, 713.
[479] Burdon, *Authority and Order*, 38.
[480] J. Wesley, "Prophets and Priests," *Works [BE]*, 4:79.
[481] J. Wesley, "Prophets and Priests," *Works [BE]*, 4:79.
[482] Burdon, *Authority and Order*, 23.
[483] Wesley, "Minutes," *Works [BE]*, 10:845.

the least of your care. Let who will receive this, so you receive the money, the revenue of a good benefice. While you minister the Word and Sacraments before God, He gives the Holy Ghost to those who duly receive them; so that through your hands likewise the Holy Ghost is in this sense given now. But you have little concern whether He be or not: So little, that you will minister no longer, He shall be given no more either through your lips or hands, if you have no more money for your labour. O Simon, Simon! what a saint wert thou, compared to many of the most honourable men now in Christendom?[484]

Wesley unapologetically spoke to the clergy, challenging their calling, their morality, and provoking them to respond to the call of Christ with humility and reverence. In this instance he was speaking to those ministers whom he believed lived for the money that accompanied the office of priest in the Church of England.[485] Wesley concluded: "And why (I will not say, do we fall short, but why) are we satisfied with falling so short of it? Is there any necessity laid upon us, of sinking infinitely below our calling?"[486] Those whom Wesley addressed in this work are precisely the ones whom the Methodist preachers were sent to provoke. According to Burdon, Wesley's "purpose was the enlivenment of the Church of England. He regarded the use of his preachers as a temporary expedient towards that end."[487] He continued: "Presumably, John Wesley anticipated that once the established church began to respond to his spiritual challenge then his workers would become redundant."[488] Ultimately, the preachers, or prophets, were called to provoke the ordinary ministers, so that they would remember their calling and fulfil their role as ordinary ministers.

Still, by what or whose authority did these "extraordinary messengers" preach? The Methodist preachers derived their authority to preach from their experience of being called by the Holy Spirit. Three requirements were necessary for a Methodist preacher to be used by the Wesleys. When asked, "How shall we try those who think they are moved by the Holy Ghost, and called of God to preach?" Wesley gave the following formula:

- Do they know God, as a pardoning God? Have they the Love of God abiding in them? Do they desire and seek nothing but God? And are they holy in all manner of conversation?
- Have they Gifts (as well as Grace) for the Work? Have they (in some tolerable degree) a clear, sound understanding? Have they a right judgement in the

---

[484] J. Wesley, *An Address to the Clergy* (London: 1756), 23.

[485] Note that Wesley includes the affirmation that the operation of the Holy Spirit was not obstructed by the minister to the receiver. God works through his instruments regardless of their character, although the minister was not himself operating in the Spirit. Morality is preferred, but not a prerequisite to the role of a priest. Morality is, however, required of the prophet. See J. Wesley, *An Address to the Clergy*, 23.

[486] J. Wesley, *An Address to the Clergy*, 31.

[487] Burdon, *Authority and Order*, 27.

[488] Burdon, *Authority and Order*, 27.

things of God? Have they a just conception of salvation by faith? And has God given them any degree of utterance? Do they speak justly, readily, clearly?
- Have they fruit? Are any truly convinced of sin, and converted to God by their preaching?

As long as these three marks concur in any, we believe he is called of God to preach. These we receive as a sufficient proof, that he is moved thereto by the Holy Ghost.[489]

This three-tiered inquiry was employed by the Wesley brothers when interviewing potential preachers. A testimony of the assurance of salvation, signs of the Holy Spirit working in their lives, and fruits of their labour were the three requirements necessary for one to be admitted as a preacher. These further support the pneumatological dimension of Wesley's ecclesiology. But there was also an implicit fourth condition: Full obedience to the leadership and direction of John and Charles Wesley. The growth of the Methodist revival and the increase of the number of preachers needed for the mission to reform the nation, the Church, and to spread scriptural holiness throughout the land required strict oversight. Because of the tension caused by the irregularity of lay-preachers, the Wesley brothers, John in particular, had to keep a firm grip on their preachers. "Wayward preachers," as Gunter claimed, could not be tolerated.[490] It was one thing for Wesley to admonish his fellow clergymen; it was another for Wesley to tolerate immoral and unfruitful lay preachers. Gunter further pointed out that every "moral failure [of the Methodist preacher] was seized by the Anglican opposition as a normative example of Methodist behavior."[491] The responsibility for leading Methodism rested on the shoulders of Wesley. As Davies stated, Wesley "*was* Methodism, in person and in power."[492] In order to ensure the integrity of Methodism, Wesley constantly had to maintain his preachers under his supervision and authority.

Despite sharp criticism from other clergy due to Wesley's use of lay preachers, a major theme of Wesley's advice to his preachers throughout his life was the importance of remaining active members of the Church of England. When asked for advice to give his preachers, Wesley said, "1. Let all our Preachers go to Church. 2. Let all our people go constantly. 3. Receive the sacrament at every opportunity...6. [Warn] against calling our Society 'a Church', or 'the Church'. [Warn] against calling our preachers 'ministers.'"[493] It was imperative that the Methodists abide in the Church of England. He believed the Methodists were peculiarly raised up, not to form a new sect, or a new church, but to revive the Church of England from within. This was the

---

[489] J. Wesley, "Minutes," *Works [BE]*, 10:177-178.
[490] W. Stephen Gunter, *The Limits of Love Divine* (Nashville, Tennessee: Abingdon, 1989), 181-201.
[491] Gunter, *The Limits of Love Divine*, 182.
[492] Davies, "Introduction" *Works [BE]*, 9:20.
[493] J. Wesley, "Minutes," *Works [BE]*, 10:867-868.

task of the extraordinary prophet, who "wholly and solely [preaches] the gospel." In *Prophets and Priests* Wesley reminded his readers of the unfortunate events in Norwich, where one of the preachers baptized a few children and where the Lord's Supper was administered by unordained Methodist preachers.[494] Wesley acknowledged that this act was contrary to Methodism's design and contrary to the role of the extraordinary prophet. He emphasized, that "Methodists…are not a sect or party; they do not separate from the religious community to which they at first belonged. They are still members of the Church; such they desire to live and die."[495] It remains unclear the extent to which Wesley viewed the practice of lay preaching as potentially stifling to unity within the Church of England, as well as the extent to which he believed that his and Hooker and Taylor's view on the role of prophet ought to be restored to church polity practice should the demand for extraordinary messengers. Nevertheless, he believed that the use of lay preachers, understood as extraordinary prophets, was consistent with the traditions of the Church of England. As he concluded the sermon, Wesley stated his wish for Methodists and Methodist preachers to remain faithful to the Church of England and not to separate from it.

> I wish all of you who are vulgarly termed Methodists would seriously consider what has been said. And particularly you whom God hath commissioned to call sinners to repentance. O contain yourselves within your own bounds; be content with preaching the gospel; "do the work of an evangelist;"…Ye were, fifty years ago, those of you that were then Methodists preachers, extraordinary messengers of God, not going in your own will, but thrust out, not to supersede, but to "provoke to jealously" the ordinary messengers. In God's name, stop there! Both by your preaching and example provoke them to love and good works.[496]

An impassioned plea to the Methodist preachers, Wesley's concluding remarks of this sermon summarized his theology of preaching and the peculiar role of the prophet within the Church. Prophets are first called of God, as "God hath commissioned." Prophets are called solely to preach and to "be content with preaching the gospel." Prophets are not called to administer the sacraments, but to "keep to [their] own station." Prophets are directed by the inspiration of the Holy Spirit, rather than "going in [their] own will." Prophets are called to live the gospel, and "by [their] preaching and example provoke [others] to love and to good works."[497] Wesley concluded by reiterating the necessity of the work of the Holy Spirit in the life of the prophet: "Be Church of England Men still; do not cast away the peculiar glory which God hath put upon you, and frustrate the design of providence, the very end for which God raised you up."[498]

---

[494] See Gareth Lloyd, *Charles Wesley and the Struggle for Methodist Identity* (Oxford: Oxford University Press, 2007), 162-179.
[495] J. Wesley, "Prophets and Priests," *Works [BE]*, 4:80.
[496] J. Wesley, "Prophets and Priests," *Works [BE]*, 4:82.
[497] J. Wesley, "Prophets and Priests," *Works [BE]*, 4:82-83.
[498] J. Wesley, "Prophets and Priests," *Works [BE]*, 4:82-83.

Conclusion

Wesley's use of lay-preachers led to criticism. In his appeals, sermons, letters, and advice Wesley affirmed his theology of preaching. According to Wesley, merging the activities of prophecy and priestly work into one minister was not scriptural, nor did it reflect the practice of the Church of England as prescribed by Hooker and Taylor. According to Rainey, there "is no doubt that Wesley claimed loyalty to the Church of England and followed the Established Church in creating his ecclesiology. He never thought that Methodism was an interruption to his doctrine of the church."[499] Employing lay preachers was a significant development in Wesley's ecclesiology—an ecclesiology which was both faithful to Anglican tradition as well as thoroughly pneumatological with respect to his view of preaching as *praedicare verbum Dei*. It was the peculiar calling by the Holy Spirit to evangelize – sensed by the individual and affirmed by Wesley and the Methodist connections – which demarcated the role of extraordinary prophets and priests. Both were viewed as ministries of the Holy Spirit, but only the latter, to Wesley, had to be authorized through ordination. Wesley was concerned that although the priests were fulfilling their role as administrators of the sacraments they were not living as if they were "called of God as was Aaron." To Wesley, God's intention for Methodist lay preachers as extraordinary messengers was the same intention that God had for extraordinary prophets like Moses. They were called of God and empowered by the Holy Spirit to publish the Word of God in proclaiming the gospel and promoting scriptural holiness. Wesley's theology of preaching and his use of lay preachers did not diminish the role of the priests, nor did it diminish the primacy of the sacraments. It did, however, broaden the scope and importance of preaching in the life of the Church. This particular nuance of Wesley's integrated ecclesiological view acknowledges and affirms lay ministry as being complementary to ordained ministry.

---

[499] Rainey, "Evangelical Theology and the Established Church," 434.

Chapter 9

What has Athens to do with Oxford? An Essay in Wesleyan Theology and Virtue Ethics

By Joseph W. Cunningham

Introduction

> The purest saint that lives below
> Doth his own sanctity disclaim,
> The wisest owns, I nothing know,
> The holiest cries, I nothing am![500]

Charles Wesley, founder of the Holy Club in Oxford along with his brother John, was largely responsible for the rise of British Methodism. Although it was John who would later organize Methodism into societies, bands, and class meetings, it was Charles' poetic creativity and hymnody which helped to nurture the religious sect within the Church of England. This was the case especially during the 1760s, which proved a pivotal period for Methodist doctrine with respect to the idea of Christian perfection. It was then that two Methodist lay preachers announced publicly that they had been perfected by grace, and that, as such, they no longer needed John Wesley's connectional leadership. The lines of verse above are compelling, if not for the significance of their source, namely, a collection of hymns and sacred poems published in 1762 during a tumultuous and defining decade for the Methodists, then more for their theological characterization of holiness in both Socratic and classical Christian terms. Wisdom as defined by Socrates, according to Plato's *Apology*, exceeds the arts of persuasion and rhetoric. Wisdom requires humility. Indeed, this is the definition of piety which Euthypro was unable to discover in his dialectic with Socrates concerning the nature of piety in relation

---

[500] C. Wesley, *Short Hymns on Select Passages of Scripture*, vol. 2 of 2 (1762), 228.

to the gods: Actions are pious neither because the gods will them nor because they must will them. True piety consists in recognizing the logical and philosophical problems of eradicating the paradox at the heart of the dilemma of such a question. True knowledge, which is essential for the life of piety, consists in the virtue of humility, as both Athens and Oxford would have it.

The purpose of this paper is to explore a possible link between Wesleyan theology and virtue ethics especially with respect to John Wesley's doctrine of Christian perfection, which has fallen from favor in a majority of non-academic Wesleyan circles despite its indisputable place as a lead theological motif in much of Wesley's corpus. One reason for the lull is clear. From the vantage of systematic theology—a methodology cultivated especially during the modern era, which can be traced through the work of Friedrich Schleiermacher among others, and which presupposes the inherent viability of ordering Christian teaching into a logically congruent framework for best understanding sacred truth—Christian perfection is difficult to reconcile. John Wesley held that believers (once justified and born again) were empowered to cease committing voluntary sins, and so to live in holiness as Christ commands in Matt. 5:48: "Be ye perfect as your father in heaven is perfect." Wesley described perfection (or entire sanctification) as freedom from willful sin in his manifesto on the subject, *A Plain Account of Christian Perfection*, published in 1777: "Christians are saved in this world from all sin, from all unrighteousness… they are now in such a sense perfect, as not to commit sin… freed from evil thoughts and evil tempers."[501]

Criticism of the doctrine has emerged adjacent to two problems, one systematic and the other epistemological. First, the notion of Christian perfection understood in light of the doctrine that humans are fully corrupted by sin presents either a paradox at best or contradiction at worst with respect to systematic theology. For instance, if humans are sinful (as the Anglo-Catholic tradition inherited by Wesley suggests), and if that nature is to us inescapable except for final glorification which lays beyond the flesh, then our nature will always hinder the kind of freedom for perfection Wesley emphasizes. Christian perfection either downplays human sinfulness or it is too optimistic with respect to humanity's ability to engage in righteous living perfected by grace. Second, the notion of Christian perfection, in which sanctification is acknowledged by spiritual testimony communicated by the divine to the human agent, raises the question of certainty. To what extent can imperfect, sinful creatures be sure that they have been sanctified? Wesley's writings on the subject of perfection are filled with distinctions. Interlocutors who criticized Wesley for sounding too "papist," that is, for downplaying sin and propagating a species of works-righteousness, were given a different response than those who attacked its ostensible antinomian underpinnings (that somehow individuals are perfected by grace despite persisting in moral turpitude). To the former, Wesley explained entire sanctification as a gift of God's grace unattainable by merit, and to the latter, a practical pattern for what

---

[501] J. Wesley, 'A Plain Account of Christian Perfection', in *Works*, 11:378.

active holiness should be like, namely, devotion to Christ and his law of love. Given Wesley's varied use of language and the paradoxical nature of the doctrine, the teaching has slipped into steady decline. Kevin Lowery comments that "one would be hard pressed to hear Wesley's view articulated today, even in the local church. The vast majority of Methodists gave up on the doctrine of perfection over a century ago..."[502] Though Lowery seems to overlook the Wesleyan academic theological community itself as a sacral body still invested in the doctrine of perfection, his remark is nevertheless on point. What Wesley once called "the grand depositum"[503] lodged by God with the Methodists is no longer embraced as such. The claim I wish to make here is that by reconsidering Christian perfection as a moral theology that resonates with the tradition of virtue ethics and its emphasis on character in relation to teleology, it provides a way forward for recovering Wesley's original vision of the soul's journey into the perfect life of God.[504]

To that end, this essay will focus on the concept of virtue as it functions in Aristotle's moral philosophy, and in particular the concept of *phroenesis*, or prudence, which to Aristotle, steers the soul toward its proper end, namely, *eudaimonia* or happiness. Secondly, we will compare the concept of practical wisdom or *phroenesis* to Wesley's doctrine of Christian perfection, specifically in terms of its description as "perfect love." In doing so, we will address some of the criticisms raised against Wesley's doctrine of Christian perfection mentioned above. The end goal is to provide an interpretation of Wesley's theology of Christian perfection through the lens of moral theology rather than a primarily systematic one.

Phroenesis

Aristotle's moral philosophy draws upon at least two fundamental concepts—essence and purpose—both of which belong to his broader science of "being *qua* being," or metaphysics. In Aristotle's philosophy, "primary substance" has ontological implications. He qualifies his understanding of substance

---

[502] Kevin Lowery, *Salvaging Wesley's Agenda: A New Paradigm for Wesleyan Virtue Ethics* (Eugene, Oregon: Pickwick Publications), xii.

[503] See John Telford, ed. *The Letters of the Rev. John Wesley A.M.*, 8 vols (London: Epworth Press, 1960), 8:238. In a letter from 1790, Wesley labelled Christian perfection 'the grand depositum which God...lodged with the people called Methodists'.

[504] Kevin Lowery makes a similar claim in his book, *Salvaging Wesley's Agenda: A New Paradigm for Wesleyan Virtue Ethics* (Princeton Monographs, 2008). However, he draws the conclusion that Wesley's ethics and its inherent "cognitivism"—that the "will" follows the "intellect" in terms of moral agency—not only resembles Aristotle (as well as Aquinas), but that it can be correlated with features of Kantian or deontological ethics. While notable similarities between them exist, one major barrier for the comparison is Kant's view of "ought" as unequivocally disinterested; the intellect inclines the will toward the good for its own sake, and not because of any affective or spiritual benefit.

using the terms "matter" and "form." Matter, according to Aristotle, refers to things in themselves, while form designates the structural relationship of "accidents," or characteristic features of things, to particular beings. Thus, matter and form together comprise individual objects as particulars, which, when experienced by human agents through the senses, lead to the formation of ideas concerning them. To him, a thing's "thing-ness" or its "what it is" can be identified empirically by examining what two or more instantiations of substance hold in common with each other. Essence, then, distinguishes particular entities from other species and, simultaneously, essence represents that which is held in common by those of the same genus. To Aristotle, a thing's essence is directed toward a *telos*, or what it's meant to do. All particular objects, from the smallest particles to the most complex organisms, exhibit some kind of design or *telos*.

Thus, as it relates to his practical (or moral) philosophy, everything has a good, including humankind. The good of being human like everything else is that we function properly and according to our essence. In particular however, it means that since humans possess the unique ability to act on more than just feeling, unlike the rest of *animae*, we befit the term good, or rather, excellent, when our lives are governed by reason. Indeed, this is what demarcates our essence from other spirited beings and inanimate modes of existence. Becoming what we were meant to be requires excelling at what we are; the good life depends upon the human being functioning well, and acting reasonably and responsibly in all possible circumstances by cultivating certain patterns of behavior that rationally accord with the good, the true, and the beautiful. This is our excellence, which he identifies as virtue (*arête*). On what grounds does Aristotle establish goodness as objectively preferable to evil? For him, experience tells us so. The happiest and wisest are those who seek justice and pursue truth for its own intrinsic reward, a path less traveled by the vicious. Along the journey, human agents develop various habits of the mind and soul that secure our love of wisdom and execution of right action. The more virtuous we become, the less tempted we are to engage in impious behavior. For Aristotle then, the end (*telos*) or perfection of our existence is happiness, a stasis of life reached when the entirety of our thought and action is governed by reason and virtue.

Of all the virtues, which ones are most important to human flourishing? Aristotle distinguished between two kinds of virtue: intellectual and practical. The former we acquire by learning from a teacher, and the latter through habitual practice. For example, moral agents develop the virtue of fortitude when given the opportunity to act courageously in concrete situations. It becomes a habit insofar as the agent repeatedly acts with bravery at the right time and place, whenever the situation may arise. Wisdom on the other hand, when understood in terms of the concept of *phroenesis*, has both practical as well as intellectual benefits. We must be taught how to identify the good, and what it looks like in practice. But it also requires contemplation and thoughtfulness which are decisively intellectual activities. Alasdair MacIntyre comments. "*Phroenesis* is an intellectual virtue; but it is that intellectual virtue without which none of the virtues of character can be exercised."[505] Without the virtue of prudence by which the agent guides him or herself away from vice, he or she cannot knowingly practice the good. Phroenesis makes possible the examined life. One may stumble his or her way into right action occasionally without *phroenesis*, but true morality requires knowledge of the good in addition to right action.

Prudence then, is cardinal among the other virtues. When it is cultivated by human agents, it signifies a broader harmony or stasis achieved. To develop prudence means that one has cultivated the ability to act in the right way, at the right time, and for the right reasons. As such being prudent is sufficient for a host of other virtues, though the converse is not always true. Virtue, according to Aristotle, is formed habitually, and refers to any praiseworthy trait of character situated between two corresponding vices, one of excess and the other of deficit. For Aristotle, the more we practice virtuous living, the more we discover meaning and purpose in doing so, and the less inclined we are toward acting in excess or defect of the virtues. The more we experience the good, the more attractive it becomes to us, because the more it benefits our potential to achieve happiness, which aligns with our purpose as rational beings. His writings suggest that one can become so inclined toward the good that indulging its vicious outliers no longer holds sway.[506] This is partly what it means to say that humans are rational beings. Having the faculty of reason distinguishes humanity's essence from other forms of life. We function properly, which is to say in accordance with our essence, when we engage in virtuous living, which is an inherently rational activity involving both the intellect and the will. The human being achieves *eudaimonia* when virtue is habitually practiced and vice continually avoided. But happiness and virtuous living both have a social dimension. When right character, proper balance of material (or external) goods, and the satisfaction of being surrounded by friends are blended, human life reaches a point of completeness or wholeness. Aristotle's conception of human nature, virtue, and purpose, especially with respect to his understanding of *phroenesis*—both an intellectual as well as practical virtue requisite for the flourishing of human nature—suggest the perfectibility of human character. The more virtuous we become, consequently, the less we're inclined toward vices of excess and defect, and the happier we are.

Perfect Love

A number of these themes resonate in Wesley's theology of Christian perfection. It's worth noting that many of Aristotle's categories for describing the journey of the soul into the life of happiness are foreign to Wesley's corpus. Wesley shows little preference for the term virtue in describing the life of perfection. But this may have more to do with eighteenth century British lan-

---

[505] Alasdair MacIntyre, *After Virtue: A Study in Moral Theory*, 3rd ed. (Notre Dame, Indiana: Notre Dame University Press, 2007), 154.
[506] Aristotle, *Nicomachean Ethics*, Book II:6.

guage and culture than any real disparity of ethics. David Morse suggests that the term "virtue" had three primary usages during the period: 1) political action guided by commitment to crown and country; 2) general benevolence, or, a general philanthropic approach to life and human nature characterized by the belief that more than self-interest drives our moral behavior, or 3) the dignity and social graces characteristic of higher society, especially among those of greater wealth, refinement, and sophistication.[507] Although Samuel Johnson defines virtue in part according to its classical roots, that is, as a kind of "goodness" or "excellence" necessary for the moral life,[508] still, Morse suggests that this was less typical of the period than the former, which identify virtue, broadly speaking, in terms of general benevolence, social refinement, and commitment to the state. On the whole, if his assessment is correct, then it may well be that Wesley avoided using the term precisely because it lacked in popular parlance the connotations of moral excellence, divine purpose, and character originally associated with Aristotle's ethics. Indeed, a "virtue" ethics of general benevolence, philanthropy, or social status, would have been at variance with Wesley's moral theology, which emphasized instead a teleology of human nature with respect to the divine. Consider Wesley's critique of three salient philosophers of the period, who each appeared to him to build "religion" or "morality" without dependence upon God.

> Rousseau, Voltaire, and David Hume, have contributed all their labours, sparing no pains to establish a religion which should stand on its own foundation, independent of any revelation whatever, yea, not supposing even the being of a God. So leaving him, if he has any being, to himself, they have found out both a religion and a happiness which have no relation at all to God, nor any dependence upon him... [Call] it "humanity", "virtue", "morality", or whatever you please, it is neither better nor worse than atheism.[509]

Ethics must be situated within a proper metaphysic, contoured by the divine, which shapes our quiddity and gives us purpose. Morality without divine purpose is like a house built on shifting sand. To both Wesley and Aristotle, the concept of God refers to an immutable, eternal foundation, on which physical and metaphysical reality is based, and which gives the good life meaning. Without such a foundation in something universal and unchanging, ethics becomes a general discussion of cultural conventions and alternating mores. For both Wesley and Aristotle, true virtue has an end: divine life, or happiness.

How does Wesley define Christian perfection and in what sense does it reflect elements of Aristotle's moral philosophy? In his sermon, "The Scripture Way of Salvation" (1765), Wesley explains entire sanctification in terms of perfect love and its consummation of the soul: "But what is perfection? The

---

[507] David Morse, *The Age of Virtue: British Culture from the Restoration to Romanticism* (New York: Palgrave, 2000), 3-4.

[508] Jack Lynch, ed. *Samuel Johnson's Dictionary: Selections from the 1755 Work that Defined the English Language* (Delray Beach, Florida: Levenger Press, 2002), 533.

[509] J. Wesley, 'The Unity of the Divine Being', in *Works [BE]*, 4:69.

word has various senses: here it means perfect love. It is love excluding sin, love filling the heart, taking up the whole capacity of the soul."[510] Although elsewhere in his writings he describes perfection as a "second blessing" supernaturally bestowed on believers and sealed by the indwelling Spirit through direct testimony—among other places in various letters and correspondence throughout the 1760s—here, it's simply love excluding sin, the perfection of which places the believer in communion with the divine. "*Constant communion with God... [as] fills their hearts with humble love...*" writes Wesley in his journal from 6 March 1760, "this is...'perfection'."[511] The more we experience the goodness of God, the more attractive it becomes to us. The more we love and serve our neighbor, the less inclined we are to indulge in behaviors that fail to align with that end. In other words, as we cultivate holiness through the Holy Spirit's empowerment, as we respond to the grace of God freely offered in Christ, believers experience freedom from the power of sin. Our telos, according to Wesley, is happiness in God, which we experience when love reigns in the soul.

In what sense, then, does Wesley's theology of entire sanctification parallel with the idea of *phroenesis*? Love, for Wesley, is not solely an affective experience. Rather, it is a disposition of soul which is cultivated as believers discover what is ultimately good and just how inherently attractive that good is. The deeper one grows in communion with the divine, the greater one's love for God and neighbor becomes.

Like the virtue of prudence to Aristotle, for Wesley, perfect love is necessary with respect to moral action, involving both the intellect and the will. As Wesley put it, love is the essence of true virtue, which believers come to embody through imitation of Christ. Consider the following quote, taken from one of Wesley's earliest published sermons, which was preached on New Year's Day 1733 at St. Mary's, Oxford: "[Love] is the essence, the spirit, the life of all virtue. It is not only the first and great commandment, but it is all the commandments in one. Whatsoever things are just, whatsoever things are pure, whatsoever things are amiable or honourable; if there be any virtue, if there be any praise, they are all comprised in this one word—love."[512] Just as for Aristotle, without practical wisdom, moral agents cannot knowingly embody right behavior or any of the other (habitual) virtues,[513] so too for Wesley, without love, believers cannot willfully practice the good as God commands. Both Wesley and Aristotle lay heavy emphasis not only on what the human agent does, but also, on what he or she becomes. For both, moral excellence requires growth in knowledge and practice of the good, not just for its own sake, as Kant would have it, but because our nature is inclined to do so and because we find it enjoyable. Like Aristotle, Wesley suggests that true morality leads to the fulfilling of our purpose in terms of happiness. "This, this

---

[510] J. Wesley, 'The Scripture Way of Salvation', in *Works [BE]*, 2:160.
[511] J. Wesley, *Works [BE]*, 21:245.
[512] J. Wesley, 'The Circumcision of the Heart', in *Works [BE]*, 1:407.
[513] See Joseph Pieper, *The Four Cardinal Virtues* (South Bend, Indiana: University of Notre Dame Press, 1966), 3-22.

alone," he claims, "is the one end of our abode here; for this alone are we placed on the earth..."[514] Consider Wesley's remarks in a sermon published just two years before he died.

> The love of Christ constrains us, not only to be harmless, to do no evil to our neighbour, but to be useful, to be "zealous of good works", "as we have time to do good unto all men", and be patterns to all of true genuine morality, of justice, mercy, and truth. This is religion, and this is happiness, the happiness for which we were made.[515]

Wesley suggests that true morality requires becoming "patterns" of justice, truth, and mercy built on the "love of Christ." This is the way to true religion and "the happiness for which we were made." Our chief end, for Wesley, is happiness in the divine, attained through the practice of holy patterns founded upon the perfect love of God and neighbor.

Wesley's description of Christian perfection as perfect love, as well as his approach which grounds morality in a teleological metaphysic, echoes some important features of Aristotelian philosophy. Both suggest that the moral life is grounded in the very stuff of reality and the One who gives it motion. Both suggest that humans have an ultimate purpose, and that we begin to flourish when the soul is properly balanced and our impulses governed. Both suggest that human agents can become so inclined toward the good or righteous living that vice or sin ceases to dominate our behavior. And both affirm the foundation of "true" wisdom for the life of virtue, which steers the soul into divine happiness. In short, constructive parallels exist between Wesley's doctrine of Christian perfection as perfect love and Aristotle's notion of *phroenesis*, which may be for use for Wesleyan moral theology and the recovery of its distinctive narrative.

Conclusion:
Reading Christian Perfection as Moral Theology

Although resolving the tension inherent to the term perfection poses systematic problems, the concept of perfection and being drawn toward union with God is consistent with other examples of moral theological discourses embedded within the Anglo-Catholic tradition. For instance, Aquinas conceives of moral agency along these lines, and views human nature as perfectible in relation to the divine, in terms of humanity's potentiality for incorporating the virtues into a lifeway reflective of God's nature. To Aquinas, faith, hope, and love are theological virtues which complement the four cardinal virtues of prudence, justice, fortitude, and temperance. Just as humans flourish when happiness is achieved through the cultivation of the virtues, Aquinas's philosophy of nature suggests that our desire to know and be known by God is ingrained within our nature as persons, and we are most whole when we cul-

---

[514] J. Wesley, 'The One Thing Needful', in *Works [BE]*, 4:358.
[515] J. Wesley, 'The Unity of the Divine Being', in *Works [BE]*, 4:67.

tivate the virtues of faith, hope, and love.[516] Love, in this instance is neither purely affective, nor is it entirely a gift extrinsic to human nature. Rather, just as Aristotle's conception of phronesis incorporates qualities of the practical as well as the intellectual virtues, Aquinas conceives of love as both gift and endeavor—both something we do and something we are empowered to do. But it also involves the intellect as well as the will, and in this respect, it has practical as well as intellectual characteristics. Love of course does not consist in speculative exercises concerning the nature of things or the beloved, but it does involve affect, which coheres with the intellect, as the latter designates the object of one's affections. Love is both an activity of the mind and an activity of the will. Like *phroenesis*, it is both practical and intellectual. To love is to be mindful of one's beloved and to express one's mindfulness of the beloved through concrete actions.

Love, as an expression of Wesley's doctrine of Christian perfection, can be understood similarly. Wesley suggests that humans are empowered by grace to love their neighbor. The desire to do so is not foreign to our nature; it is what we were created for in the beginning. Humanity was fashioned for knowledge, love, and enjoyment of God and fellowship with one another. Similar to the way in which both Aristotle and Aquinas understand the intellect as always already bent toward the good and the true, for Wesley, when God's love is shed abroad in the heart through religious encounter rooted in worship and community, humanity begins to realize that potentiality which has always been part and parcel to our nature as human beings. Thus, on the one hand love perfected is both gift and endeavor, and the more we engage in concrete actions which esteem the beloved and draw us into closer union with the divine, the more we see just how inherently attractive divine love is. As this happens, as love is cultivated within the soul, vice and sin become less desirable to us, and the less tempted we are to engage in them. Understanding perfect love as such, while it does not immediately resolve the systematic or epistemological problems discussed above, does provide groundwork for thinking through the moral and pragmatic significance of the teaching.

William James suggests that the value of experiential religious truth is inextricably tied to three factors: "immediate luminousness," "philosophical reasonableness," and "moral helpfulness."[517] The two critiques discussed earlier in the essay (the systematic and the epistemological) pose serious challenges to Wesley's doctrine of Christian perfection, when understood primarily through the lens of systematic theology. However, when read through the lens of moral theology, Christian perfection as perfect love provides a constructive way of thinking about human agency in relation to the divine, which resonates with classical discourse on the virtues. Christian perfection, as both Athens and Oxford would have it, describes the souls journey into the divine life, where true knowledge consists in virtuous or pious intentions and behaviors, embodied within our person as praiseworthy traits of character

---

[516] See Josef Pieper, *Faith, Hope, Love* (San Francisco: Ignatius Press, 1997).

[517] William James, *The Varieties of Religious Experience*. Reprint. (New York: Random House, 1929), 19.

habituated and guided by wisdom (for Aristotle) and love (for Wesley). To hold that human agency is perfectible by grace does not require that one reject the doctrine of sinfulness, but it does require that sinfulness be understood beyond the lines of genetic disease inherited by humans from two original parents, and especially in terms of a central and generational human predicament facing all human beings: alienation from God, brokenness, and the real possibility of anguish and despair, an ongoing spiritual pandemic into which every son and daughter is born. The doctrine of perfection asserts that, insofar as humanity becomes rapt in the beauty of divine love by grace through faith—when intellect and will are oriented toward the beloved mindfully—the predicament no longer stifles our flourishing as freed spiritual beings in relation to others seeking the same freedom. Evidence of perfected living consists in humility, and the disinclination toward the appellation of perfection. Although this does not resolve the epistemological question of certainty as to the objectivity of perfection, which remains a central problematic in Wesleyan theology,[518] it does provide a moral compass for those seeking personal assurance of the phenomena of perfection. John Wesley's views on perfection, understood in terms of the concept of perfect love, refract elements of a much older moral tradition which emphasizes teleology in relation to essence and the possibility of moral excellence with respect to happiness as end and the virtues (especially perfect love) as means.

---

[518] For a recent study on this problematic, see William J. Abraham, *Aldersgate and Athens: John Wesley and the Foundations of Christian Belief* (Waco, Texas: Baylor University Press, 2010). Abraham engages Wesley in relation to contemporary approaches in theological epistemology. He lays important groundwork for considering the possibilities and challenges of a uniquely Wesleyan epistemology capable of contributing to wider philosophical discussions concerning reason and religious experience.

Part V

Interreligious

Chapter 10

John Wesley's Engagement with Islam: Exploring the Soteriological Possibilities in light of a Diversity of Graces and Theological Frameworks[519]

By Kenneth J. Collins

"From everyone to whom much has been given, much will be required." Luke 12:48a NRSV

Introduction

The Wesleyan tradition, as an important representative of the Christian faith, may have the theological wherewithal to consider the soteriological footprint of Islam in terms of the basic theological frameworks that John Wesley, himself, employed in his practical theology as he looked well beyond the walls of the church. As such we shall consider the Muslim faith in light of Wesley's own theological constructs in the form of all of the following: prevenient grace, a covenant theology that embraces the distinct Adamic dispensation (of works) and every subsequent dispensation of the covenant of grace, the distinction of the faith of a servant, the faith of a child of God, the paradigm of the phrase "fearing God and working righteousness," as well as a consideration of the Abrahamic covenant and its significance for Muslims. After an

---

[519] This work was originally presented (in a slightly expanded form) at the Wesley and Methodist Historical Studies section of the Oxford Institute of Methodist Theological Studies that met in Oxford, England in August, 2013.

examination of these elements we shall bring to bear not only Wesley's own assessment of what he called Mahometanism but also the Christological judgments of the Koran, itself, in order to arrive at a balanced judgment with respect to the universal possibilities of grace as well as their more limited saving actualizations.

The Promise of Prevenient Grace

As a good Anglican whose theology was steeped in an Augustinian understanding of original sin, John Wesley was a quintessentially Western theologian who articulated a doctrine of prevenient grace to restore measures of freedom that were never judged to be lacking in some of the theologies of the eastern fathers.[520] Indeed, in a way similar to John Calvin, Wesley employed the language of total depravity in his sermon "The Way to the Kingdom," for example, to depict the depth and extent of sin, that is, when he considered a person in "the natural state," unassisted by the grace of God: "Thou art corrupted in every power, in every faculty of thy soul, that thou are *totally* corrupted in every one of these, all the foundations being out of course."[521] Put another way, in Wesley's theology the universality of his largely Augustinian understanding of original sin is matched by the universality of prevenient grace such that none are left in an utterly depraved state, apart from all measures of the grace of God.[522] In the sermon "On Working Out Our Own Salvation," Wesley explains:

> For allowing that all souls of men are dead in sin by nature, this excuses none, seeing there is no man that is in a state of mere nature; there is no man, unless he has quenched the Spirit, that is wholly void of the grace of God. No man living is entirely destitute of what is vulgarly called "natural conscience." But this is not natural; it is more properly termed "preventing grace."[523]

---

[520] For more on this theme see Kenneth J. Collins, "John Wesley's Critical Appropriation of Tradition in His Practical Theology" in *The Wesleyan Theological Journal*, vol. 35 no. 2 (Fall 2000): 69-91. For the influences of the eastern fathers on Wesley's theology see Randy L. Maddox, "John Wesley and Eastern Orthodoxy: Influences, Convergences and Differences" in *The Asbury Theological Journal*, vol. 45 no. 2 (Fall 1990): 29-53.

[521] Albert C. Outler, ed., *The Works of John Wesley*, Vols. 1-4. *The Sermons* (Nashville: Abingdon Press, 1984), 1:225. ("The Way to the Kingdom") Some of the material in this section on prevenient grace is drawn from my *Theology of John Wesley* as is used by permission. See Kenneth J. Collins, *The Theology of John Wesley: Holy Love and the Shape of Grace* (Nashville: Abingdon Press, 2007), 73-81. Used by permission of Abingdon Press.

[522] See Umphrey Lee, *John Wesley and Modern Religion* (Nashville: Cokesbury Press, 1936), 124-25.

[523] *Works [BE]*, 3:207. ("On Working Out Our Own Salvation") Three works on prevenient grace make important contributions to Wesley studies: Charles A. Rogers, "The Concept of Prevenient Grace in the Theology of John Wesley" (Dissertation, Duke University, 1967); Herbert McGonigle, *John Wesley's Doctrine of Prevenient Grace* (Derby's, London: Moorley's Bookshop, 1995); James Gregory Crofford, "Streams of

Wesley supported his doctrine of prevenient grace by an appeal to both Scripture and tradition, that is, by reference to the Gospel of John ("The true light, which enlightens everyone, was coming into the world." John 1:9), and to the Anglican *Thirty-Nine Articles*. However, this use of specifically Christian resources in no way limited the scope of this grace. Thus, Wesley asserted that prevenient grace, based upon the salvific work of Jesus Christ, is applied to all people, Christians and non-Christians alike, through the ministrations of the Holy Spirit.[524] "Every man has a greater or less measure of this," Wesley declares, "which waiteth not for the call of man."[525] Again, this grace is "free for all," not limited to the accidents of geography or culture, and it is "free in all to whom it is given," not dependent on any human power and merit.[526] It is inclusive not exclusive; freely given not merited. Moreover, this first glimmer of grace marks the entrance upon the path that leads to salvation, properly speaking, as is evident in Wesley's following observation:

> Salvation begins with what is usually termed (and very properly) preventing grace; including the first wish to please God, — the first dawn of light concerning his will, and the first slight transient conviction of having sinned against him. All these imply some tendency toward life; some degree of salvation; the beginning of a deliverance from a blind, unfeeling heart, quite insensible of God and the things of God.[527]

The Benefits of Prevenient Grace

In his writings Wesley points out five benefits that are conveyed universally to humanity by prevenient grace which together mitigate some of the worst effects of the fall.[528] First of all, in his commentary on Romans 1:19, Wesley asserts that a basic knowledge of God, chiefly in the form of the divine attributes (such as omnipotence, eternity, etc.), is revealed to all men and women as a result of the prevenient agency of the Holy Spirit. Once again, humanity has not been left in the natural state, devoid of all grace and therefore knowing nothing of God, but all people have at least some understanding of God, however clouded or scant this knowledge may be. In his *Notes Upon the New Testament*, Wesley explains: "For what is to be known of God -- Those great principles which are indispensably necessary to be known, 'is manifest

---

Mercy: Prevenient Grace in the Theology of John and Charles Wesley" (Ph.D. Thesis, University of Manchester, 2008).

[524] *Works [BE]*, 2:286. ("The Good Steward").
[525] *Works [BE]*, 3:207. ("On Working Out Our Own Salvation").
[526] Cf. "Free Grace" *Works [BE]*, 3:545-52.
[527] *Works [BE]*, 3:203-04. ("On Working Out Our Own Salvation").
[528] For a thorough discussion of these benefits Cf. Charles Allen Rogers, "The Concept of Prevenient Grace in the Theology of John Wesley" (Ph.D. dissertation, Duke University, 1967), 196. Note, however, that I have added a fifth category, "the restraint of evil," to the four of Rogers. Moreover, some of the material in this section on the benefits of prevenient grace is drawn with some modifications from Kenneth J. Collins, *Theology of John Wesley*, 77-81.

in them; for God hath showed it to them' -- By the light which enlightens every man that cometh into the world."[529] Since this knowledge is universal and independent of special revelation some scholars contend that it forms the basis for a natural theology.[530] Others are quick to point out, however, that though a *theologia naturalis* is indeed in the offing, it never occurs apart from *grace*--a grace that may or may not even be acknowledged in the celebration of reason and its powers.

Second, since men and women, apart from the grace of God, are spiritually dead, they have neither the ability nor the inclination to comprehend the dictates of God's holy law, the same law that was inscribed on their hearts at creation and which is expressive of the image of God. Nevertheless, Wesley affirms that after the fall God did not leave men and women in this utterly dejected state, but reinscribed, in some measure, a knowledge of this moral law upon their hearts. He writes:

> But it was not long before man rebelled against God, and by breaking this glorious law well nigh effaced it out of his heart; ... And yet God did not despise the work of his own hands; but being reconciled to man through the Son of his love, he in some measure re-inscribed the law on the heart of his dark, sinful creature.[531]

Third, in his "Thoughts Upon Necessity," produced in 1744, Wesley reveals that the ultimate origin of conscience is neither nature nor society, but God Almighty. "It is undeniable, that he has fixed in man, in every man," he writes, "his umpire conscience; an inward judge, which passes sentence both on his passions and actions, either approving or condemning them."[532] And in his sermon, "The Scripture Way of Salvation," produced in 1765, Wesley closely identifies the operations of conscience with prevenient grace in particular. Beyond this, in his sermon "On Conscience," written a couple of decades later, the seasoned Wesley continues to argue that although in one sense conscience may be viewed as natural, since this faculty appears to be universal, yet, properly speaking, "it is not natural; but a supernatural gift of God, above all his natural endowments."[533]

---

[529] John Wesley, *Explanatory Notes Upon the New Testament* (Salem, Ohio: Schmul Publishers), 363. (Romans 1:19).

[530] M. Elton Hendricks, "John Wesley and Natural Theology [Prevenient Grace]" in *Wesleyan Theological Journal*, vol. 18 no. 2 (Fall 1983): 12. Moreover, Hendricks contends that "Wesley's approval of the natural theology of Bishop Butler is instructive and would establish *prima facie* a case for Wesley as natural theologian in the absence of any other evidence." Cf., 12.

[531] *Works [BE]*, 2:7. ("Original, Nature, Properties and Use of the Law") See also Wesley's piece, *Predestination Calmly Considered* in which he writes: "His first step is to enlighten the understanding by that general knowledge of good and evil. To this he adds many secret reproofs, if they act contrary to this light..." Cf. Thomas Jackson, ed., *The Works of John Wesley*, vol. 9 of 14 (Grand Rapids, Michigan: Baker Book House, 1978), 233. Hereafter abbreviated as *Works*.

[532] *Works*, 10:473.

[533] *Works [BE]*, 3:105. ("Spiritual Idolatry").

Fourth, since Wesley taught a doctrine of original sin similar in many respects to the Protestant Reformers, he denied that human beings possess natural free-will.[534] In other words, apart from grace, humanity is a mass of sin. Roman Catholicism, on the other hand, (and in a way similar to Eastern Orthodoxy) contended that though free will had been weakened by the fall, it had not been extinguished or lost,[535] a point alluded to earlier.[536] What kept Wesley's theology clear of semi-Pelagianism, on the one hand, as he faced Rome, and from determinism (the elimination of moral responsibility etc.), on the other hand, as he faced Wittenberg and Geneva, was the affirmation that a certain measure of free-will is supernaturally restored to all people by the Holy Spirit (based upon the work of Christ), who apart from such a restoration are not free, soteriologically speaking. For example, in his treatise, "Predestination Calmly Considered," written in 1752, Wesley observes:

> But I do not carry free-will so far: (I mean, not in moral things;) Natural free-will, in the present state of mankind, I do not understand: I only assert, that there is a measure of free will supernaturally restored to every man, together with that supernatural light which "enlightens every man that cometh into the world."[537]

Beyond this, as Albert Outler has correctly noted, Wesley's sophisticated understanding of a graciously restored free-will, the presence of prevenient grace, separated his theology, in an important respect, even from that of Jacobus Arminius as well. For example, "Arminius held that man hath a will to turn to God *before* grace prevents him," Outler writes, "whereas for Wesley it is the Spirit's prevenient motion by which 'we ever are moved and inspired to *any* good thing.'"[538] And this consideration gives added credence to Wesley's claim made at the Methodist conference in 1745 that he and his preachers had come "to the very edge of Calvinism" by ascribing all good to the grace of God and by denying natural free-will and merit.[539]

Fifth, prevenient grace expressed as a limited knowledge of God's attributes, as an understanding of the moral law, as the faculty of conscience, and as a measure of free will supernaturally restored has the cumulative effect,

---

[534] *Works*, 10:229.

[535] H. Orton Wiley, *Christian Theology*, vol. 2 (Kansas City: Beacon Hill Press, 1940-1943), 104. In this context, Wiley has in mind principally Tridentine Catholicism.

[536] In fact, John Cassian, who founded two monasteries near Marseilles and whose *Institutes* had an impact on the Benedictine Rule, tried to find a compromise between the position of Augustine and Pelagius. This gifted monk contended that though all people are sinful as a result of the fall, their wills are simply weakened but not totally corrupted. Men and women are, therefore, free enough to cooperate with grace. See also Wiley, *Christian Theology*, 2:104.

[537] *Works*, 10:230.

[538] *Works [BE]*, 2:157, n.3. ("The Scripture Way of Salvation").

[539] *Works*, 8:285. George Croft Cell's work *The Rediscovery of John Wesley* is well known for having championed the thesis that Wesley's theology was similar in some important respects to that of John Calvin. Cf. George C. Cell, *The Rediscovery of John Wesley* (Lanham, Maryland: University Press of America, 1984).

which can be distinguished from each of the preceding instances, of restraining human wickedness, of placing a check on human perversity. In fact, in his "Sermon on the Mount, Discourse the Third," Wesley describes "the braking effect" which prevenient grace (and providence) has on human evil, in this instance with respect to the hatred directed against the sons and daughters of God. He writes:

> If we were of the world, the world would love its own: but because ye are not of the world, [...] therefore the world hateth you. Yea (setting aside what exceptions may be made by the preventing grace or the peculiar providence of God) it hateth them as cordially and sincerely as ever it did their Master.[540]

And again, in his notes on Romans 1:24, Wesley points out that God withdrew "his restraining grace" from the obstinate and rebellious, from those who remained in idolatry.[541]

Prevenient Grace and the Muslim Community

In light of the preceding it is evident that Wesley affirmed the universality of prevenient grace, along with its five specific benefits, and therefore that such graces mark the Muslim community as well. Moreover, the *benefits* of prevenient grace such as knowledge of the attributes of God, a measure of the knowledge of the moral law, conscience, a freedom that is associated with personhood and responsibility, and the braking effect of such grace on human evil all represent not cooperant grace but free grace. In other words such grace, in the form of restored *faculties*, highlights in a preeminent way the work of God alone. Indeed prevenient grace is given, to use Wesley's own words, in a manner "which waiteth not for the call of man."[542]

Although prevenient grace is universal, and it marks the *beginning* of salvation in Wesley's estimation nevertheless such grace, it must be noted, is not salvific, properly speaking. Understood in a broad way prevenient grace represents the prior activity of God at any point along the *ordo salutis*, underscoring that the Most High is always ahead, so to speak.[543] In a second, more focused sense, however, prevenient grace can be conceived as that grace which literally goes before, properly speaking, the saving graces of justification and regeneration. And so the question in terms of the Muslim community, in light of Wesley's own theological constructs, has now become: Are Muslims recipients of more than prevenient grace, even of those graces that make holy? Put an-

---

[540] *Works [BE]*, 1:526. ("Sermon on the Mount, Discourse the Third").
[541] Wesley, *NT Notes*, 364. (Romans 2:24).
[542] *Works [BE]*, 3:207. ("On Working Out Our Own Salvation"). Note, however, that "irresistibility" in this context pertains not to the call or overtures made to these faculties (that can be resisted) but to the re-establishment of these faculties that constitute responsible personhood and accountability. For more on this topic see, Kenneth J. Collins, *The Theology of John Wesley*, 81-82.
[543] The broad and narrow sense of prevenient grace is developed by Albert Outler, See his comments on his introduction to Wesley's sermon, "On Conscience." *Works [BE]*, 2:479. ("On Conscience").

other way, may it rightly be claimed that Muslims are justified and born of God?

The Import of Covenant Theology

Like the Puritans William Ames and William Perkins, John Wesley understood that salvific graces are communicated through a covenant relationship established by God. However, unlike Ames and Perkins, Wesley parsed the distinction of a covenant of works and a covenant of grace somewhat differently.[544] Whereas many of the Puritans considered the moral law to be the primary feature of the covenant of works, Wesley rejected this judgment most likely because it failed to recognize the gracious nature of the moral law itself which is holy, just and good (Rom. 7:12).[545] In Wesley's estimation, as expressed for example in his sermon, "The Righteousness of Faith," produced in 1746, the dividing line between the covenant of works and the covenant of grace does not mirror the distinction between Moses and Christ but rather that of Adam before the fall on the one hand and all of humanity since the fall (the Mosaic and Christian dispensations) on the other hand. Put another way, it is only the covenant made with Adam in paradise (and in innocence) that is rightly termed a covenant of works. The covenants represented by Moses and Christ are *both* gracious.[546] As such it is proper in Wesley's judgment to distinguish the Mosaic dispensation from the Christian one, both of which fall under the designation of a covenant of grace. This means, of course, that in Wesley's practical theology he is by and large concerned with the gifts, graces and strengths of distinct *dispensations* that carry much of his soteriological concern.[547]

So then, in order to assess the soteriological status, so to speak, of the Muslim community using Wesleyan theological materials it is helpful at the outset to recognize the priority of dispensations in his thinking that devolve upon Moses and Christ. Indeed, Wesley grappled with the question of the possibility of redemptive graces beyond the church (though not beyond the agency of the Holy Spirit) chiefly in terms of the servant metaphor (faith of a servant/faith of a child of God) as well as with respect to his careful employment of the Apostle Peter's judgment "Of a truth I perceive that God is no respecter of persons: But in *every nation* he that feareth him, and worketh

---

[544] For a consideration of the influence of covenant theology on John Wesley's soteriological judgments, see Stanley J. Rodes, "From Faith to Faith: An Examination of the Servant-Son Metaphor in John Wesley's Theological Thought" (Ph. D. Thesis, University of Manchester, 2011).

[545] See Wesley's sermon "On the Original, Nature, Properties and Use of the Law," in *Works [BE]*, 2:4-19.

[546] *Works [BE]*, 1:203. ("The Righteousness of Faith"). See also Rodes, "From Faith to Faith," 73-89.

[547] Granted the Old Testament can be perverted and misunderstood as a covenant of works in which obedience to the law is viewed as the path to justification.

righteousness, is accepted with him" (Acts. 10: 34-35).[548] Clearly both of these elements must be understood in the context of the two dispensations already defined. In other words, the metaphor of "the faith of a servant," and the language of "those who fear God and work righteousness," (which gather up his soteriological interests especially in terms of extent) are dependent upon Wesley's distinction of the Mosaic and Christian dispensations and they have little meaning apart from that dispensational framework.[549] As Rodes puts it, "he [Wesley] restricted his employment of the servant-son metaphor to those who were, *soteriologically*, clearly under the Jewish dispensation or under the Christian dispensation."[550]

This last observation then helps to explain, in part, why Wesley left the Abrahamic covenant (which is of great interest to Muslims) largely undeveloped in this theology, especially in terms of its soteriological implications. For although he affirmed that Abraham is the "father of the faithful,"[551] "the father of all them that believe,"[552] and though he even declared that the covenant entered into with Abraham was an "evangelical covenant,"[553] and a "gospel covenant,"[554] nevertheless Wesley specifically pointed out that "Christ is not in any of these instances the direct or immediate object of Abraham's faith,"[555] such that he had to conclude that "neither Abraham, David nor any Jew, was greater than John [the Baptist]."[556] In other words, in this instance "he which is least in the kingdom of God ... is greater than he [Abraham]."[557] Simply put, it is not the Abrahamic covenant that informs the paradigm of the faith of a servant and the language of one who "fears God and works righteousness," with their broad soteriological implications, but the dispensations of Moses and Christ.

---

[548] *The Holy Bible: King James Version.* 1995 (electronic ed. of the 1769 edition of the 1611 Authorized Version.) (Ac 10:34-36). Bellingham WA: Logos Research Systems, Inc.

[549] Rodes, "From Faith to Faith," 28, 100-106.

[550] Rodes, "From Faith to Faith," 222. In other words one could be a "soteriological" Jew, though not a literal one, due to one's relation to God that is not only "legal" but is also marked by fear.

[551] *Works [BE]*, 2:8 ("The Original, Nature, Properties and Use of the Law").

[552] *Works*, 10:240. ("Predestination Calmly Considered").

[553] *Works*, 10:191. ("A Treatise on Baptism").

[554] *Works*, 10:194. ("A Treatise on Baptism").

[555] Reginald W. Ward, and Richard P. Heitzenrater, eds., *The Works of John Wesley*, vol. 23. *Journals and Diaries VI* (Nashville: Abingdon Press, 1988), 69.

[556] Kenneth J. Collins, and Jason Vickers, eds., *The Sermons of John Wesley: A Collection for the Christian Journey* (Nashville: Abingdon Press, 2013), p. 616 ["On Christian Perfection"].

[557] *Works [BE]*, 2:108. ("Christian Perfection").

Two Dispensations: One Gracious Covenant

When Wesley employed the language of "Mosaical dispensation"[558] or "legal dispensation,"[559] he was not simply thinking historically in terms of the giving of the law to ancient Israel at Sinai, but he was also thinking *soteriologically*.[560] In other words, gentiles (those to whom the law was *not* historically given) may yet be in the legal dispensation due to their relation to God which is preeminently marked by fear. Indeed, Wesley contrasted "the Pentecost of Sinai, in the Old Testament, and the Pentecost of Jerusalem, in the New"[561] which taken together he referred to as "the two grand manifestations of God, the legal and the evangelical; the one from the mountain, and the other from heaven; the terrible [evoking fear] and the merciful one [evoking love]."[562] As such those under the legal dispensation, soteriologically speaking, will include both Jew and gentile and therefore Muslims as well. Beyond this it must be recognized that gentiles as well as Jews may utilize the moral law of the Old covenant in an improper fashion, that is, not viewing it as the gracious gift that it is but instead making it the principal vehicle for all sorts of attempts at self-righteousness and self-justification.

It is precisely the way in which Wesley contrasted these two dispensations, the Mosaic and the Christian, that bespeaks of his well-worked metaphor of the faith of a servant and the faith of a son. Thus, in his observations on Deuteronomy 34:12, Wesley points out that "Moses was faithful as a servant, but Christ as a son."[563] However, not only are these two dispensations emblematic of this vital soteriological metaphor but they are also expressed, at least in some sense, in the typology that Wesley employed in his sermon, "The Spirit of Bondage and of Adoption," in which he distinguished between the *natural*, the *legal* and the *evangelical*, a movement along the path of salvation that marks a transition from ignorance to fear and on to holy love.[564] More importantly for the task at hand, Wesley's parsing of the dispensations, soteriologically speaking, not only informs the metaphor of the faith of a servant/ faith of a son but also the metaphor itself in turn becomes one of his principal means, in terms of theological structures, through which Wesley thought through the whole matter of justification and those graces that are properly described as "saving."

---

[558] John Wesley, *Explanatory Notes Upon the Old Testament*, 3 vols. (Bristol: William Pine, 1765). See the note on Joshua 1:1.

[559] John Wesley, *Explanatory Notes Upon the New Testament* (London: William Bowyer, 1755). See the note on Gal. 4:2-3.

[560] Rodes, "From Faith to Faith," 175-84.

[561] Wesley, *NT Notes*. See Acts. 2:1.

[562] Wesley, *NT Notes*. See Acts. 2:1. Bracketed material is mine.

[563] Wesley, *OT Notes*. See Deuteronomy 34:12. See also Wesley's comments on Hebrews 3:5-6 in his *NT Notes*.

[564] *Works [BE]*, 1:248-266. ("The Spirit of Bondage and of Adoption").

Justification

For the sake of clarity it is important to recognize at the outset that Wesley, in a manner similar to John Fletcher, defined justification in a least four different ways. The first sense underscores the *universality* of the atoning work of Christ, in other words that provision has been made for *all*, that is, sin has been forgiven and God is *already* reconciled. In this context, however, justification does not necessarily imply regeneration in the Christian sense. The second way stresses the importance of *receiving* and *applying* this justification[565] to the individual life such that believers can affirm not simply in a general manner that Christ died for the sins of the whole world (think of Spangenberg's questions to Wesley in Georgia!) but also in a more personal fashion, reminiscent of Wesley at Aldersgate, that Christ "had taken away *my* sins, even *mine*, and saved *me* from the law of sin and death."[566] The third sense of justification developed by Wesley is intimately tied with the whole matter of assurance and the final way has to do with what Wesley on occasion referred to as final justification (which he initially rejected but which he later came to accept) before the throne of Christ in glory, a justification that is manifested in *works*.[567]

The sense of justification that upheld Wesley's soteriological standards and therefore the promises of the gospel as well, and the one that is most often found in his writings, is the second sense enumerated above that Wesley at times specifically referred to as "the Christian sense." Thus, for example, in his sermon "Justification by Faith," produced in 1746, Wesley observes: "in whatever moment a man believes (in the Christian sense of the word) he is justified, his sins blotted out, 'his faith counted to him as righteousness.'"[568] In a similar fashion, Wesley points out in his comments on Acts 10:4 that although Cornelius had a measure of faith before the Apostle Peter arrived, "in the Christian sense Cornelius was then an unbeliever."[569] Moreover, it is this Christian sense of the term that is referred to when Wesley declares that justification (the work that God does for us) is ever *conjoined* with regenera-

---

[565] Wesley republished (with modifications) Richard Baxter's *Aphorisms of Justification* and cited favorably this second sense of justification as follows: "Through Christ hath satisfied the law, yet is it not his will that any man should be justified or saved thereby who hath not some ground in himself of personal and particular right and claim thereto, nor that any should be justified by the blood only as shed or offered except it be also received and applied." See Randy L. Maddox, ed., *The Works of John Wesley: Doctrinal and Controversial Treatises I* (Nashville: Abingdon Press, 2012), 12:65.

[566] Reginald W. Ward, and Richard P. Heitzenrater, eds., *The Works of John Wesley: Journals and Diaries I* (Nashville: Abingdon Press, 1988), 18:250.

[567] See Rupert E. Davies, *The Works of John Wesley: The Methodist Societies, I: History, Nature and Design* (Nashville: Abingdon Press, 1989), 9:65. See also Collins, *Theology of John Wesley*, from which some of these comments are taken.

[568] Gerald R. Cragg, ed., *The Works of John Wesley: The Appeals to Men of Reason and Religion* (New York: Oxford University Press, 1975), 11:117.

[569] Wesley, *NT Notes*, Acts 10:4.

tion (the work that God does in us) as is evident in his sermon "On Sin in Believers," written in 1763:

> In doing this I use indifferently the words "regenerate," "justified', or "believers"; since, though they have not precisely the same meaning (the first implying an inward, actual change; the second a relative one; and the third the means whereby both the one and the other are wrought) yet they come to one and the same thing, as everyone that 'believes' is *both* "justified" *and* "born of God"[570]

Since justification in the Christian sense and regeneration are associated, never one without the other,[571] then this means that justification is also associated with the marks of the new birth that bespeak of both the promises and standards of redemption.

The Faith of a Servant Metaphor and Justification[572]

In terms of its relation to justification in the *Christian sense*, Wesley employed the faith of a servant metaphor in two key ways: first of all, after initially affirming that assurance is the *common*, not rare, privilege of a child of God,[573] Wesley links the faith of a servant to the spirit of bondage. This is the *broad* usage of the metaphor and it includes many people, both inside and outside the walls of a church. Accordingly, Wesley still did not identify nor confuse the faith of a servant, and its measure of acceptance (a degree of faith and grace), with the assurance that one's sins are forgiven; since being under "the spirit of bondage," a servant, properly speaking, lacks justifying faith. Indeed, in a letter to Thomas Davenport, drafted in 1781, Wesley counsels the suffering gentleman who was then under a spirit of fear that "You have now *received the spirit of bondage*. Is it not the forerunner of the Spirit of adoption? He is not

---

[570] *Works [BE]*, 1:319-320. Emphasis is mine. Laura Bartels Felleman failed to distinguish this second sense of justification (she was employing the term largely in the first "universal" sense of the term). As a result of this move, Bartels Felleman was not able to recognize that much more is entailed in the term justification in the *Christian sense* as employed by John Wesley than she has allowed. Logically this same ongoing mistake can be expressed in the form of "affirming the consequent," that is, of not taking into account all that is entailed in the *Christian sense* of justification. Put another way, such an approach did not allow Bartels Felleman to affirm Wesley's soteriological standards, and with them, their implied promises as well. See Laura Bartels Felleman, "John Wesley and the 'Servant of God'," *Wesleyan Theological Journal*, vol. 41 no. 2 (Fall, 2006): 72-86.

[571] For a view that denies justification and regeneration are ever conjoined, see Randy L. Maddox, "Continuing the Conversation," *Methodist History*, vol. 30 no. 4 (July 1992): 241.

[572] The material in this section, with some slight modifications, is drawn from my book, *The Theology of John Wesley*, 133-136. Used by permission of Abingdon Press.

[573] Frank Baker, ed., *The Works of John Wesley: The Letters II* (New York: Oxford University Press, 1982), 26:254-55. (To Charles Wesley; July 31, 1747)

afar off. Look up!...He is nigh that justifieth!"[574] Such advice clearly reveals, once again, that those under the spirit of bondage do indeed lack justifying faith in the Christian sense. More important, a few years later in his sermon, "On the Discoveries of Faith," Wesley specifically links the spirit of bondage with the faith of a servant indicating that this faith has yet to *receive* the forgiveness of sins. Wesley observes: "Exhort him to press on by all possible means, till he passes 'from faith to faith'; from the faith of a *servant* to the faith of a *son*; from the *spirit of bondage* unto fear, to the spirit of childlike love."[575]

What then are the traits of the spirit of bondage displayed in the sermon "The Spirit of Bondage and of Adoption" written in 1746, and that were later identified with the faith of a servant? Those under a spirit of bondage, Wesley argues, feel sorrow and remorse; they fear death, the devil, and humanity; they desire to break free from the chains of sin, but cannot, and their cry of despair is typified by the Pauline expression: "O wretched man that I am, who shall deliver me from the body of this death?"[576] In fact, in this sermon Wesley specifically identifies "this whole struggle of one who is 'under the law'" with the spirit of bondage and with the spiritual and psychological dynamics of the seventh chapter of Romans.[577]

Second, Wesley recognized that in some exceptional cases those who are justified and regenerated (and hence children of God) may lack an assurance that their sins are forgiven due to either ignorance or bodily disorder.[578] These too have the faith of a servant. This is the narrow usage of the metaphor. This means, then, that Wesley defined the faith of a servant in at least two key ways. The first, which is a *broad* usage and occurs repeatedly in Wesley's writings, *excludes* justification, regeneration and assurance and corresponds to the spirit of bondage detailed above. The second, which is a narrow usage and seldom occurs, corresponds to the exempt cases and exceptions just noted and *includes* justification and regeneration but not assurance. Interestingly enough, although the faith of a servant in this second sense is obviously Christian (saving) faith since it includes justification and regeneration, Wesley still did not refer to it as the *proper* Christian faith since it lacks assurance.

---

[574] John Telford, ed., *The Letters of John Wesley, A.M.*, 8 vols. (London: The Epworth Press, 1931), 5:95. Hereafter abbreviated as *Letters*. (To Thomas Davenport, December 2, 1781).

[575] *Works [BE]*, 4:35-36. Emphasis is mine. (On the Discoveries of Faith).

[576] *Works [BE]*, 1:258. ("The Spirit of Bondage and of Adoption").

[577] *Works [BE]*, 1:258. Observe that the servants of God are awakened, but they see not a God of love, but One of wrath. It is, therefore, important not to confuse the issue of awakening with regeneration (and conversion).

[578] In addition, Wesley wrote to Dr. Rutherforth in 1768: "Therefore I have not for many years thought a consciousness of acceptance to be essential to justifying faith." Cf. *Letters*, 5:359. See also Starkey, *The Work of the Holy Spirit: A Study in Wesleyan Theology* (Nashville, Tennessee: Abingdon Press, 1962), 68-69.

The preceding discussion of Wesley's distinctions pertaining to assurance can now be outlined into three major groups as follows:

Faith of a Child of God	Faith of a Servant (Broad)	Faith of a Servant (Narrow)[579]
Under the Spirit of Adoption	Under the Spirit of Bondage	Not under the Spirit of Bondage
Have the Witness (Spirit)	Lack the Witness	Lack the Witness
Justified and Born of God	Accepted (But Not Justified and Born of God in the Christian Sense)	Justified and Born of God
Have the Witness of the Spirit	Lack the Witness Due to Sin (Many People; Common)	Lack the Witness Due to Ignorance or Bodily Disorder (Few People; Exceptions)

By 1771 Wesley had come to a greater appreciation of the faith of a servant and its degree of acceptance; and he had realized that in exceptional cases one may even be justified and yet lack assurance due to either ignorance of the gospel promises or due to bodily disorder. Nevertheless, the theme which Wesley chose to develop during the last period of his life was none other than a strong identification of assurance with the proper (real) Christian faith. To illustrate, in January 1787, Wesley acknowledged that "To believe Christ gave Himself for me is the faith of a Christian,"[580] and a year later he not only once again clarified the distinction between the faith of a servant and that of a son, but he also maintained that assurance is an integral component of the proper Christian faith. In his sermon "On Faith," Wesley reasons:

> Thus the faith of a child is *properly and directly* a divine conviction whereby every child of God is enabled to testify, "The life that I now live, I live by faith in

---

[579] Wesley indicates that the dividing line between the faith of a servant and that of a child of God has to do specifically with the direct witness of the Holy Spirit: "He that believeth, as a child of God, 'hath the witness in himself.' This the servant hath not.' See *Works [BE]*, 3:498. ("On Faith").

[580] *Letters*, 7:361-62. (To Theophilus Lessey, January 1787) Wesley's response to Mr. Fleury, who had claimed that Wesley pretended to extraordinary inspiration, was to associate the witness of the Spirit (assurance) as vital to the Christian faith: "I pretend to no other inspiration than that which is common to all real Christians, without which no one can be a Christian at all." Cf. *Works [BE]*, 9:392.

the son of God, who loved me, and gave himself for me." And *whosoever hath this*, the Spirit of God witnesseth with his spirit that he is a child of God.[581]

Even more significantly, there is nothing in Wesley's often-quoted letter to Melville Horne in 1788 which detracts from this identification and emphasis. Thus, in this correspondence, Wesley maintains that the servants of God who lack assurance are not thereby condemned, a commonplace by now, but he then goes on to assert once more that "we preach assurance as we always did, as a *common* privilege of the children of God...."[582]

The Language of "Fearing God and Working Righteousness" and Justification

Just as Wesley employed the faith of a servant metaphor in a twofold way: one that excluded justification (associated with the spirit of bondage) and one that embraced it (the exceptions or exempt cases) so too did he utilize the language of "fearing God and working righteousness" in similar manner. To illustrate, Wesley used this language, in its *broad* sense, to describe those who were contrite in heart but not necessarily born of God and who were about to unite with the Methodists by joining a class meeting. Indeed, Wesley gloried in the fact that one did not have to chronicle a conversion experience or confess that Jesus is the Messiah in order to be among the Methodists. He elaborates:

> I have never read or heard of, either in ancient or modern history, any other church which builds on so broad a foundation as the Methodists do; which requires of its members no conformity either in opinions or modes of worship, but barely this one thing, to fear God, and work righteousness. [583]

On occasion Wesley exhorted those that "fear God and work righteousness" continually "to cry to God, that he would reveal his Son in your hearts, to the intent you may be no more *servants* but *sons*; having his love shed abroad in your hearts, and walking in 'the glorious liberty of the children of God.'"[584]

Moreover, though the only requirement to become a Methodist was a desire to "flee the wrath which is to come," to remain a Methodist, however,

---

[581] *Works [BE]*, 3:497-498. (On Faith) Emphasis is mine. For examples of what Wesley meant by "full assurance," cf. Wesley, *NT Notes*, 638; *Works [BE]*, 3:549, 4:36; *Works [BE]*, 22:436.

[582] Robert Southey, *The Life of John Wesley* (New York: W. B. Gilley, 1820), 1:258. Emphasis is mine. That Wesley maintains that assurance is the *common* privilege of the sons and daughters of God suggests that it is rare when assurance, marked by doubt and fear, does not soon follow the new birth.

[583] Reginald W. Ward, and Richard P. Heitzenrater, eds., *The Works of John Wesley*, Vol. 24. *Journals and Diaries VII* (Nashville: Abingdon Press, 2003), 152. The "fearing God" in this context may be equivalent to the kind of fear described in Wesley's typology found in the sermon, "The Spirit of Bondage and of Adoption," that is, in terms of ignorance → fear → love. See *Works [BE]*, 1:248-266.

[584] *Works [BE]*, 3:500 ("On Faith"). Emphasis is mine.

class members had to keep the *General Rules of the United Societies* which included the following: 1) doing no harm, 2) doing good, and 3) attending upon "all the ordinances of God."[585] These same three rules emerged elsewhere in Wesley's writings in the context of *repentance*. This last factor demonstrates quite clearly that the very purpose of the class meeting was to foster repentance from an old way of life to a new one. Again, one did not have to have the faith of a child of God to join the Methodists. One need only "fear God and work righteousness." In this broad sense such language does *not* imply justification and regeneration, properly speaking.

Wesley, however, also utilized this distinct language in a second, more *narrow*, way to refer to those who were indeed the children of God, who knew that their sins were forgiven, and who had the direct witness of the Holy Spirit. Wesley explains:

> I believe a consciousness of being in the favour of God (which I do not term plerophory, or full assurance, since it is frequently weakened, nay, perhaps interrupted, by returns of doubt or fear) is the *common privilege* of Christians, fearing God and working righteousness.[586]

Even more emphatically Wesley clearly links those who "fear God and work righteousness," with those who are nothing less than *real Christians*, in other words, with believers who are justified, born of God and have a measure of assurance. In his sermon, "On Divine Providence," for example, produced in 1786, Wesley observes:

> Within the third, the innermost circle, are contained only the real Christians; those that worship God, not in form only, but in spirit and in truth. Herein are comprised all that love God, or, at least, truly fear God and work righteousness; all in whom is the mind which was in Christ, and who walk as Christ also walked.[587]

Beyond this, interestingly enough, Wesley wrote about those who "fear God, and work righteousness *evangelically*," demonstrating once again the high measure of grace that this phrase can depict, even that of a child of God who is redeemed in nothing less than the Christian sense of this important terminology.

Wesley's Difficult Statements about "Mohametans"

Before Wesley's own soteriological standards in the form of justification, the metaphor of the faith of a servant and the biblical language of "fearing God and working righteousness," can be applied to the Muslim faith, it is important to note that the language of Wesley's own observations on "Mahome-

---

[585] *Works [BE]*, 9:70-73.
[586] *Letters*, 5:358. (To Dr. Rutherforth). Emphasis is mine.
[587] *Works [BE]*, 2:543. ("On Divine Providence").

tans" was often negative.[588] For example, he declares in his sermon, "The General Spread of the Gospel": "A little, and but a little, above the Heathens in religion, are the Mahometans. But how far and wide has this miserable delusion spread over the face of the earth!"[589] And again Wesley points out: "How many, even of good sort of people, of them whose lives are innocent, are as ignorant of themselves, of God, and of worshipping him in spirit and in truth, as either Mahometans or Heathens!"[590] However, Wesley mitigates the harshness of his statements with respect to Muslims in his sermon "On Living Without God," written less than a year before his death. In it he explains:

> Let it be observed, I purposely add, 'to those that are under the Christian dispensation,' because I have no authority from the Word of God 'to judge those that are without.' Nor do I conceive that any man living has a right to sentence all the heathen and **Mahometan** world to damnation. It is far better to leave them to him that made them, and who is 'the Father of the spirits of all flesh;' who is the God of the Heathens as well as the Christians, and who hateth nothing that he hath made.[591]

Though Wesley maintained that "Mahometans" were ignorant of God and the nature of true religion, he nevertheless cautioned the Methodists against condemning this people to loss, to an eternity apart from the glorious presence of God. Accordingly, judgment and utter condemnation of the Muslim community by Christians (to take on the prerogatives that belong to God alone) was inappropriate in Wesley's eighteenth century Britain, and it remains inappropriate today. That much at least is clear. Nevertheless the application of Wesley's theological standards and frameworks to Muslims may yet be warranted, if in a twenty-first century global setting of informational exchange it can be presumed that the Muslim community has at least some knowledge of the gospel and its promises.

The Application of Wesley's Soteriological Standards and Frameworks to Muslims

So then there are two major positions on the question of whether Wesley's soteriological standards in the form of the metaphor of the faith of a servant and the language of "fearing God and working righteousness," (terminology that is best understood in the larger context of justification in the Christian sense) can be properly applied to Islam. The first view argues that these

---

[588] For more on this topic of the question of the truth of other religions see Randy L. Maddox, "Wesley and the Question of Truth or Salvation through Other Religions" in *Wesleyan Theological Journal*, vol. 27 (Spring-Fall 1992): pp. 10-12.

[589] *Works [BE]*, 2:486 ("The General Spread of the Gospel").

[590] *Works [BE]*, 4:124 ("On a Single Eye"). For Wesley's other negative statements about "Mahometans" see, *Works*, 11:159; *Works [BE]*, 12:186; *Works [BE]*, 3:470. ("On Attending the Church Service"); and *Works [BE]*, 12:185-86.

[591] *Works [BE]*, 4:174-75. ("On Living Without God").

standards are indeed applicable to Muslims simply because Wesley employed the metaphor of the faith of a servant and the distinct language of "fear God and work righteousness," in a very general way to *every* nation, a judgment that surely must include Muslims. Indeed, Wesley's discussion of the "infant state" of the faith that will in the end be properly saving appears to embrace the Muslim community as well. In his sermon, "On Faith," for example, Wesley reasons:

> But what is the faith which is properly saving; which brings eternal salvation to all those that keep it to the end? It is such a divine conviction of God, and the things of God, as, even in its infant state, enables every one that possesses it to 'fear God and work righteousness.' And whosoever, *in every nation*, believes thus far, the Apostle declares, is 'accepted of him.' He actually is, at that very moment, in a state of acceptance. But he is at present *only a servant of God, not properly a son.* Meantime, let it be well observed, that 'the wrath of God' no longer 'abideth on him.'[592]

This soteriological judgment, entailed in this first major position, can be expressed in the following chart, if indeed the standards are applicable:

The Faith of a Muslim
(Are the Soteriological Standards Applicable?)

YES (Mosaic Dispensation; Legal)	NO (Christian Dispensation; Evangelical)	YES (Mosaic Dispensation; Legal)	NO (Christian Dispensation; Evangelical)
Faith of a Servant (Broad)	**Faith of a Servant (Narrow)**	**Fear God and Work Righteousness (Broad)**	**Fear God and Work Righteousness (Narrow)**
Under the Spirit of Bondage	Not under the Spirit of Bondage	Under the Spirit of Bondage	Not under the Spirit of Bondage
Lack the Witness	Lack the Witness	Lack the Witness	Have the Witness
Accepted (But Not Justified and Born of God in the Christian Sense)	Justified and Born of God	Accepted (But Not Justified and Born of God in the Christian sense)	Justified and Born of God

---

[592]*Works [BE]*, 3: 497. ("On Faith"). Emphases are mine. See also Philip Schaff, *The Creeds of Christendom*, vol. III (Grand Rapids, Michigan: Baker Book House, 1983), 499. Notice here that Wesley specifically connects the phrase "fear God and work righteousness" with the faith of a *servant*.

Lack the Witness Due to Sin (Many People; Common)	Lack the Witness Due to Ignorance or Bodily Disorder (Few People; Exceptions)	Lack the Witness Due to Sin (Many People; Common)	Have the Witness as *Real Christians*, soteriologically speaking

Moreover, this first view can be supported by distinguishing between an historical Jewish dispensation (in which the Jews were given the Mosaic law) from a *soteriological* understanding of this same dispensation in the form of one who, whether Jew or not, is "under the law," due to illumination and awakening, as expressed in the typology of natural, legal, evangelical found in the sermon, "The Spirit of Bondage and Of Adoption."[593]

The second major position, however, contends that Wesley's metaphor of the faith of a servant as well as the language of "fear God and work righteousness" are not properly applied to the Muslim community. In other words, these standards are not, after all, employed in a *soteriological* way as the first view suggests. To illustrate, In Wesley's sermon, "On Faith," (Heb. 11:6), written in April 1788, he distinguishes several kinds of faith in an ascending order: a materialist, a deist, a heathen, a Jew, John the Baptist, a Roman Catholic, a Protestant. More to the point, observe precisely where Wesley places the faith of a Mahometan in this typology in the following observation drawn from this same sermon:

> The next sort of faith is the faith of Heathens, with which I join that of Mahometans. I cannot but prefer this before the faith of the Deists; because, though it embraces nearly the same objects, yet they are rather to be pitied than blamed for the narrowness of their faith. And their not believing the whole truth, is not owing to want of sincerity, but merely to want of light. When one asked Chicali, an old Indian Chief, 'Why do not you red men know as much as us white men?' he readily answered, 'Because you have the great Word, and we have not.'[594]

And since later in this same sermon Wesley clearly distinguishes the faith of a heathen from that of a servant ("There is no reason why you should be satisfied with the faith of a materialist, a heathen, or a deist; nor indeed with that of a servant"[595]) it is reasonable to conclude that the faith of a heathen which typifies the faith of a "Mahometan," in the end, does not partake of either the Mosaic or Christian dispensation, soteriologically speaking, but that it is at best understood more generally as simply enjoying the prevenient grace of God that is given universally to all nations. In this second view, the failure to receive the deeper graces which these two dispensations just cited enjoy is due, in Wesley's estimation at least, to a want of light, to a *lack of knowledge and understanding* with respect to the promises of the gospel. Moreover, these promises, when viewed in another way, are nothing less than the standards of

---

[593] *Works [BE]*, 1:248-66. ("The Spirit of Bondage and of Adoption").
[594] *Works [BE]*, 3:494 ("On Faith").
[595] *Works [BE]*, 3:498 ("On Faith").

salvation manifested in Jesus Christ. This means, then, that Wesley set aside his own Christian worldview as he looked toward Islam and proceeded in a largely phenomenological way. That is, he considered what in reality were the "live options" for practicing Muslims whose birth, family ties, education, socialization, and culture had not offered them knowledge of Christ. The judgment entailed in this second major position can be expressed in the following chart, if indeed the soteriological standards are *not* applicable:

The Faith of a Muslim (Are the Soteriological Standards Applicable?)
NO (Beyond the Mosaic and Christian Dispensations)
The Faith of a Heathen (Distinguished from the Faith of a Servant)
Ignorant of the Gospel Promises
"How it will please God, the Judge of all, to deal with *them*, we may leave to God himself."

And what is it that may prevent the Muslim community from receiving the illumination that may lead to saving grace, from hearing the gospel that would render them responsible for the light so received?[596]

Possible Impediments to Receiving Justifying Graces in the Muslim Community

There may be at least two impediments to the reception of justification in its saving sense (in other words as it is conjoined with regeneration and the marks of the new birth) in the Muslim community. The first difficulty has to do with the Christology of the Koran itself. Indeed, the Koran is replete with verses that specifically deny the divinity of Christ in a way similar to that of Arius centuries earlier. The following material, then, drawn from the Koran itself, clearly evidences a low Christology:

- "Unbelievers are those who declare: 'God is the Messiah, the son of Mary.'"[597]
- And of Allah it is written: "he is the Creator of the heavens and the earth. How should He have a son when He had no consort?"[598]
- "Those who say: 'The Lord of Mercy has begotten a son,' preach a monstrous falsehood, at which the very heavens might crack, the earth break asunder, and the mountains crumble to dust."[599]

---

[596] For more on the Christology of the Koran see Kenneth J. Collins, *The Theology of John Wesley*, 113-120.
[597] N.J. Dawood, ed., *The Koran* (London: Penguin Books, 1990), 81. (Sura 5:17).
[598] Ibid., p. 102. (Sura 6:101.).

- "God forbid that He Himself should beget a son!"[600]

In light of this and other pertinent evidence, the question must finally be addressed: Does God/Father have a Son or not? The Koran clearly says "No"; the New Testament, on the other hand, repeatedly says, "Yes." It is difficult, if not impossible, to reconcile these views.[601]

The second impediment concerns the church, itself, which is composed, at least in part, of those whose lives give evidence of dullness, superstition and sin. Indeed, Wesley refers to the lives of Christians as the "grand stumbling block"[602] set before Muslims that prevents them from hearing the gospel aright. Naturally Wesley was critical of his own Anglican church in this regard, for one thing because it was near at hand, but he reserved some of his sharpest opprobrium for the Greek Church, which today is known, more popularly, as Eastern Orthodoxy. Wesley's censure is worth quoting at length:

> Proceed we now to the Christian world....The gross, barbarous ignorance, the deep, stupid superstition, the blind and bitter zeal, and the endless thirst after vain jangling and strife of words, which have reigned for many ages in the Greek Church, and well-nigh banished true religion from among them, make these scarce worthy of the Christian name, and lay an insuperable stumbling-block before the Mahometans.[603]

Among other things, Wesley astutely realized that the use of icons by the Eastern Church could easily despoil dialog with the Muslim community before it ever had a chance to begin.[604] Indeed, from the days of Muhammad in the seventh century to the present day, Muslims have repeatedly rejected the use of icons and images to portray the divine (in a way not very dissimilar

---

[599] Ibid., p. 219. (Sura 19:88). The Koran also intimates that the Jews attach particular significance to Ezra as revealed in the following: "The Jews say Ezra is the son of God, while the Christians say the Messiah is the son of God. Such are their assertions, by which they imitate the infidels of old. God confound them! How perverse they are! p. 136. (Sura 9:29-30)

[600] Ibid., p. 216. (Sura 19:35).

[601] For more on this topic see Kenneth J. Collins, *The Theology of John Wesley*, 117.

[602] *Works [BE]*, 2:495 ("The General Spread of the Gospel").

[603] *Works [BE]*, 12:186-87. See also Collins, *The Theology of John Wesley*, 118 from which some of this material is taken. Used by permission of Abingdon Press.

[604] *Works*, 10:176 ("The Origin of Image-Worship Among Christians"). For a defense of the use of icons from the Eastern Orthodox tradition, Cf., St. Theodore the Studite, *On the Holy Icons*, trans. Catherine P. Roth (Crestwood, New York: St. Valdimir's Seminary Press, 2001). The justification of the use of icons in terms of a doctrine of the incarnation, here as elsewhere, is actually based upon a specious argument. It makes the subtle and not-often-noticed shift from "person" to "thing." However, in its best sense the doctrine of the incarnation, richly evident in scripture, helps the church to understand, at least in some sense, the divine nature of the *person* of Christ, a divinity that is embodied ("The Word became flesh" John 1:14), though apparently not present in a block of wood or gold paint.

from Jewish judgment) since such artifacts, these human creations, can over time undermine a monotheistic faith in *practice*, in aberrant and superstitious forms of folk religion. Wesley, however, unlike the Muslim community, was not an iconoclast, arguing against the use of all images, but he did at least recognize the serious danger in this area not only for Christian life but also for its witness.[605]

Conclusion

From the preceding evidence it is clear, on the basis of Wesley's soteriological frameworks, that the condemnation of Muslims to eternal loss cannot and should not be affirmed. To be sure, Muslims are recipients of God's prevenient grace, a grace that marks the very beginning of salvation. Are Muslims, however, the recipients of more than prevenient grace? The answer to that question, as we have seen, is dependent upon how one understands the metaphor of a faith of servant and the language of "fear God and work righteousness" and their applicability to Muslims who as "heathens" (according to Wesley's own designation) may fall outside the Mosaic and Christian dispensations, though they may, after all, be included "soteriologically," if they have at least a measure of knowledge of Christ and his promises. There is therefore at least some basis, then, according to this last view to affirm that Muslims have the faith of a servant in a broad sense as well as "fear God and work righteousness" in that same sense.

Beyond this, however, to affirm that Muslims are redeemed, properly speaking, that they are marked by the presence of the Holy Spirit of the living Christ reigning in their hearts may be problematic, though Wesley does offer some measure of hope even in this context. For example, in a letter to Thomas Whitehead, written on February 10, 1748 Wesley surmised:

> 'The benefit of the death of Christ is not only extended to such as have the distinct knowledge of His death and sufferings, but even unto those who are inevitably excluded from this knowledge. Even these may be partakers of the benefit of His death, though ignorant of the history, if they suffer His grace to take place in their hearts, so as of wicked men to become *holy*.'[606]

Again is his sermon, "On Charity," written in 1784, Wesley mitigates some of the harshness found in the judgments made by Christians even in his own day. He observes:

> Accordingly that sentence, 'He that believeth not shall be condemned,' is spoken of them to whom the gospel is preached. Others it does not concern; and

---

[605] Ibid. Moreover, when Wesley considered the Second Commandment, that is, the prohibition against making a graven image, he cautioned: "Our religious worship must be governed by the power of *faith*, not by the power of *imagination*." See Wesley, *OT Notes*, (Exodus 20:3).

[606] *Letters*, 2:118. (To Thomas Whitehead). Emphasis is mine. That the wicked become holy is evidence that Wesley has the Christian understanding of justification (and regeneration) in mind.

we are not required to determine anything touching their final state. How it will please God, the Judge of all, to deal with *them*, we may leave to God himself. But this we known, that he is not the God of the Christians only, but the God of the heathens also; that he is 'rich in mercy to all that call upon him', 'according to the light they have';[607]

Add to these elements, what impediments may stand in the way of Muslims coming to saving faith, such as the low Christology of the Koran, and it is clear that the way forward, in its initial phases, should entail greater dialog between these two great monotheistic faiths such that they can both, in a spirit of grace and humility, come to a greater understanding of each other's religious tradition. With mutual dialog in place and with the illumination that will be left in its wake, in terms of greater knowledge of both the gospel and the Koran, what will likely emerge from this engagement is a mutual responsibility in which Wesley's theological frameworks will not only be more greatly understood but also their application will become far less problematic. In the end whatever judgments are entertained, the following maxim can at the very least be affirmed by the church that is ever faithful in its witness to the good news of Jesus Christ to a larger world: those who hear the gospel are thereby accountable for their response to the gospel.

---

[607] *Works [BE]*, 3:295-296. ("On Charity") See also Wesley, *NT Notes*, Acts 17:28. Here again Wesley considers the Muslim, for example, not through the perspective of Christian consciousness but through an Islamic one. In other words, how do things appear phenomenologically, so to speak, from within the life, culture and socialization of one who is outside the Christian worldview? For more on this topic, see Randy L. Maddox, "Wesley and the Question of Truth or Salvation through Other Religions" in *Wesleyan Theological Journal*, vol. 27 (Spring-Fall 1992): 7-29.

About the Contributors

Ron Benefiel is Dean of the School of Theology and Christian Ministry and Professor of Sociology and Theology at Point Loma Nazarene University in San Diego, California. He is the author of numerous essays and articles on Wesleyan theology, ministry, and higher education including "The Ecology of Evangelical Seminaries" in *Theological Education* (2008) and "Simplicity: The Other Side of Complexity" in *Holiness Today* (2011).

Kent Brower is Vice Principal and Senior Lecturer in Biblical Studies at Nazarene Theological College, Manchester. He is the author of numerous books, including *Holiness in the Gospels* (2005), *Holiness and Ecclesiology in the New Testament* (2007), and he is joint editor of the *Global Dictionary of Wesleyan Theology* (2013).

Kenneth J. Collins is Professor of Historical Theology and Wesley Studies at Asbury Theological Seminary in Wilmore, Kentucky. He is the author of *The Scripture Way of Salvation: The Heart of John Wesley's Theology* (1997), *The Theology of John Wesley: Holy Love and the Shape of Grace* (2007), and *Power, Politics and the Fragmentation of Evangelicalism* (2012), and numerous other books and articles.

Joseph W. Cunningham is an Assistant Editor of *Wesley and Methodist Studies*, annually published by the Manchester Wesley Research Centre and the Oxford Centre for Methodism and Church History. He is the author of *Perceptible Inspiration: John Wesley's Pneumatology* (2014) and teaches in the department of philosophy at Saginaw Valley State University in Saginaw, Michigan.

Phil Meadows is Lecturer in Missiology and Wesley Studies at Cliff College in Calver, Derbyshire. He is the author of numerous works on Wesleyan theology and ministry, including *Wesleyan DNA of Discipleship* (2013).

Thomas A. Noble is Professor of Theology at Nazarene Theological Seminary in Kansas City, Missouri. He is also a Senior Research Fellow at

Nazarene Theological College, Manchester. His most recent publication is called *Holy Trinity: Holy People: The Theology of Christian Perfecting* (2013).

Henry Rack is the Emeritus Bishop Fraser Senior Lecturer in Ecclesiastical History at The University of Manchester. He is the author or editor of numerous works on the history of Methodism, including *Reasonable Enthusiast: John Wesley and the Rise of Methodism* (3rd edition, 2002) and volume 10 of the *Bicentennial Edition of the Works of John Wesley* (2011).

David Rainey is a Senior Lecturer in Theology and Senior Research Fellow at Nazarene Theological College, Manchester. His most recent publications include, "The Established Church and Evangelical Theology: John Wesley's Ecclesiology" in *International Journal of Systematic Theology* (2010) and "Jurgen Moltmann: Creation and the Restructuring of Trinitarian Panentheism" in *As Long as Earth Endures* (2014).

Ian Randall is a Senior Research Fellow at Spurgeon's College, London. He is the author of *Evangelical Experiences: A Study in the Spirituality of English Evangelicalism, 1918-1939* (1999), *Rhythms of Revival: The Spiritual Awakening of 1857-1863* (2010), and several other books and articles.

Joseph Wood is a Sessional Lecturer in Theology at Nazarene Theological College, Manchester. His recent publications include "William White, John Wesley, and the 'Sheep without a Shepherd': Towards a New Understanding of John Wesley's Ecclesiology" in *Wesley and Methodist Studies* (2012) and "Diaconal Dilemmas: The Development of the Diaconate in the Church of the Nazarene" in *Theology and Ministry* (2013).

www.ingramcontent.com/pod-product-compliance
Lightning Source LLC
Chambersburg PA
CBHW021842220426
43663CB00005B/361